Frances Morris is an art historian, curator, and writer.
She was director of Tate Modern, London, from 2016
until 2023, having begun working at Tate in 1987 and going
on to play a key role in reconceptualizing the exhibition
displays and internationalizing the museum's collection.
Her exhibitions include retrospectives of Louise Bourgeois
(2007), Yayoi Kusama (2012), and Agnes Martin (2015).
Morris often worked with and spoke to Phyllida Barlow,
and in 2024 she completed two other projects related
to the artist: the exhibition *Phyllida Barlow: unscripted* at
Hauser & Wirth Somerset and the definitive monograph
Phyllida Barlow: Sculpture, 1963–2023.

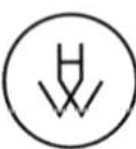

In the Studio, a new series from Hauser & Wirth Publishers, gives readers a behind-the-scenes view of artists at work. Each book focuses on a major figure of twentieth- or twenty-first-century art, offering an introduction to their influences, materials, and techniques. Written by leading scholars and critics and generously illustrated, *In the Studio* titles are the perfect companion for art lovers and newcomers alike.

Forthcoming volumes explore the life and work of Jack Whitten and Lee Lozano.

In the Studio

Phyllida Barlow

Frances Morris

Hauser & Wirth Publishers

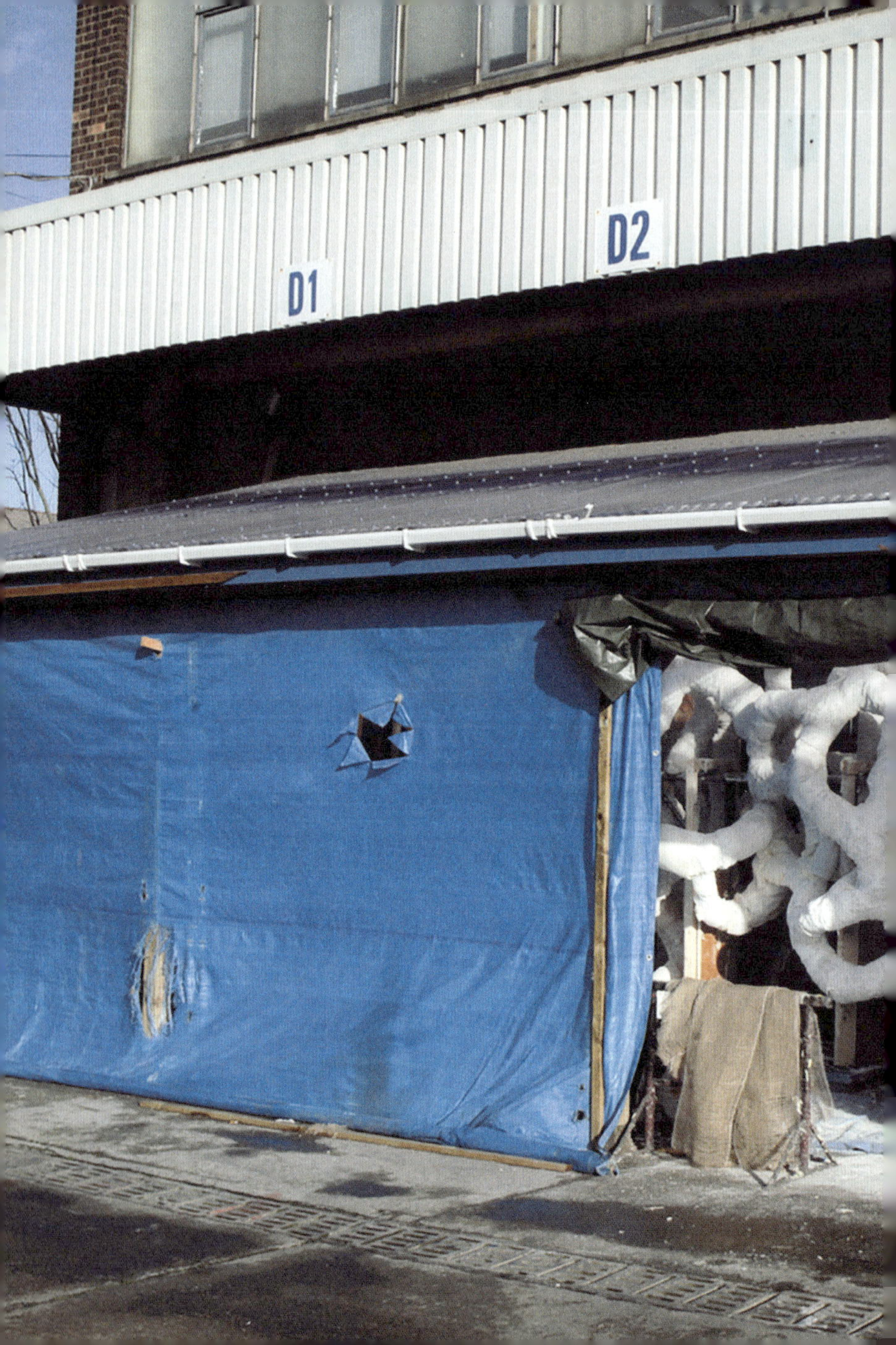

D1
D2

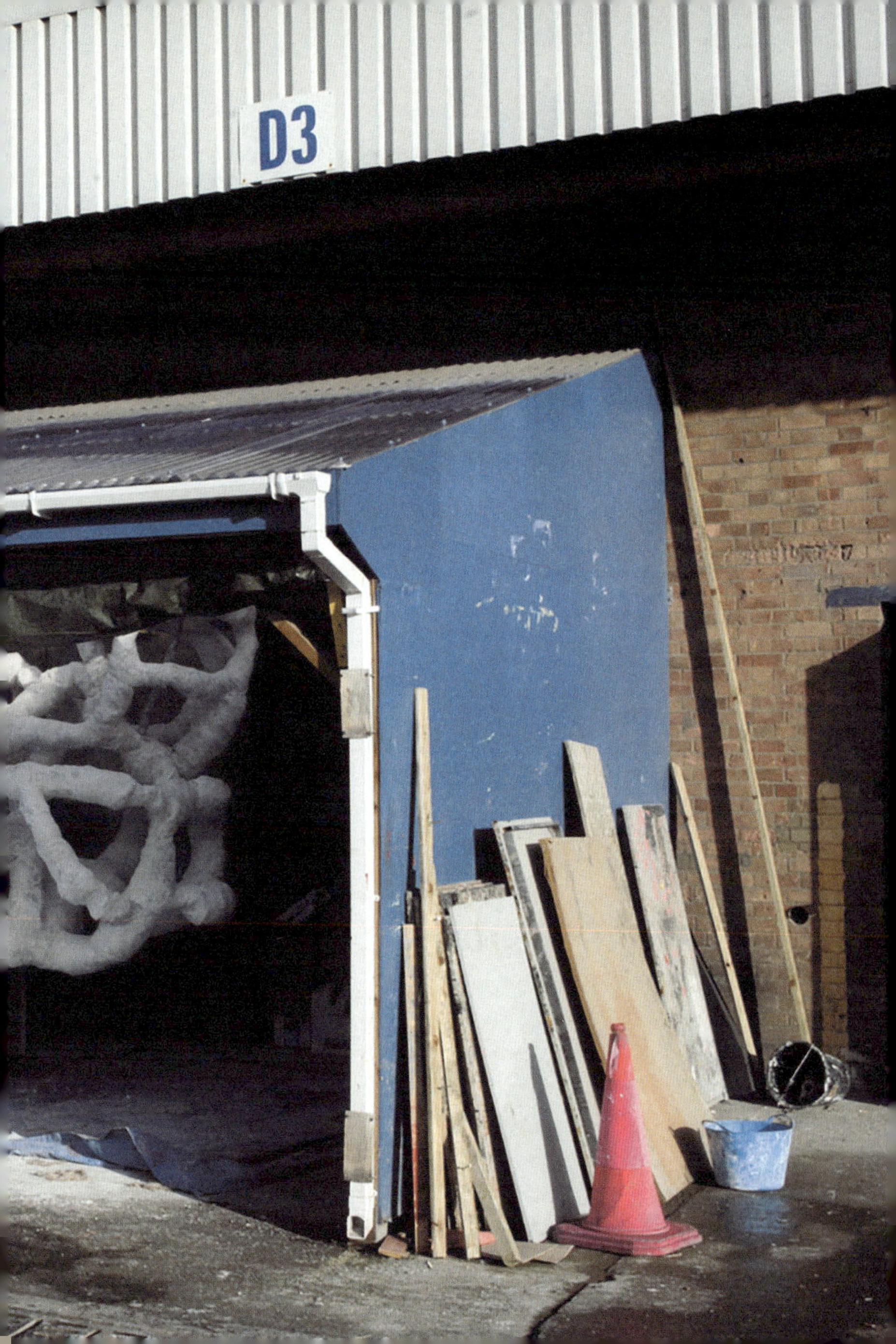
D3

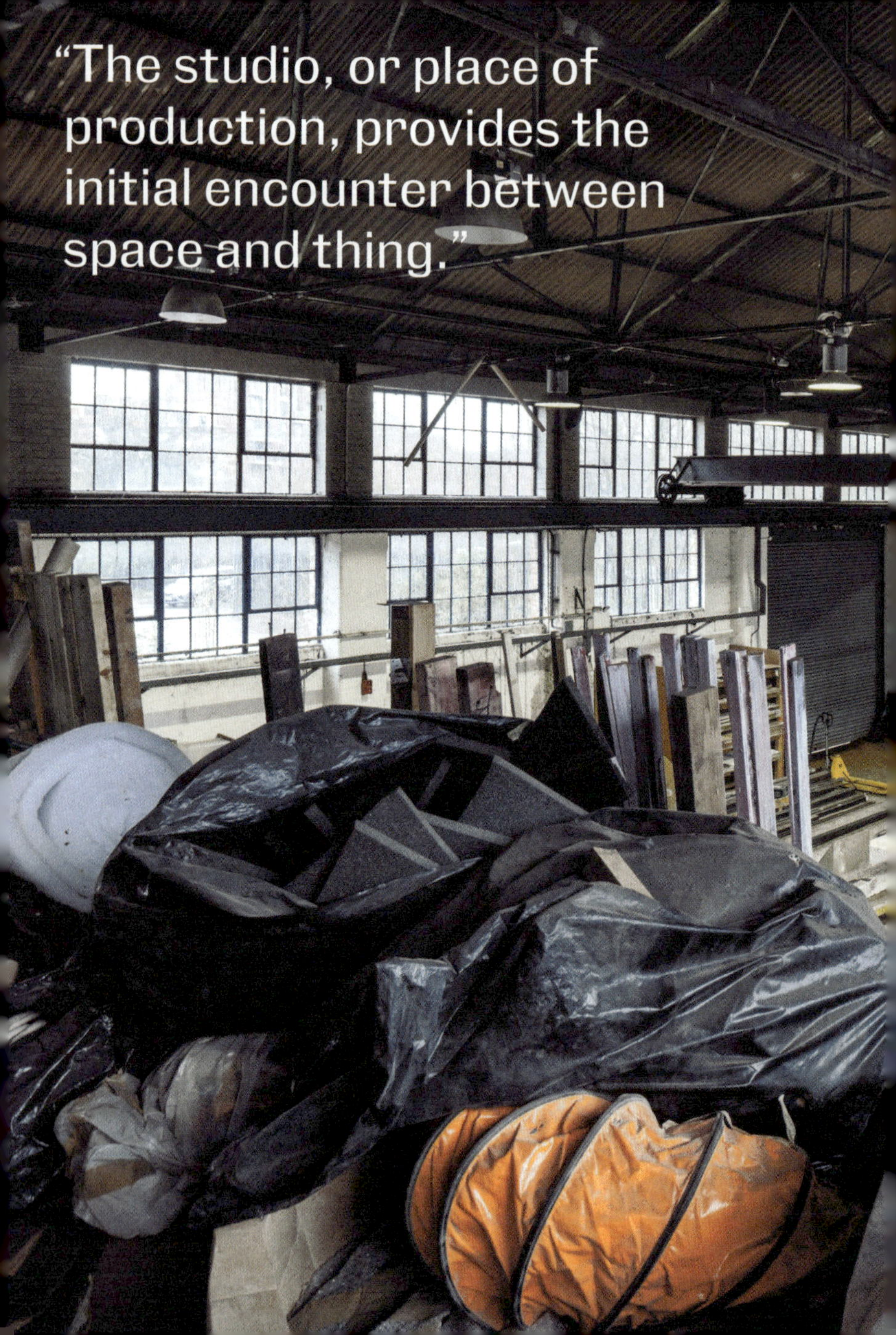
"The studio, or place of production, provides the initial encounter between space and thing."

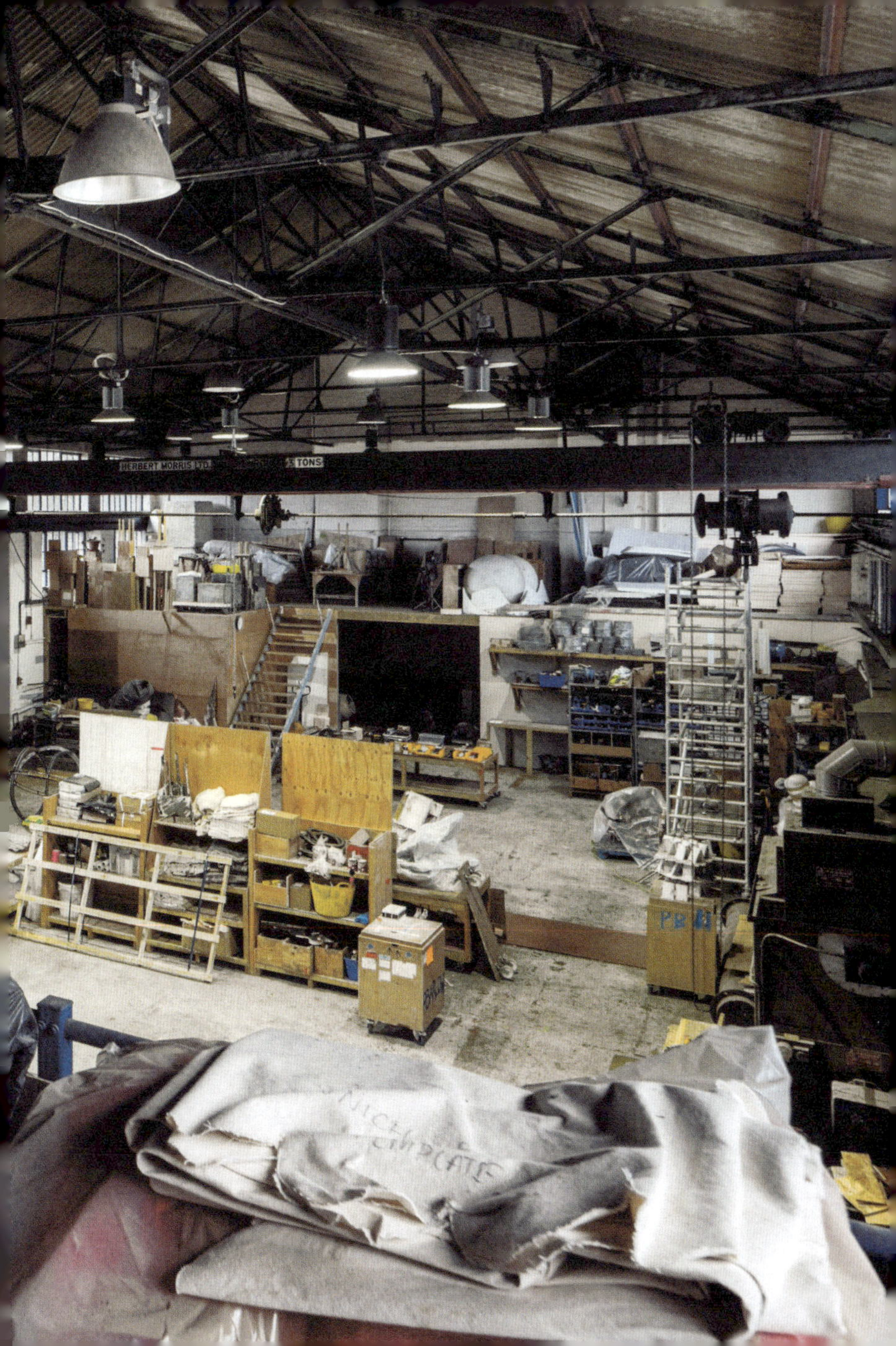

HERBERT MORRIS LTD.
5 TONS

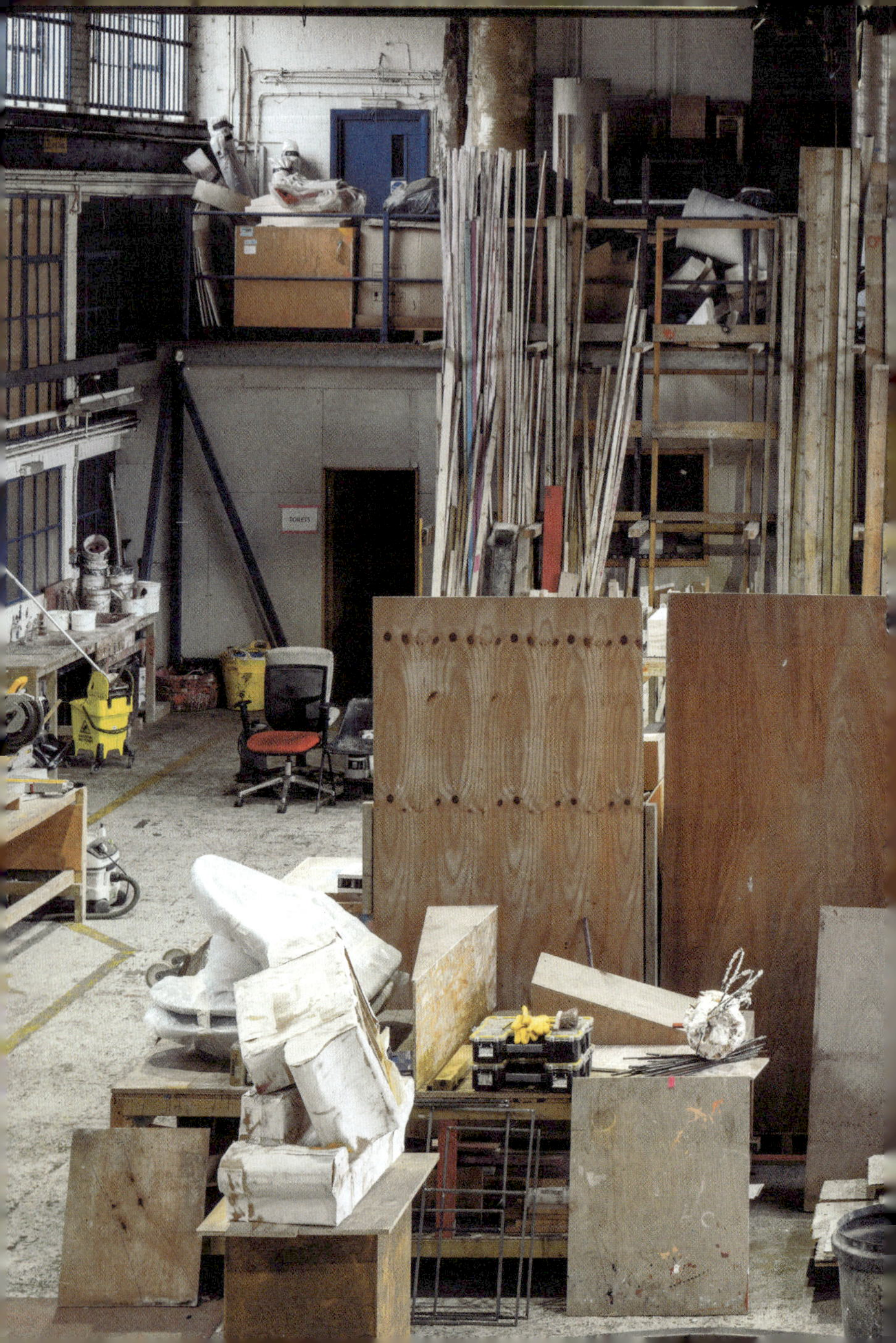

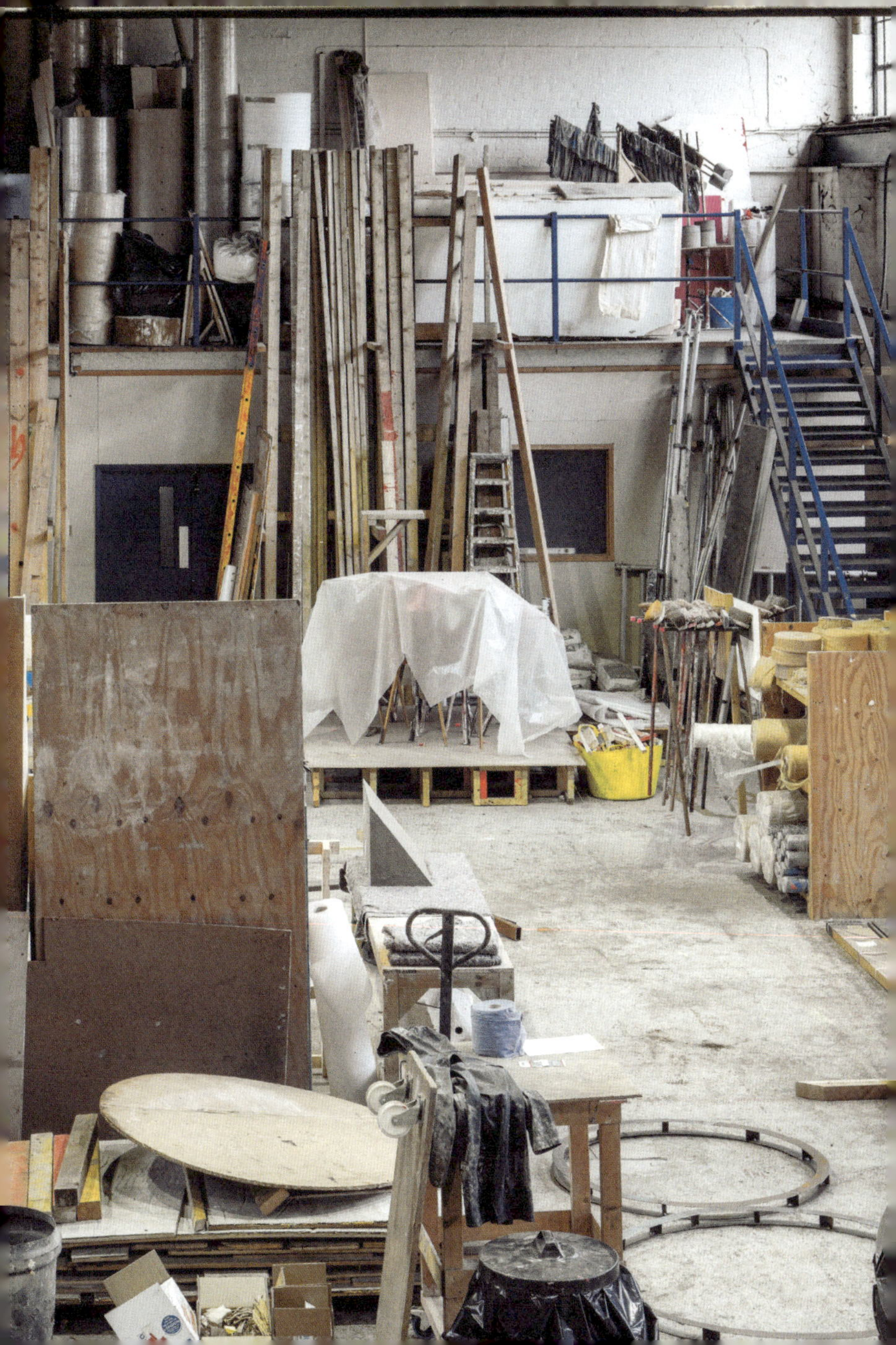

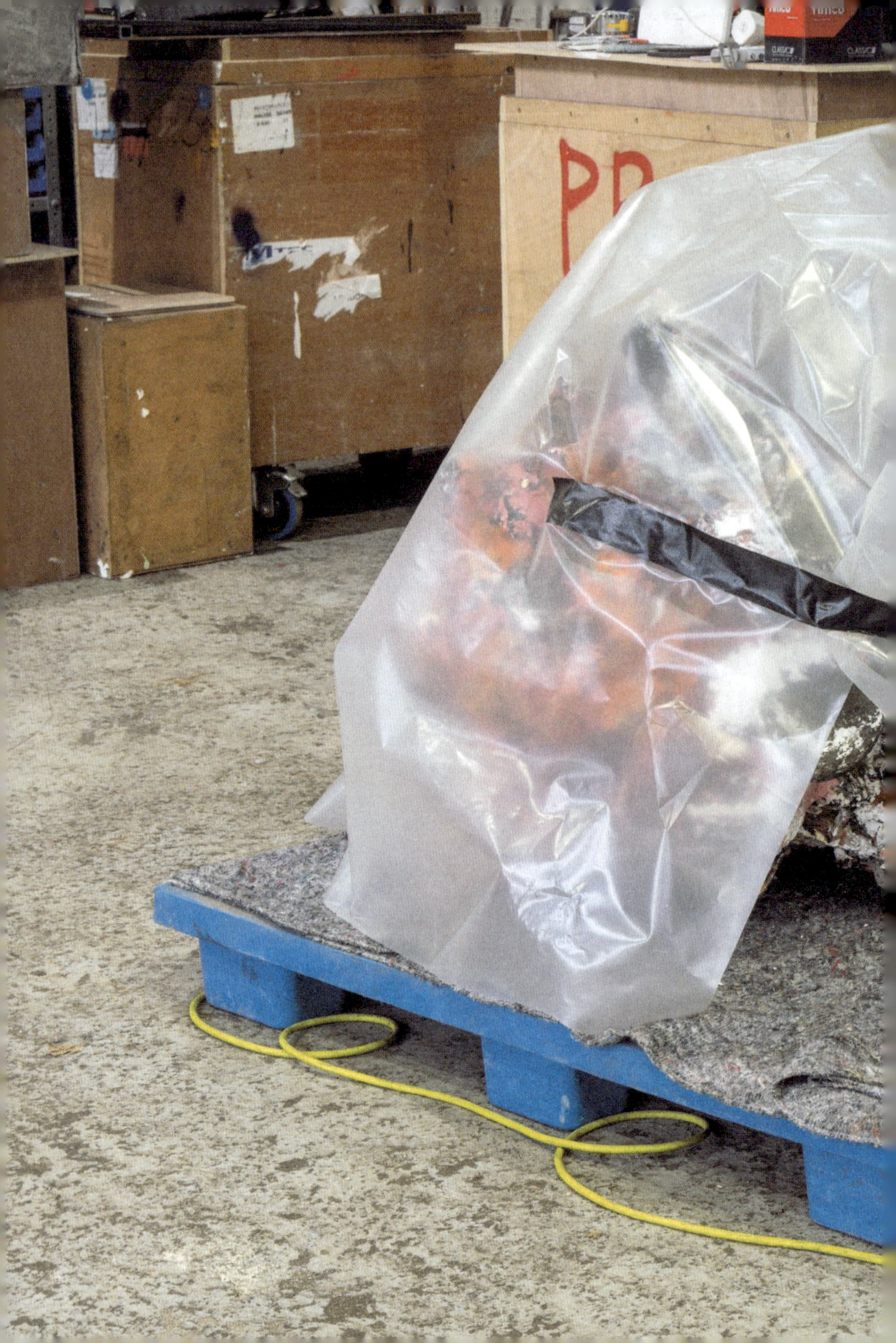

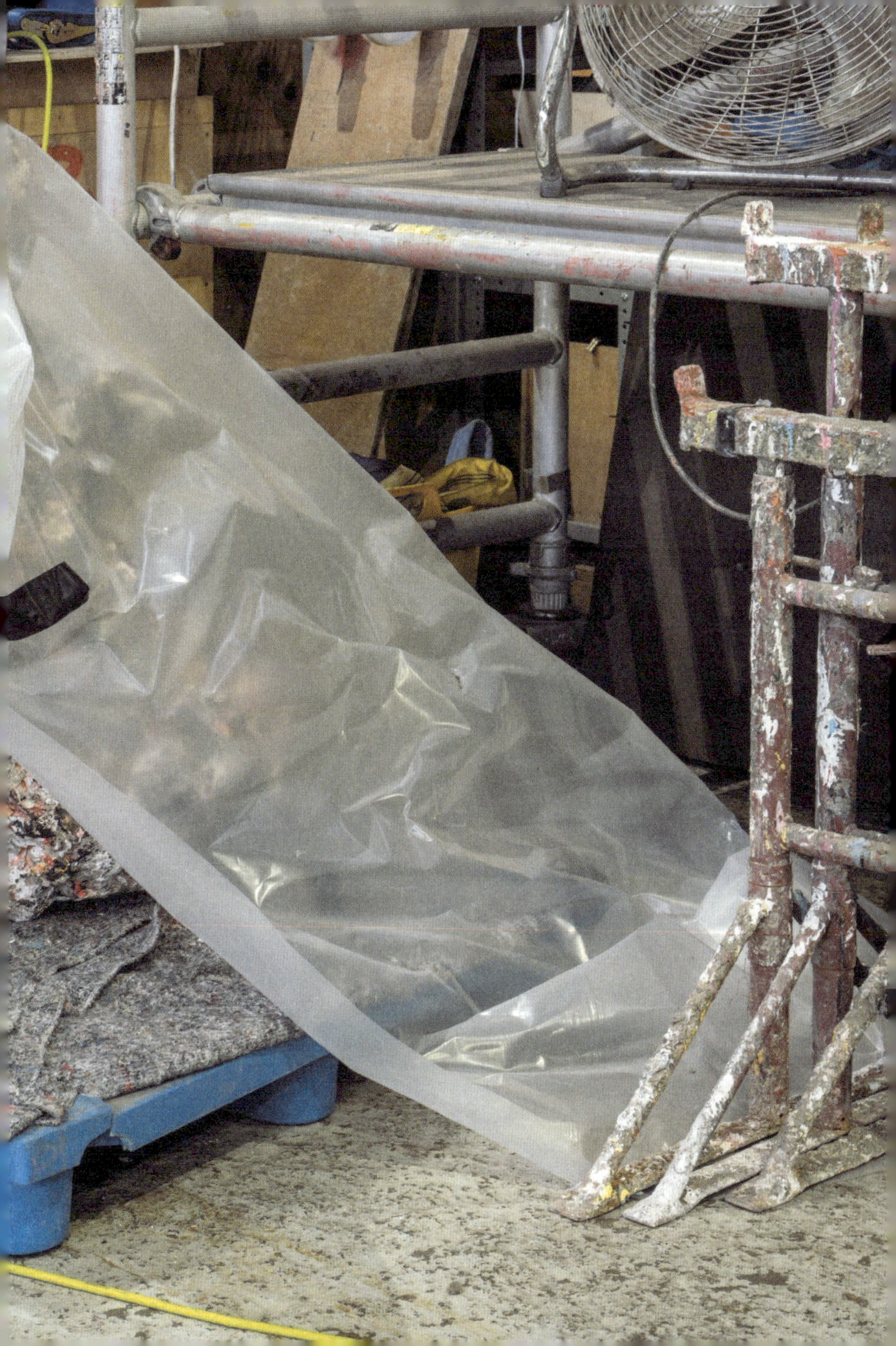

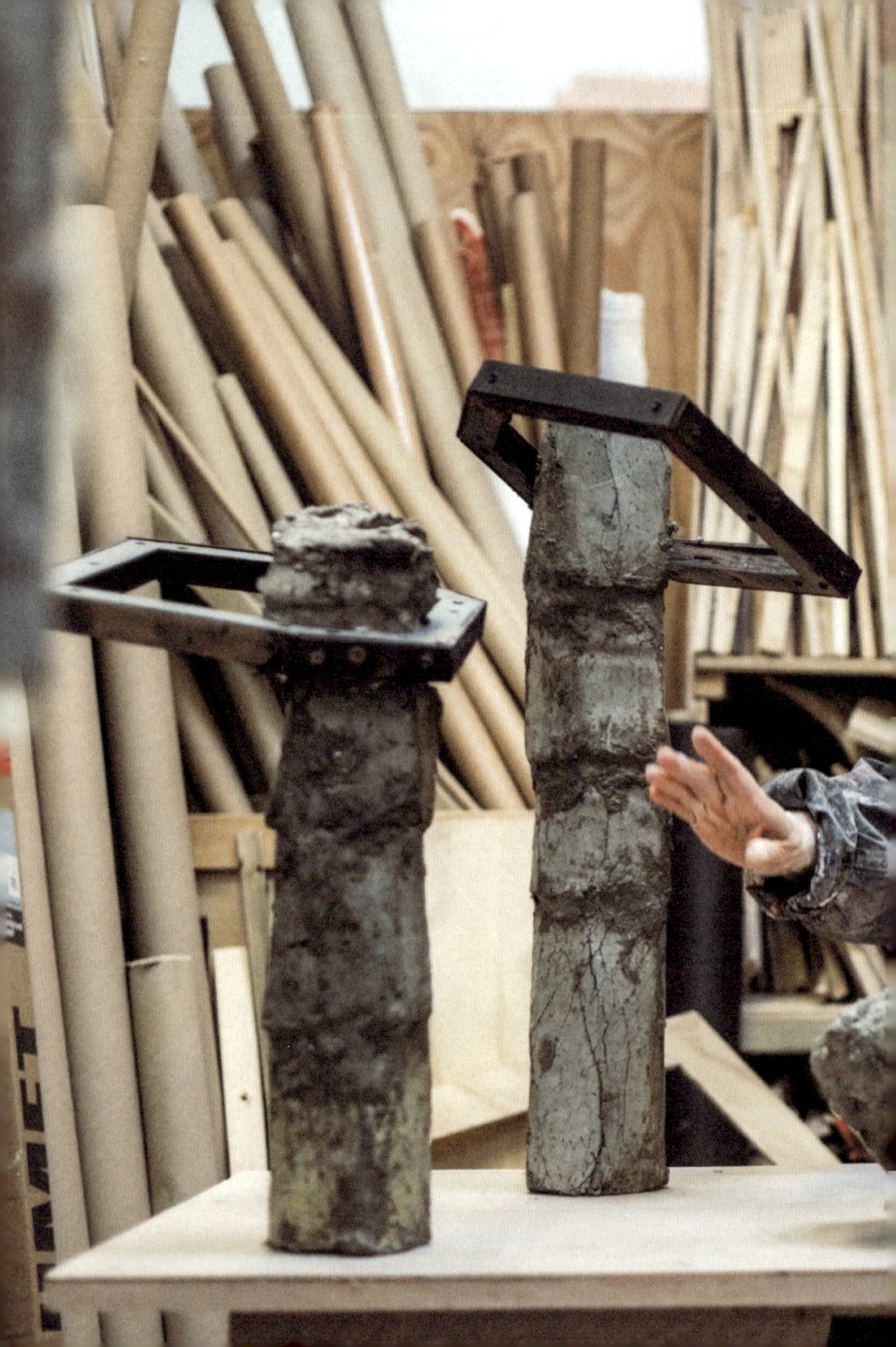

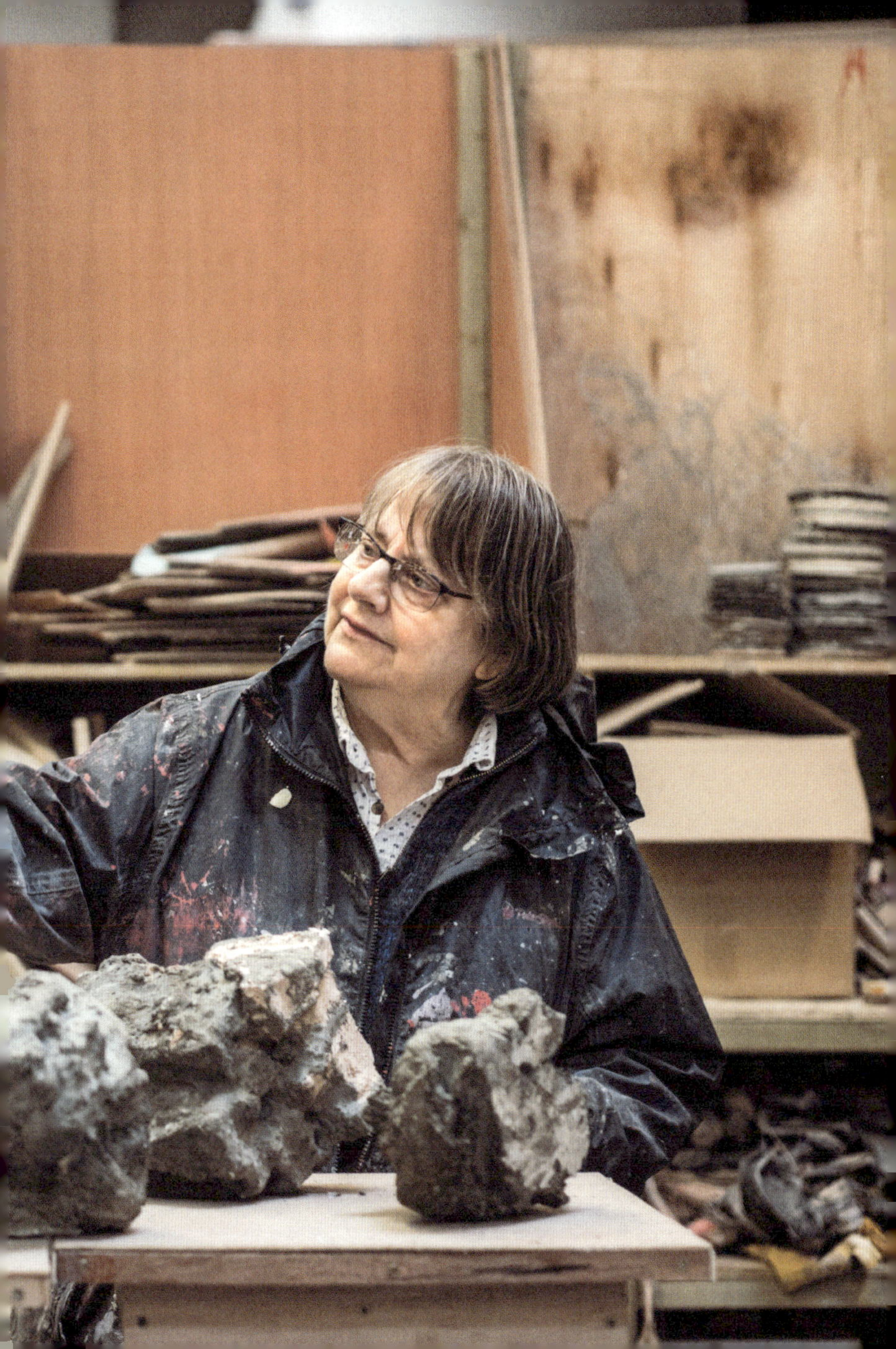

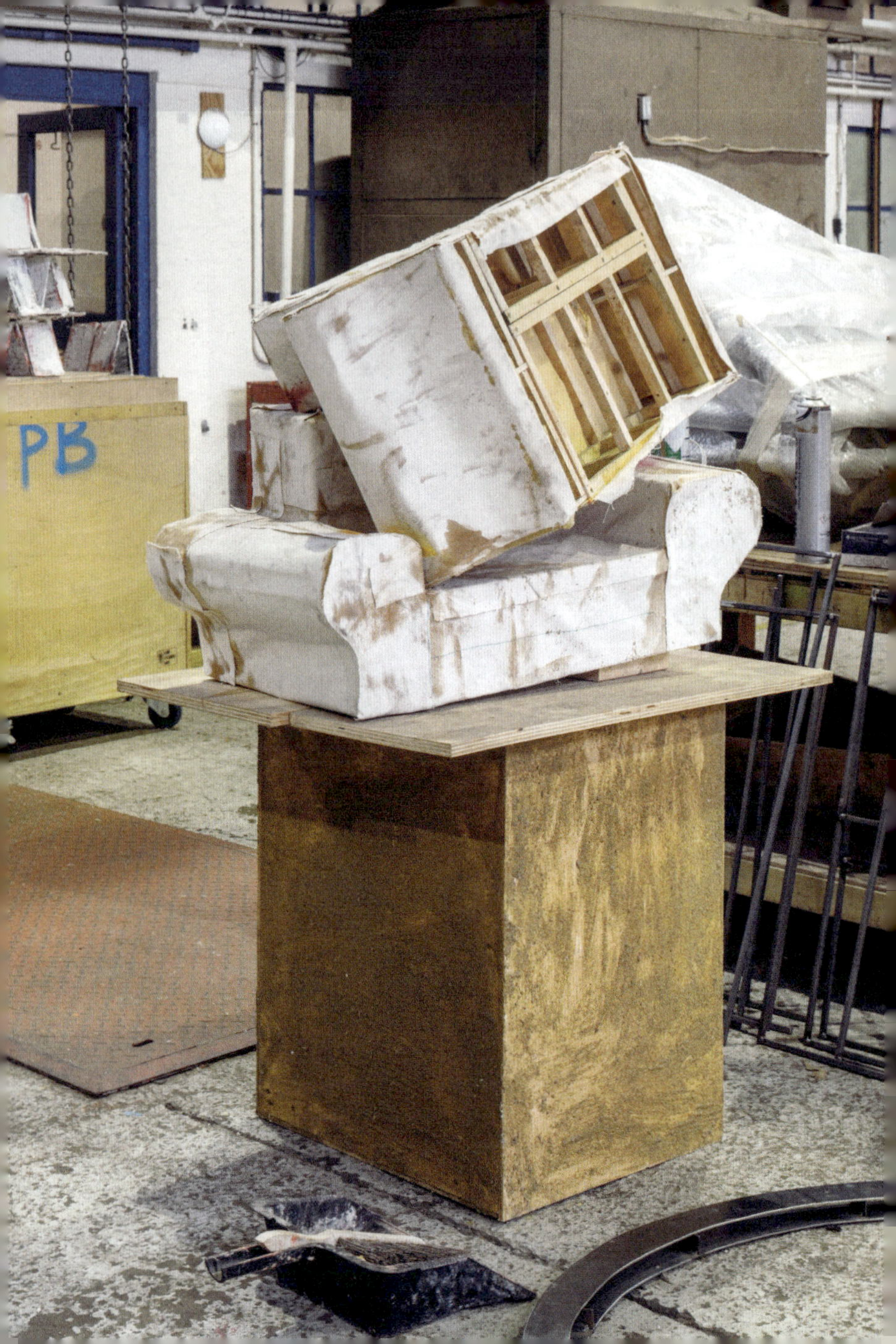

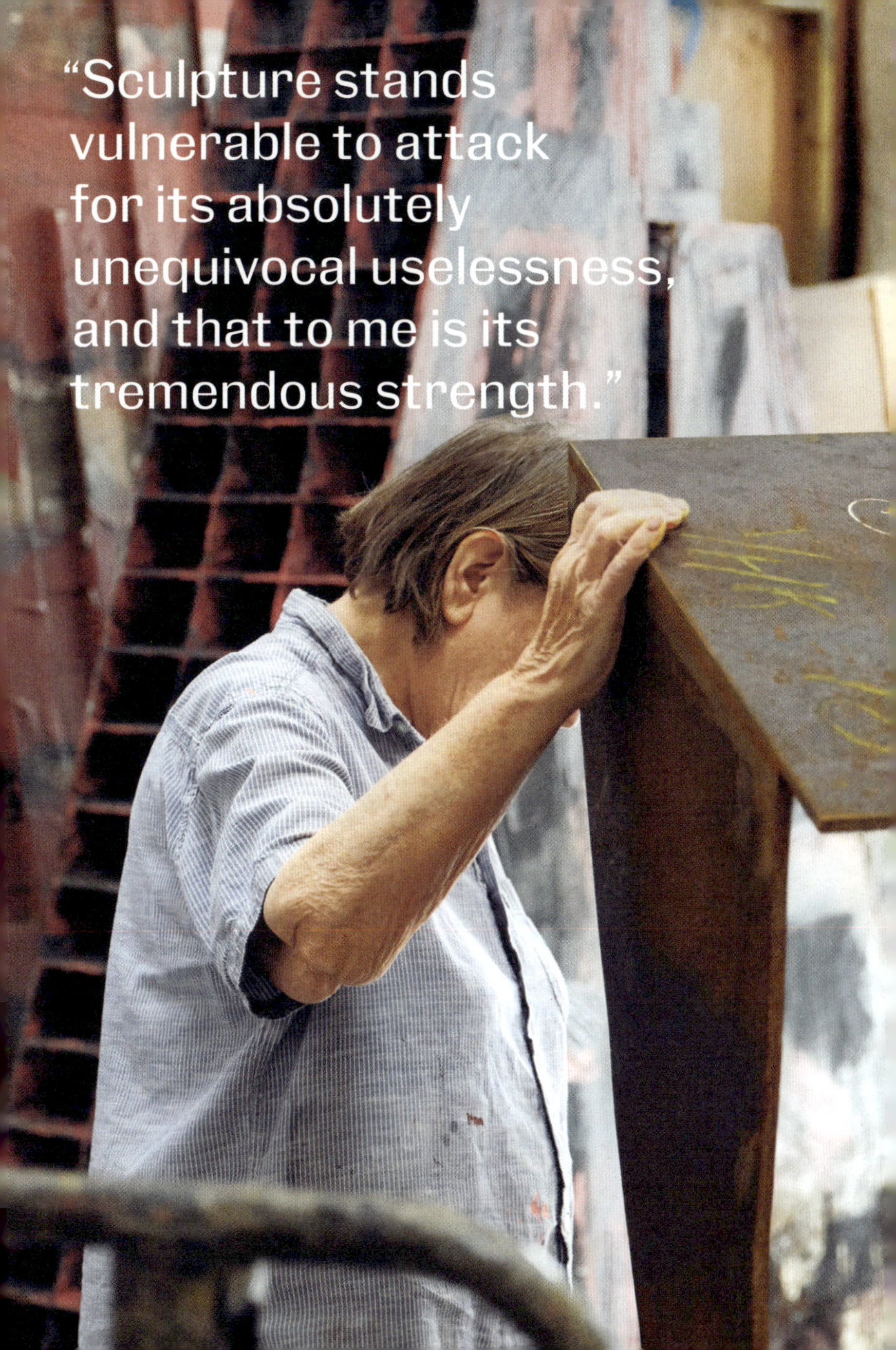

"Sculpture stands vulnerable to attack for its absolutely unequivocal uselessness, and that to me is its tremendous strength."

Contents

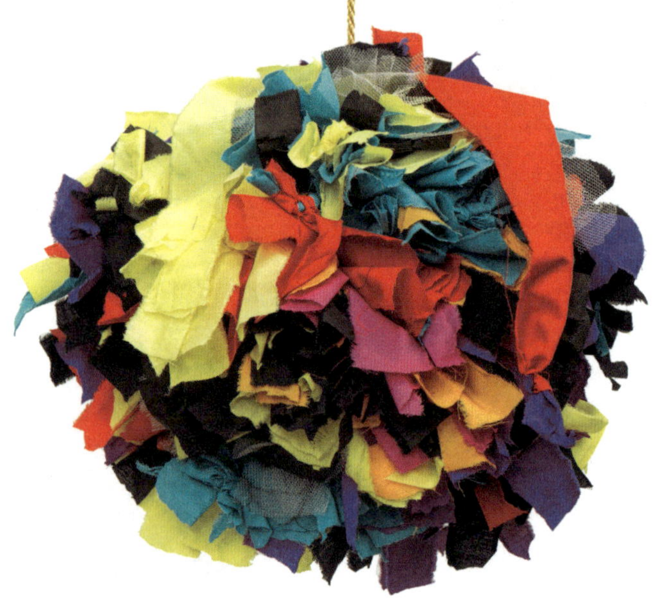

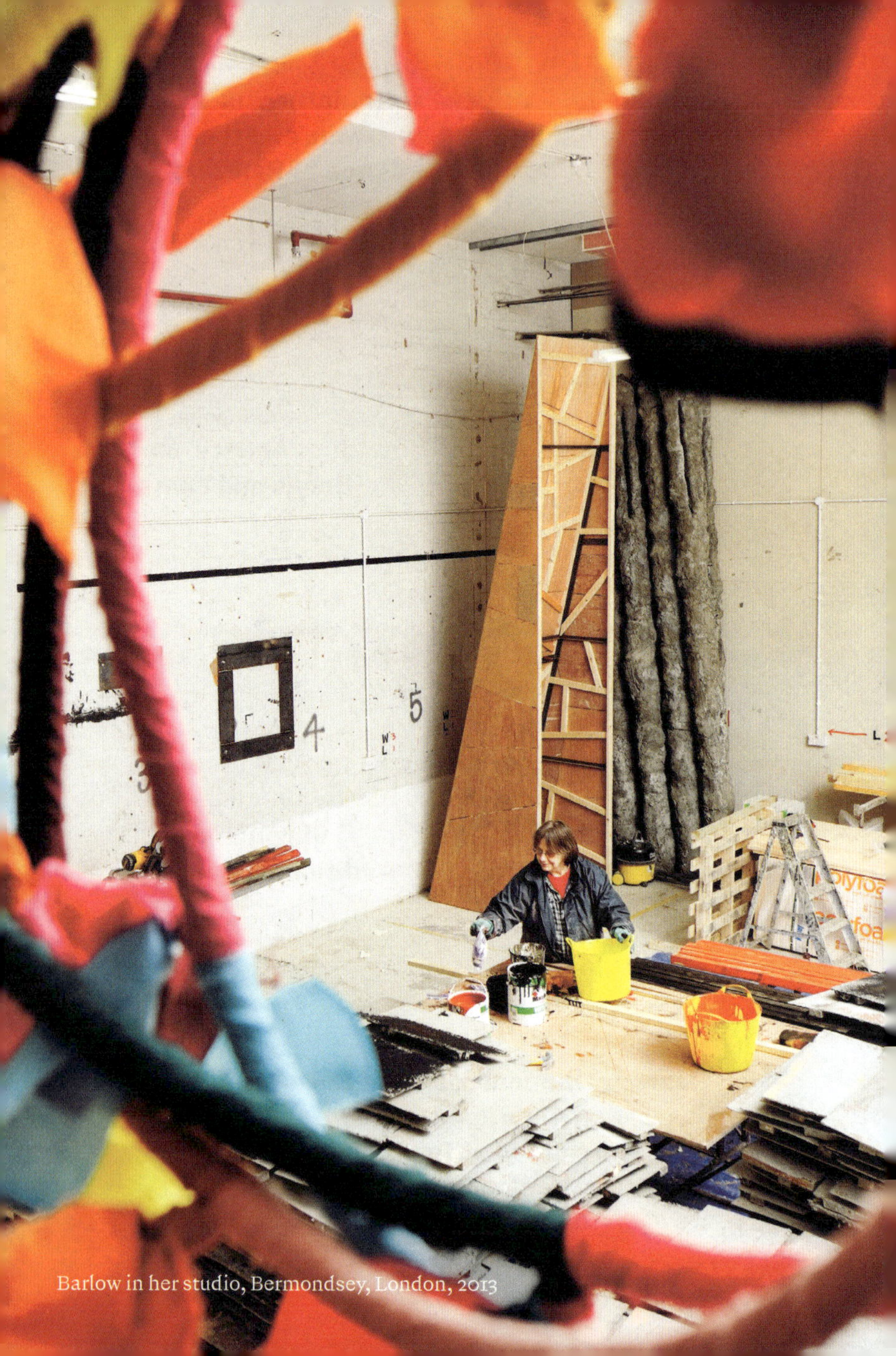

Barlow in her studio, Bermondsey, London, 2013

Ambition and Adventure

Liberated, in 2009, from a long and eminent career in teaching, Phyllida Barlow (1944–2023) set the art world on fire in the last decade and a half of her life, captivating a growing audience with a crescendo of sculptural activity. One great public project unfolded after another. Her resonant titles—among them *BRAKE, STREET, SWAMP, BLUFF, Cast, RIG, brink, siege, HOARD, GIG, dock, mix, set, tryst, demo, folly, quarry, prop, tilt, cul-de-sac, frontier, act, glimpse, STREET, BREACH*—evoke, collectively, a kind of madcap, improvised adventure. So it must have seemed to the artist herself, as she accepted, with relish for risk, every new opportunity to occupy—even take over—museums, galleries, and sculpture parks, not to mention a cemetery and a theater or two. These sites were often freighted with their own histories and bound by their own conventions; Barlow consistently worked against their grain, pushing her work beyond the limits of the last project and into new realms. She recycled ideas as well as materials, treading a moving carpet of innovation, at times reaching a dead end, at others making headway. She made brilliant forays into the worlds of opera and dance, bringing to life a language of staging and performance she had previously rehearsed in her gallery work with objects that resembled sets and props. And finally, in a project revealed only after her death, she created seven wonderfully capricious public sculptures, *PRANK* (2023; p. 20), conjuring into existence a cast of demonic cartoon characters that remain as her epithet. They manifest so much of her drive, her sense of the absurd, and her desire to encourage us to look at the world again and anew.

Barlow's career from 2010 on became a very public affair, but in truth her practice always began in the studio, and her head

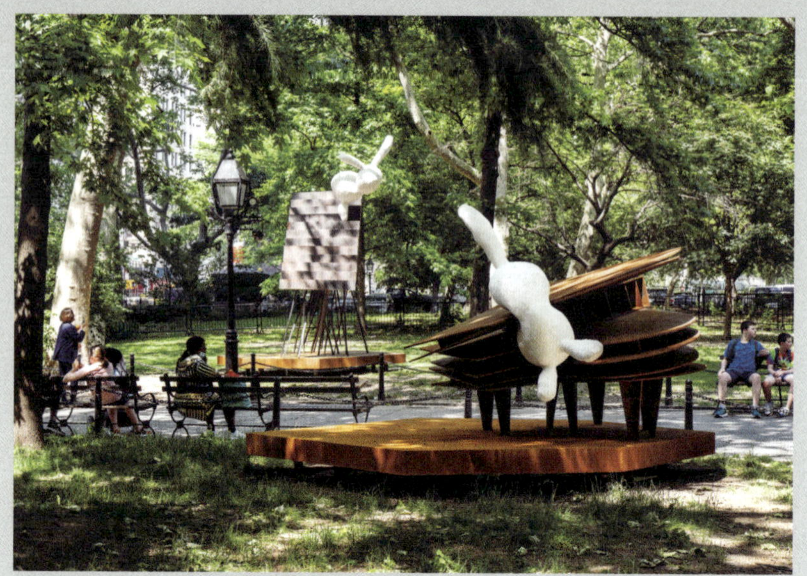

PRANK (2023)

Responding to a commission to make a suite of outdoor works for City Hall Park in New York, Barlow created what would be her last completed project: a family of seven enigmatic and slightly malevolent characters who cavort, perch, or hang precariously onto steel structures that resemble items of domestic architecture and furniture. Their bulbous, rubbery bodies and distinctive bunny ears are reminders of earlier work by Barlow, as are the references to her familiar vocabulary of stairs, lockers, and sofas, demonstrating how she continued to repurpose imagery and form over her long career.

Alongside its strong evocation of Surrealism's biomorphism, *PRANK* feels informed by traditions of popular culture—from animated cartoons to pantomime—and speaks to the expansive range of cultural references at play in her work.

and her soul felt most at home within its walls. Whether in
the basement of the family's capacious and shabby Victorian
terraced house in north London, or in one or another of
the industrial-scaled spaces she went on to rent north and
then south of the Thames, the studio was her sanctuary.
It was a place for exploration through making, often with
no prescribed outcome. She found this open-endedness
profoundly generative, and it paved the way for the detailed
planning and development of projects soon to be staged
out in the world.

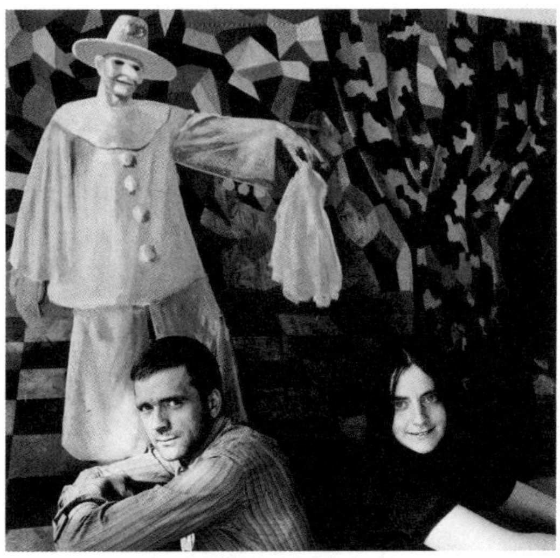

Barlow with her husband Fabian Peake in front of his
painting *Pierrot's Message* in 1971

The early years of Barlow's career as an artist were
marked by conflicting priorities: not only did she bring
up five children with her husband, artist and writer Fabian
Peake, but she also took on time-consuming teaching
commitments. Back then, invitations to exhibit were few
and far between. As far as art was concerned, she worked

for the sake of working; when she felt most in need of
showing what she was making, she evolved unique guerilla
tactics, surreptitiously inserting work into everyday
situations, whether on the streets outside her home or
in a friend's living room (pp. 26–33), to allow it to dialogue
with the real world beyond the seclusion of the studio.

Barlow's entire career was propelled by an active response
to the world as she found it; her exploratory installations
in urban and rural locations during the 1980s are eloquent
commentaries on the times in which she lived. Shortly after
the end of World War II, when she was a young child, her
family had moved to London from Newcastle upon Tyne
in the north of England. Her father would drive Phyllida
and her siblings through the streets of London's East
End, where she saw a city wounded and decrepit in the
aftermath of the Blitz: terraced streets with gaping holes
where whole houses had stood; the detritus of staircases
and toilet cisterns, wallpaper and fireplaces hanging from
inner party walls laid bare by incendiary bombs; and piles
of rubble, fertile ground for nature to begin, over time, to
do its work of renewal: everywhere in this world of grayness
and devastation, she recalled, the scene was shot through
with flashes of brilliant purple-flowering buddleia bushes.

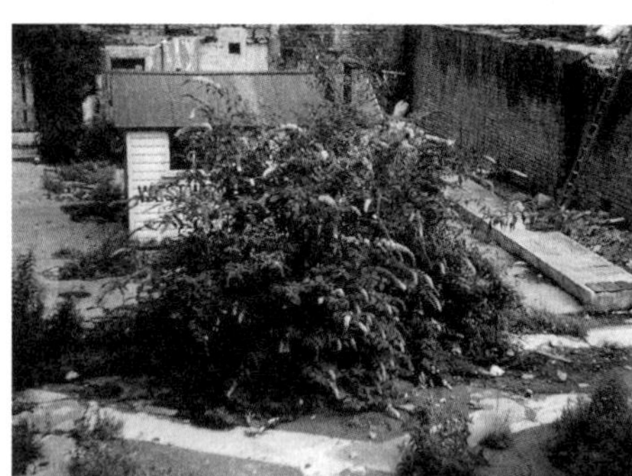

Buddleia bushes in
Cripplegate, London,
after the Blitz bombings
of 1940–41

         Life and Work

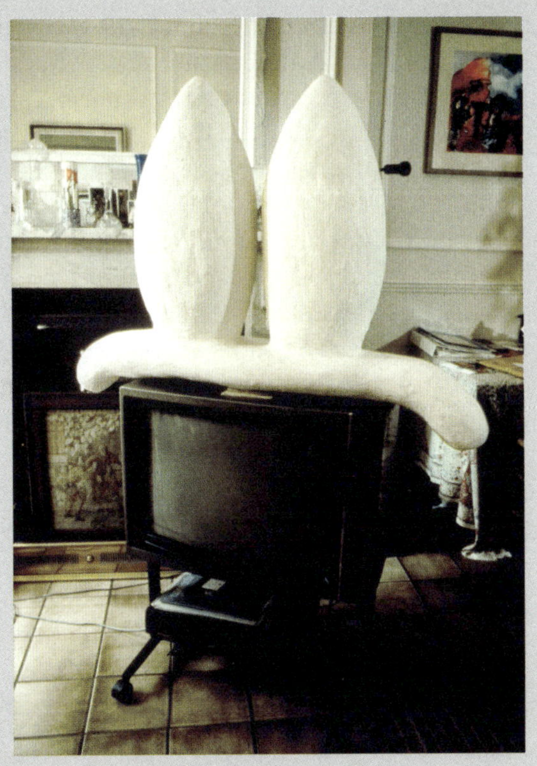

Object for the television (1994)

This is the only surviving example of the enigmatic
sculptures Barlow made in the early 1990s to address
her frustration with the lack of exhibiting opportunities
and her desire to make objects for places other than her
studio (pp. 26–33). The origins of the strange, bulbous
object placed on top of the television and reminiscent
of rabbit ears is not known, but it was an image that was
to return in many guises in Barlow's oeuvre. When first
exhibited, *Object for the television* was covered in slices
of white bread, which the artist subsequently decided
to remove.

These early experiences of London led Barlow to a particular
way of looking at the world and, as she acknowledged,
shaped the look of her art. A fear of annihilation remained
omnipresent with the onset of the Cold War, and Barlow
retained a fascinated attention to the permacrisis that
unfolded globally over her lifetime. Her work evolved
alongside a corrosive fear of nuclear holocaust, accompanied
by daily news of wars across many continents, conflicts
of race and faith, and the catastrophic impacts of
environmental disasters. The woes of the twentieth and
twenty-first centuries insistently interrupted her family life
at home, her comfortable and cultured upbringing (Barlow
was a great-great-granddaughter of Charles Darwin) shaped
by vivid personal experiences both happy and traumatic,
as well as by inherited memories from a long family history.

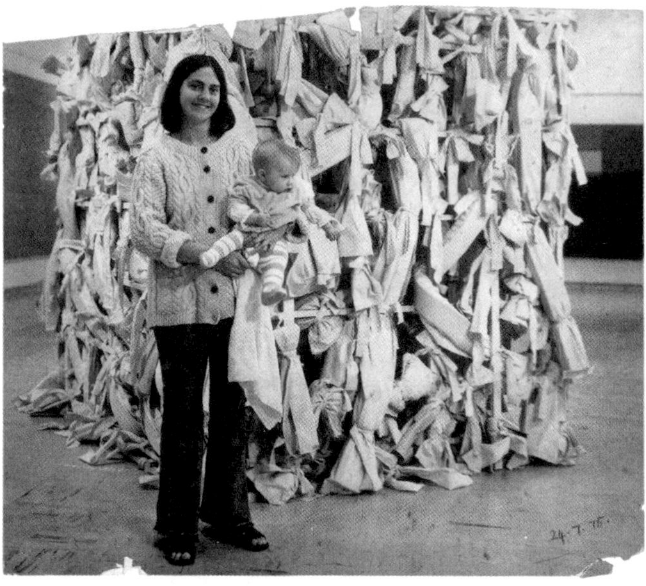

Barlow in front of her work *Shedmesh*, holding her daughter
Clover Peake, at Camden Arts Centre, London, 1975

                          Life and Work

Barlow was reluctant to psychoanalyze herself, just as she resisted the imposition of any theoretical framework on her sculpture. Her work has always eluded categorization: from early on she remained staunchly independent in her artistic outlook, and more interested in challenging certainties than in constructing rules. In the mid-twentieth century, at a time when artists were quick to jump on bandwagons, Barlow was a loner, charismatic but unclubbable, driven by curiosity and open-mindedness, and fearless. She operated in the slipstream of artistic currents, refusing to align herself with either abstraction or figuration, co-opting painting as part her sculptural language, and working happily with formally incompatible languages such as geometric and biomorphic forms. "Lies, borrowing, shadow, suspicion, premonition, acting, pastiche, figment, almost, not quite," and, not least, "approximation" were her words to describe how she negotiated the turbulent tidal flows that churned between art and life.

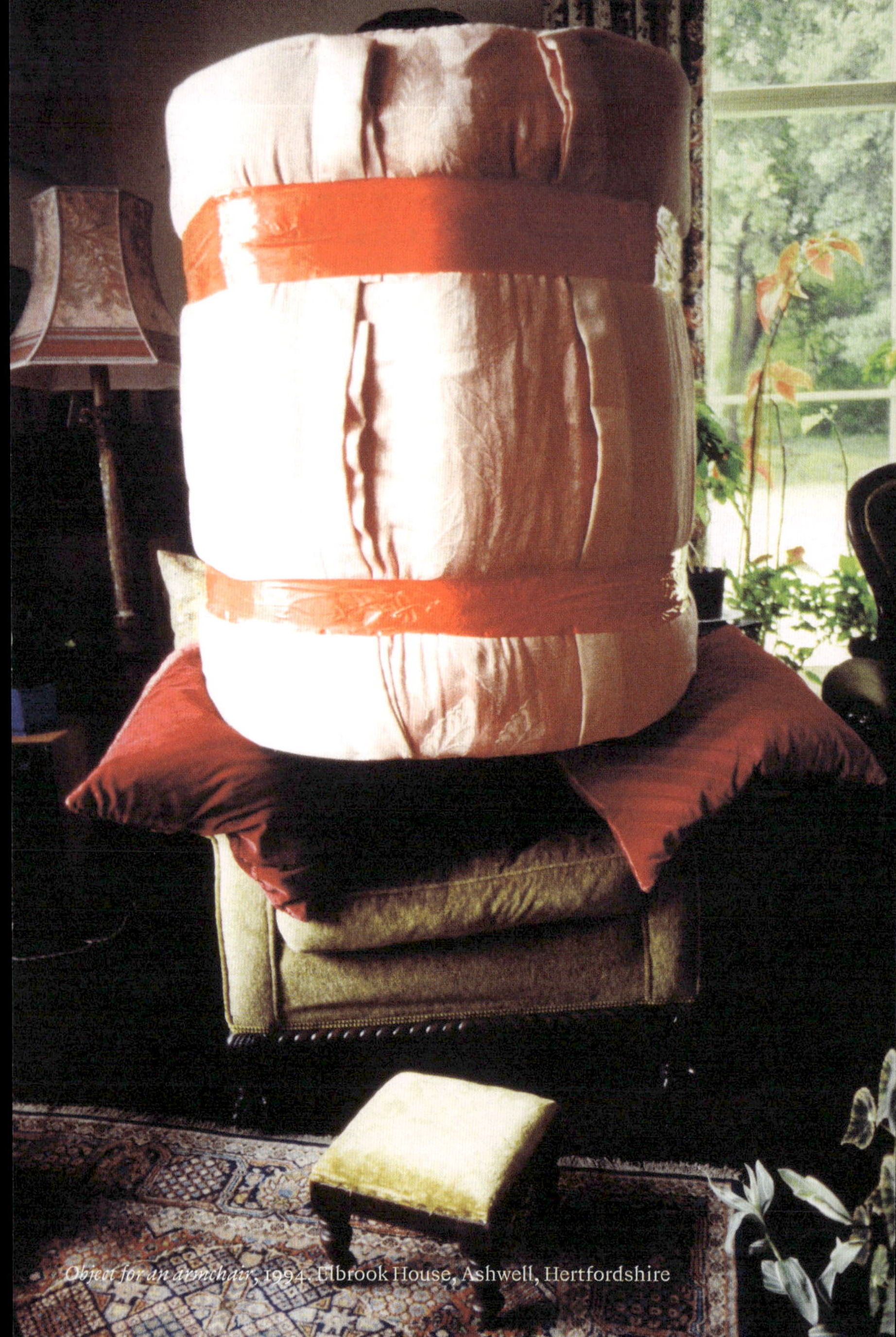

Object for an armchair, 1994, Ulbrook House, Ashwell, Hertfordshire

Objects for ... (1994–99)

The series *Objects for ...* comprises strange, unidentifiable but evocative fabrications made from textiles, plaster, and other easy-to-source materials. For *Object for a street grit bin* (1995), she wrapped a loaf of bread in aluminum foil. Each of these works was a temporary intervention designed to disrupt the familiar. The tactical juxtaposition of disparate objects and settings speaks to Barlow's interest in Surrealism and the absurd, and brings to mind the Comte de Lautréamont's famous Surrealist maxim "as beautiful as the chance encounter of a sewing machine and an umbrella on an operating table."

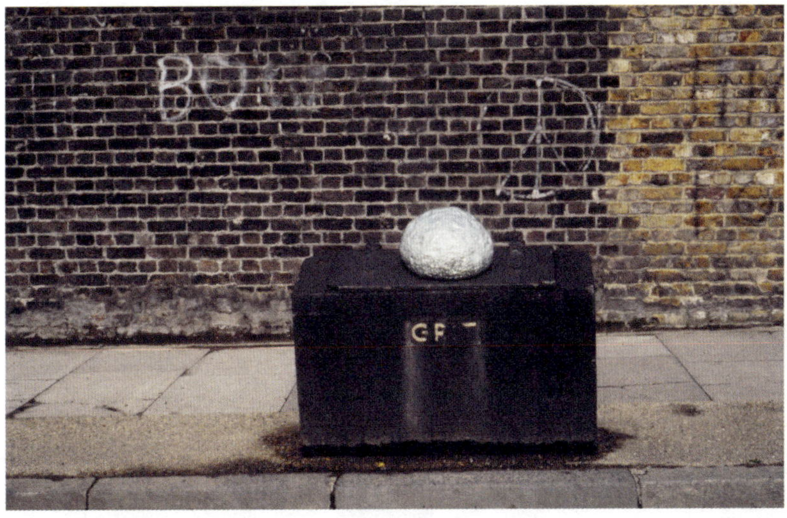

Object for a street grit bin, 1995. York Way, London

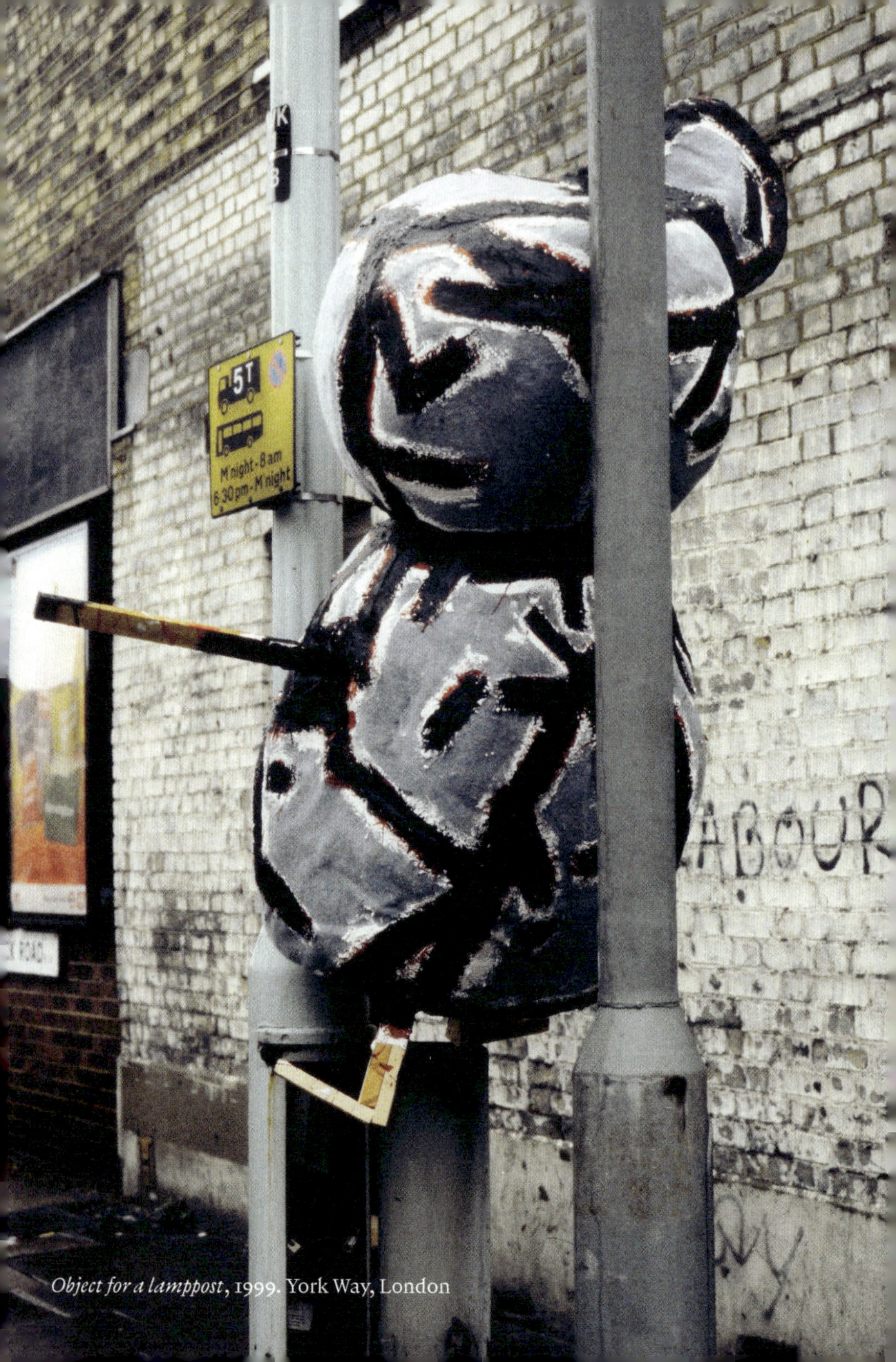

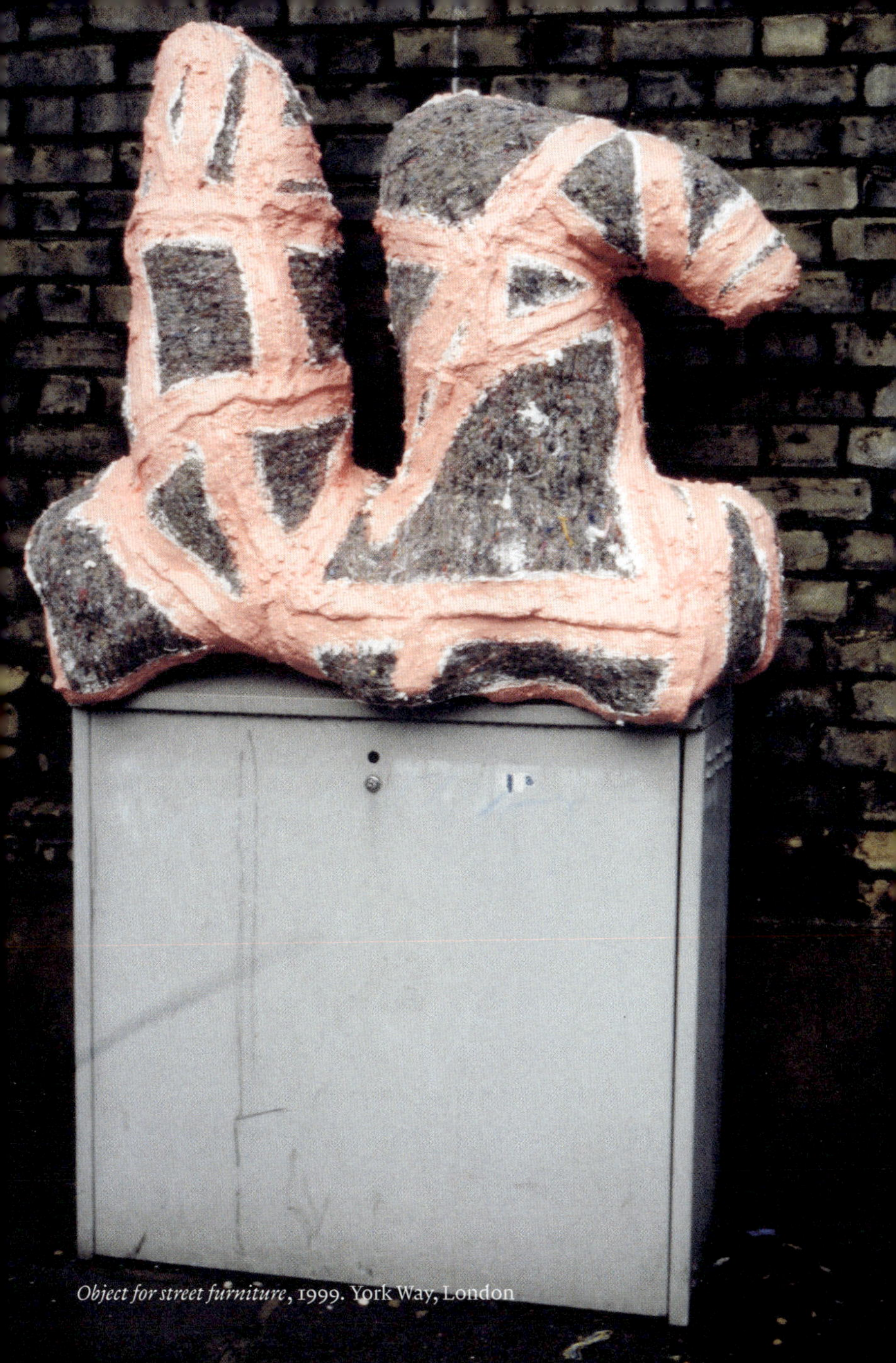

Object for street furniture, 1999. York Way, London

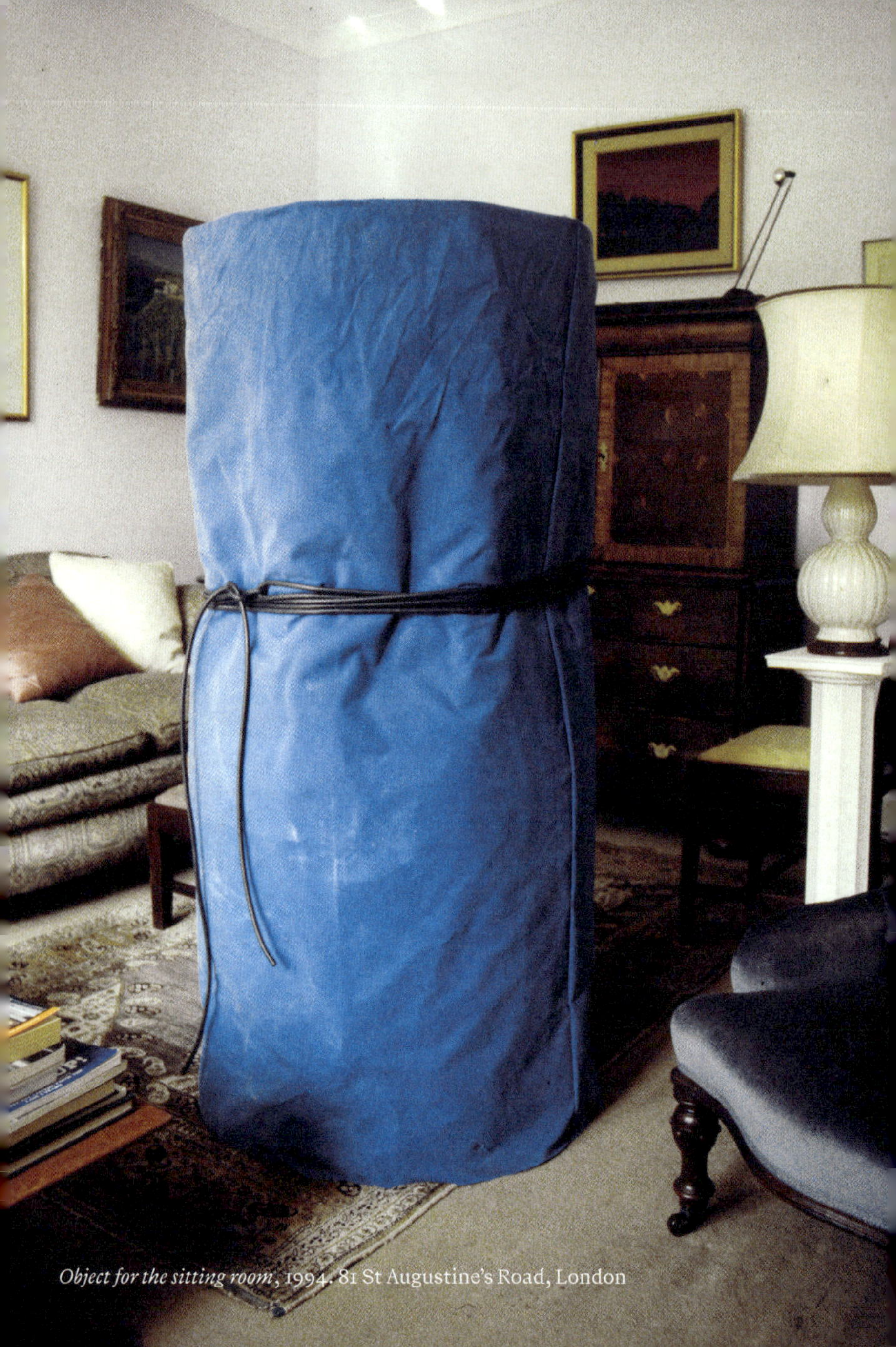

Object for the sitting room, 1994. 81 St Augustine's Road, London

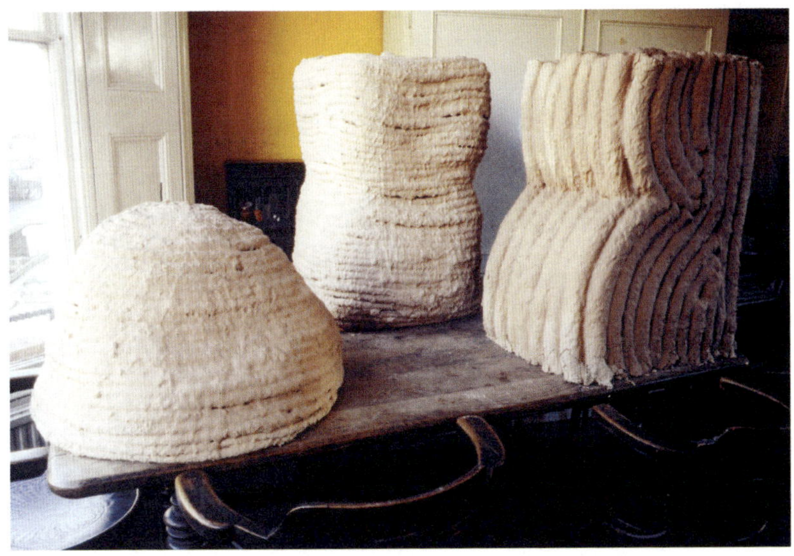

Objects for a table, 1994

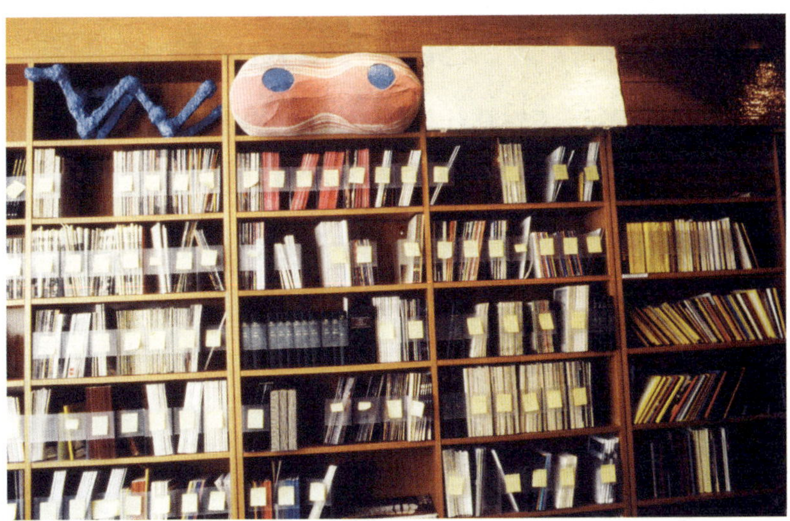

Objects for a library, 1995, at the Henry Moore Institute, Leeds

"What happens when you don't have exhibitions? Well, you get on with it, you just do it. You signed up for life, and maybe you don't know where to put things when you've done them. … So I began to make things that would be kind of uninvited guests to both domestic spaces and then spaces on the street."

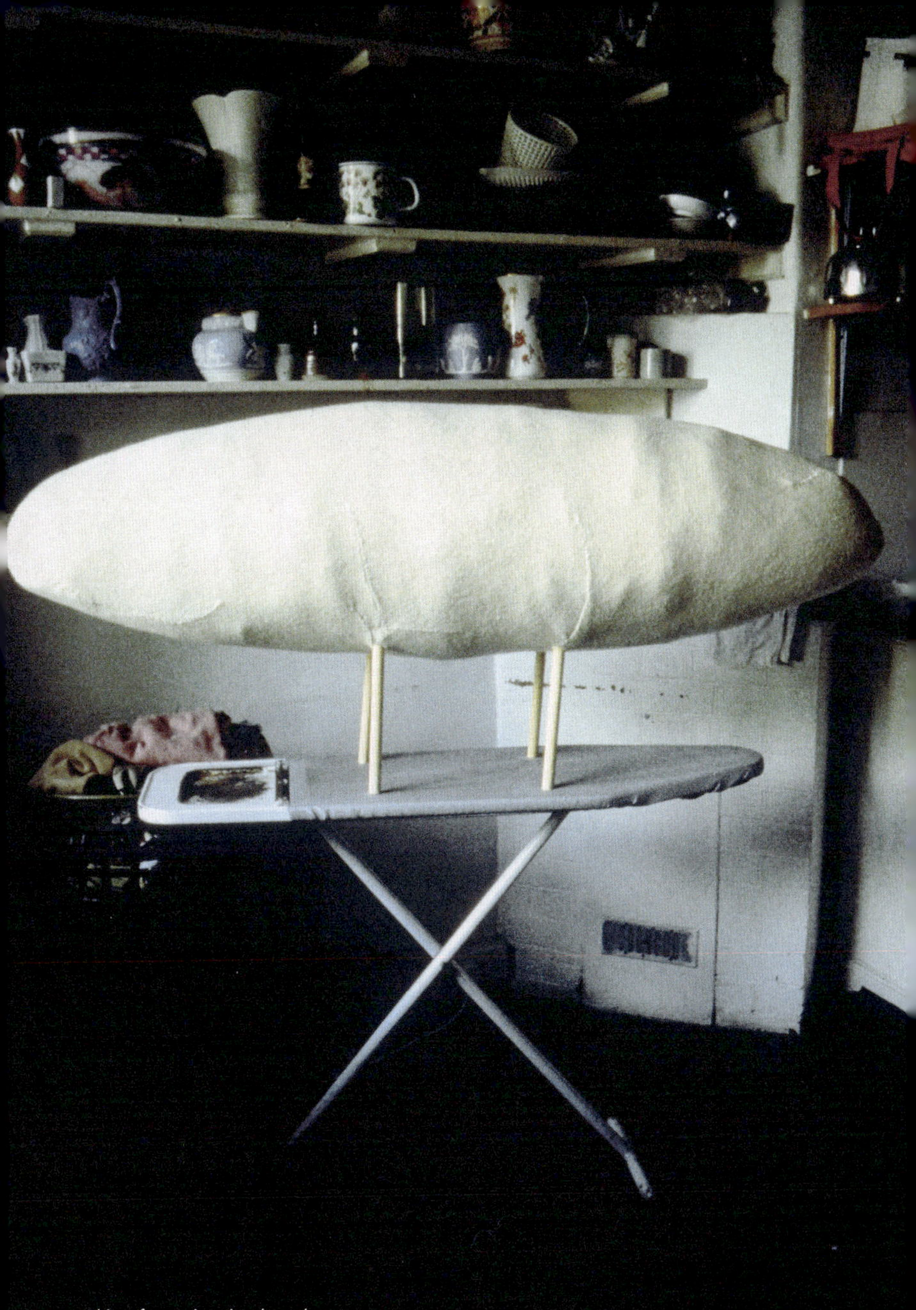
Object for an ironing board, 1994

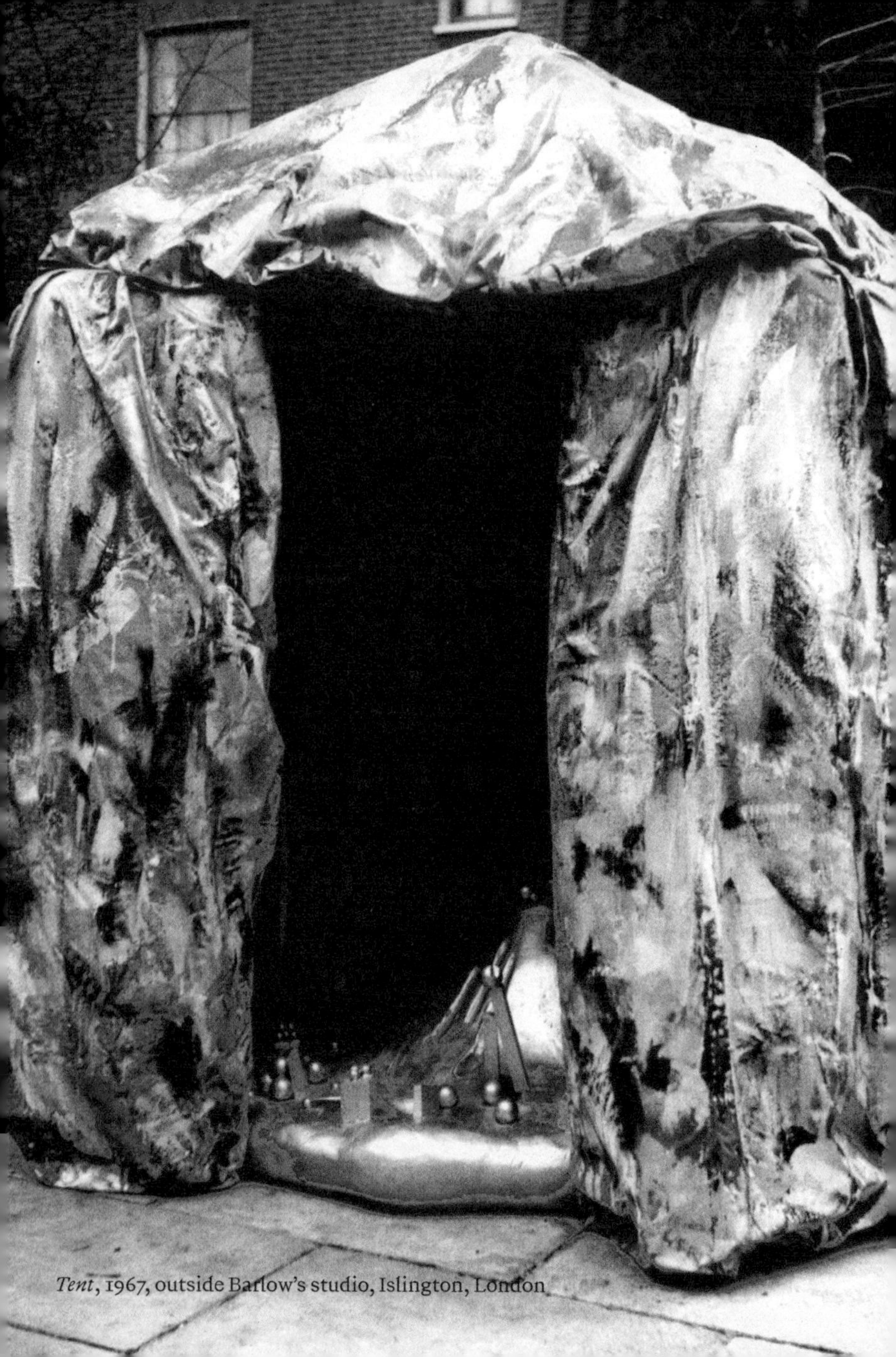

Tent, 1967, outside Barlow's studio, Islington, London

Beginnings

After briefly considering studying zoology, Barlow arrived at Chelsea School of Art in 1960, aged sixteen, keenly committed to pursuing painting. She had already experienced inspirational weekends at the Samuel Palmer School of Fine Art in Kent, where painting had been viewed as serious training for the complex adventure of looking at the world. At Chelsea, though, she was disappointed. She found the teaching dull, governed by incomprehensible rules and regulations, taught in an atmosphere both moralizing and misogynistic. After Anthony Hatwell, a sculptor teaching at the school, drew her attention to her emphasis on the tactile over the pictorial, she shifted her focus from painting to sculpture.

Similar rules held sway, though, in the teaching of sculpture at Chelsea. As a woman, Barlow was denied entry to the metalworking shop. Although she found the ritual of working in clay from the life model frustrating, she relished the material's tactility and malleability, its swift transformation from soft to hard. She also valued the time invested in mastering practical skills and sculptural techniques, and she found liberating role models and teachers in a number of tutors there, including the sculptors Robert Clatworthy and Elisabeth Frink. Most crucial for Barlow, however, was the arrival of George Fullard, a working-class war veteran from the north of England, who took over as head of sculpture in her final year. Fullard immediately abolished compulsory life-drawing classes and exhorted his students to look beyond nature and turn instead toward the gritty urban context of postwar London; he encouraged scavenging and bricolage as ways of working more appropriate to the modern world of the 1960s. Fullard drew students' attention to extraordinary works by European artists both pre- and postwar, and to recent creative endeavors in avant-garde film, slapstick, animation, literature, and theater—parallel yet interconnected realms available to open-minded artists like Barlow as sources of information and inspiration.

Barlow's student work from the Slade School of Fine Art in London, where she went on to study for three years starting in 1963, survives only in a few photographs. They show a practice already distinctive and original, unashamedly in dialogue with other artists yet animated by a keen awareness of new ways of looking at the world. Artists at the time were reluctant to speak of influences, but Barlow was open and articulate about the artists who moved her and stimulated her emerging practice, just as she was about those whose work she found dispiriting and forgettable. She was—at first—drawn to an earlier generation of mostly French postwar artists who had confronted the impossibility of representing the human figure in conventional terms, so wounded and scared was humanity in the aftermath of war. The "ugly sculptures" she admired included Jean Fautrier's scarified faces (p. 58), Alberto Giacometti's febrile and etiolated standing figures, and Germaine Richier's hybrids of man and beast (p. 58). Fascinated by these powerful, visceral works, Barlow could find little of interest in the New Generation sculpture spearheaded by Anthony Caro that was in the mid-1960s emanating from London's Saint Martin's School of Art and making waves internationally. Barlow looked elsewhere and across history, from the ancient stelae of Mesopotamia to the prewar avant-garde. She was strongly drawn to artists such as Salvador Dalí, Marcel Duchamp (p. 58), and Pablo Picasso (p. 51), who often worked in contrary directions to the mainstream,

                    Life and Work

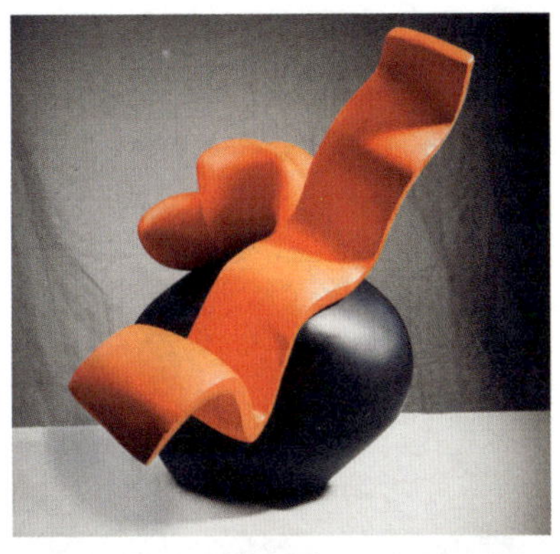

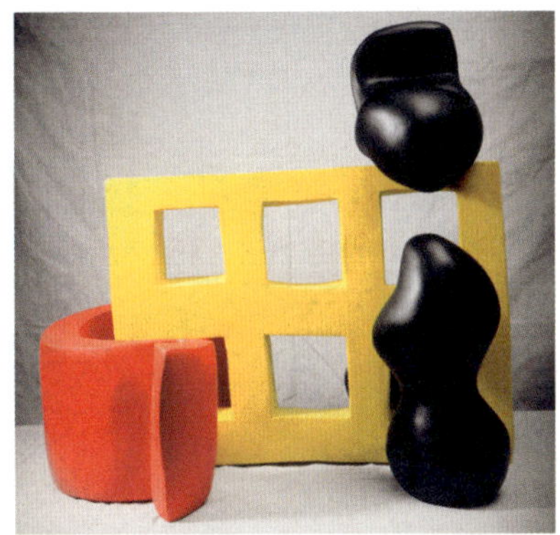

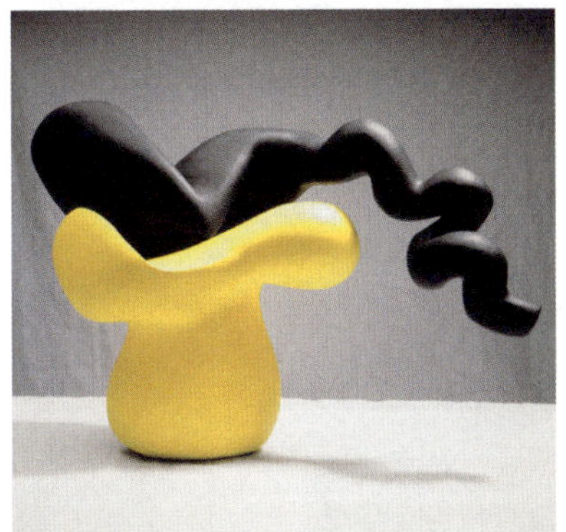

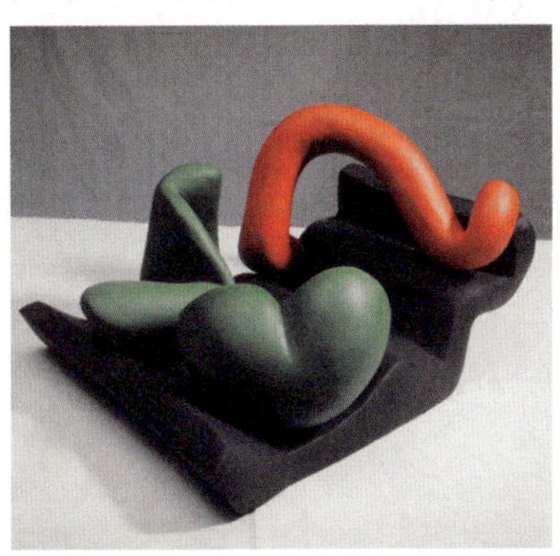

Works from *Untitled (Series of 10)*, 1965

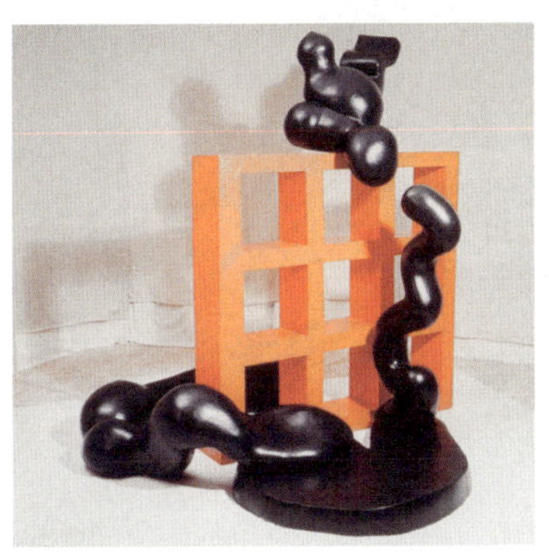

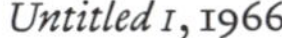

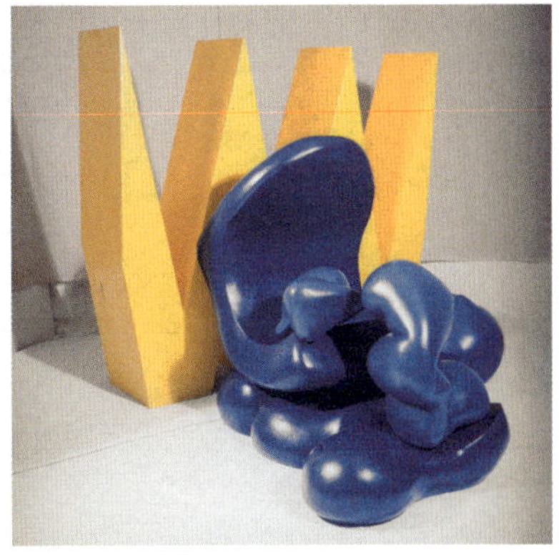

Untitled 1, 1966

Untitled 2, 1966

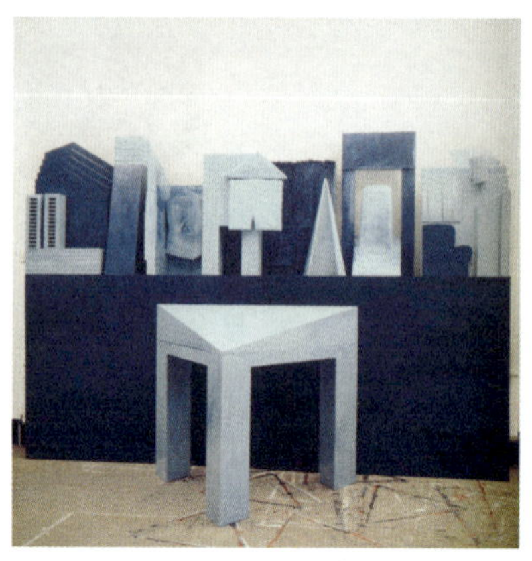

View, 1971

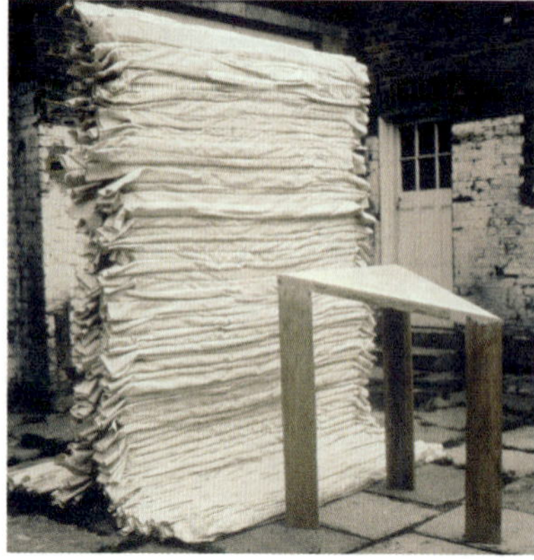

Untitled Table, ca. 1976

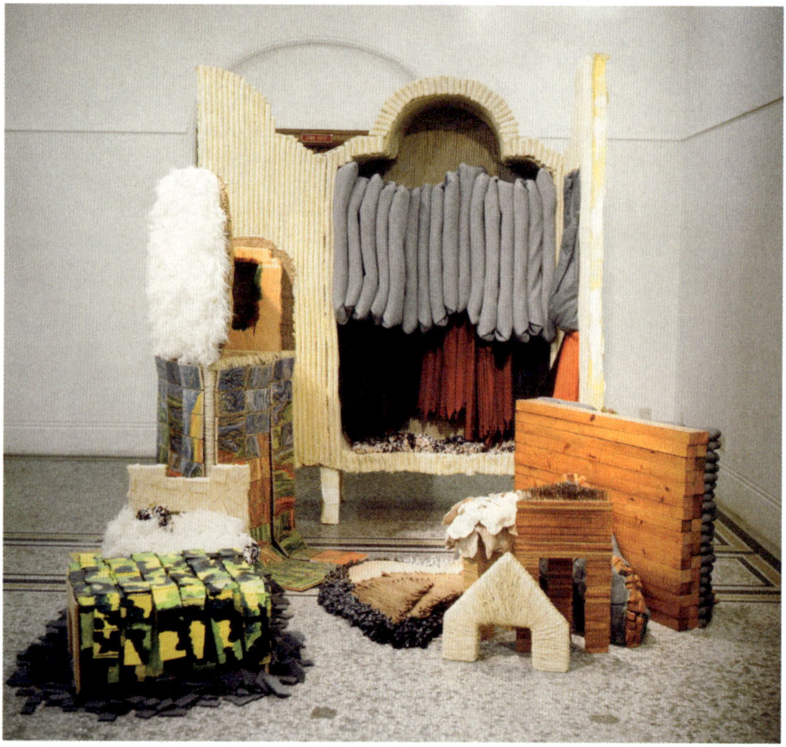

Wardrobe, 1971, at Camden Arts Centre, London

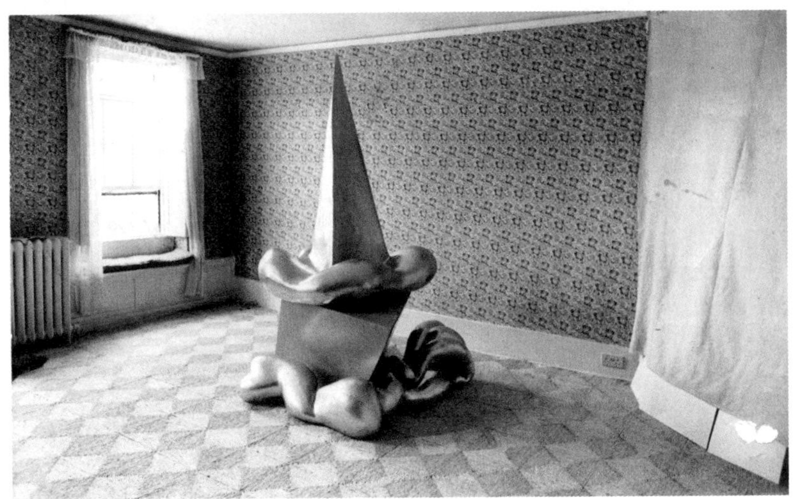

untitled, 1966

always breaking new ground. The biomorphic vocabulary
Barlow used in her early work was clearly a response to
artists like Jean (Hans) Arp (p. 54), and to Joan Miró's
unstable and sensuous work of the 1930s, but Barlow had
a Dalí-esque propensity to juxtapose the biomorphic with
irreconcilable forms, including geometric structures with
sharp angles and regular dimensions.

The hugely influential diagram (p. 50) drawn in 1936 by
Alfred H. Barr Jr., the founding director of the Museum of
Modern Art in New York, to delineate the evolving genealogy
of modern art, shows two distinct trajectories toward the
present, one through Cubism, de Stijl, and Constructivism,
the other through Expressionism, Dada, and Surrealism.
Both lines of inheritance arrived simultaneously at
parallel yet antithetical end points: geometric abstraction
and nongeometric abstraction. By the time Barlow left
the Slade in 1966, this stark divide had revealed itself

once again, with the near simultaneous emergence of
Minimalism in the work of artists such as Donald Judd and
Tony Smith, and what, misleadingly, became known as
post-Minimalism, typified by artists like Eva Hesse (p. 52)
and Louise Bourgeois (p. 56). The latter adopted almost
diametrically opposed positions to the former, in relation
not only to geometry but also to materials and processes.
Barlow refused to see these two dominant tendencies
as at odds with one another and continued to be drawn
both ways, to the hard geometries of architecture and
domestic furniture, for example, as well as to soft fabric
and collapsing structures. Antagonistic forces, of stability
and flux, reverberate through her subsequent work, an
ongoing orchestration of confrontation between paired
and opposite elements.

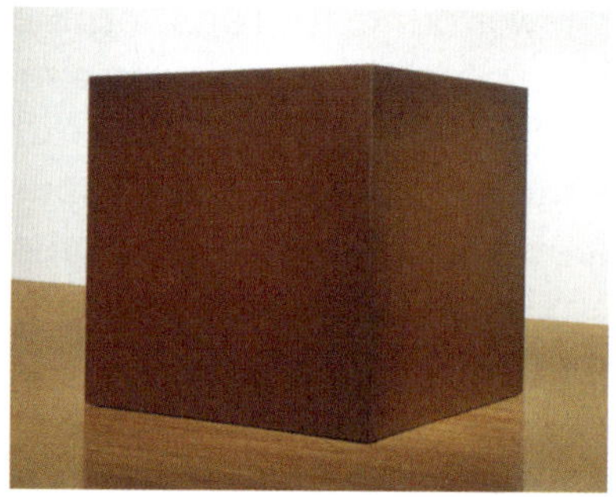

Tony Smith, *Die*, 1962

For twenty years after graduating in 1966, Barlow
worked in this vein with energy and dedication, yet without
the encouragement of audiences, critics, or gallerists.
She taught and participated very occasionally in group
exhibitions. Her isolation, her lack of affiliation with any
group or tendency, might have been lonely; it also allowed
Barlow to respond freely to whatever new ideas came her

Life and Work

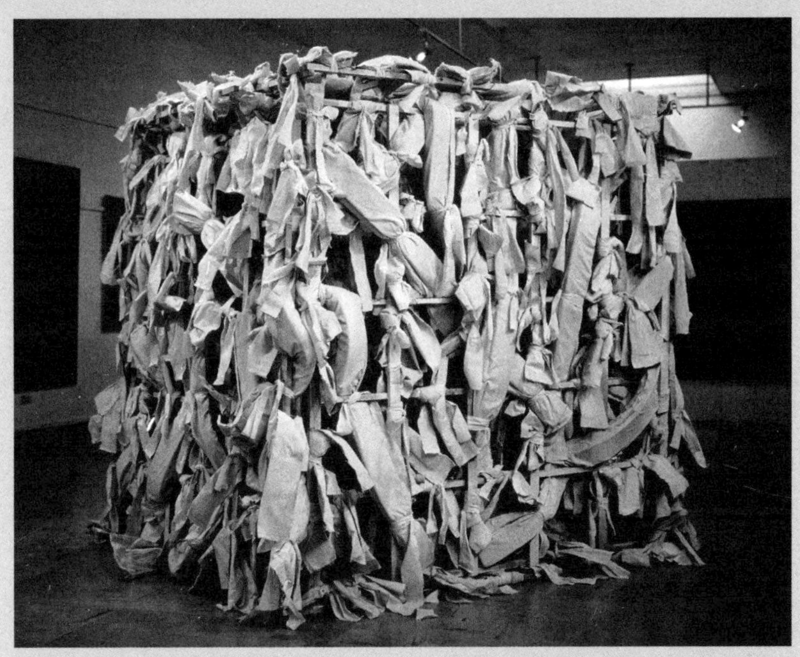

Shedmesh (1975)

Widely regarded as a sign of Barlow's "coming of age," *Shedmesh* was a statement of intent, signifying the artist's staunch independence from the established legacies of US Minimal artists and the so-called New Generation sculptors in the UK. Deliberately working with the form of the cube—the Minimalist archetype—Barlow built hers not from steel but from repurposed stretchers, tied together with strips of torn canvas and upholstery foam, pointedly countering Minimalism's preference for industrial fabrication and pristine finishes. Incorporating materials associated with painting and forms associated with sculpture, *Shedmesh* disregarded modernism's insistence on the specificity—and exclusiveness—of each medium and the associated tenet of "truth to materials."

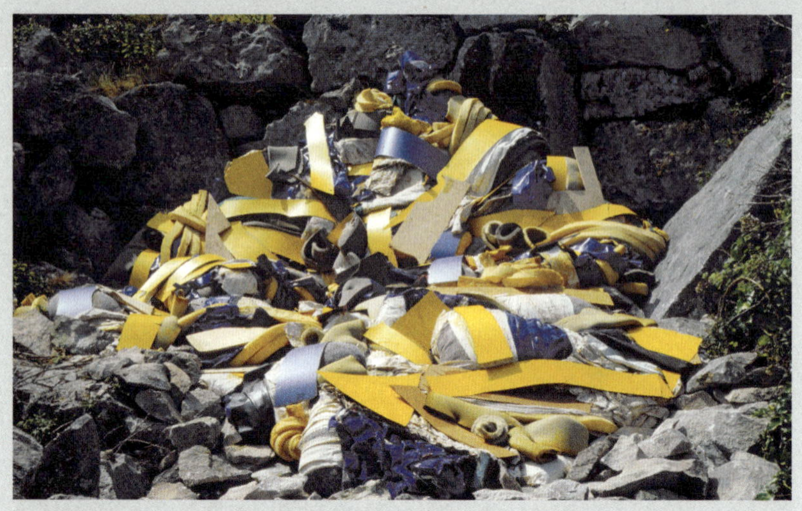

Fill (1983)

In 1983 the sculptor Phillip King invited artists to make work for the disused Tout Quarry in Portland, Dorset, as part of the site's transformation into a sculpture park. While several artists responded by working with the history and materiality of the site itself, Barlow chose to weave together discarded home furnishings and building materials, also incorporating studio debris. Her chosen location was a deep cavity left over from the extraction of stone, where she allowed her brilliantly colored, jarring, and sprawling woven fabric to fall into place. Barlow's specific references were not to the traditions of quarrying or the uses of limestone but to the environmental degradation of the site, littered as it was with discarded waste materials and marked by what she called the "natural graffiti" of lichen and moss. With its allusions to landfill, Barlow's work did not meet the expectations of the commissioning body and she was asked to remove it shortly after the opening.

way, from nearby or afar. Works such as *Shedmesh* (1975) are fully informed and consciously in critical conversation with American and European innovators.

As Barlow went on to make her first works in landscape settings, with pieces like *Fill* (1983), she was positioning herself at a distance from British artists like Hamish Fulton and Richard Long who were fast establishing international recognition by "taking to the hills" via works centered on the activity of walking. Barlow's own interventions in the British countryside, often using large quantities of cheap, synthetic waste materials, were encouraged by the epic endeavors of emerging US land artists such as Robert Smithson, as well as by the new generation of European artists including Michelangelo Pistoletto, of the emergent Italian Arte Povera group, who by the late 1960s were effectively promoting more open-ended and experimental practices, often working with non-art, or "poor," materials.

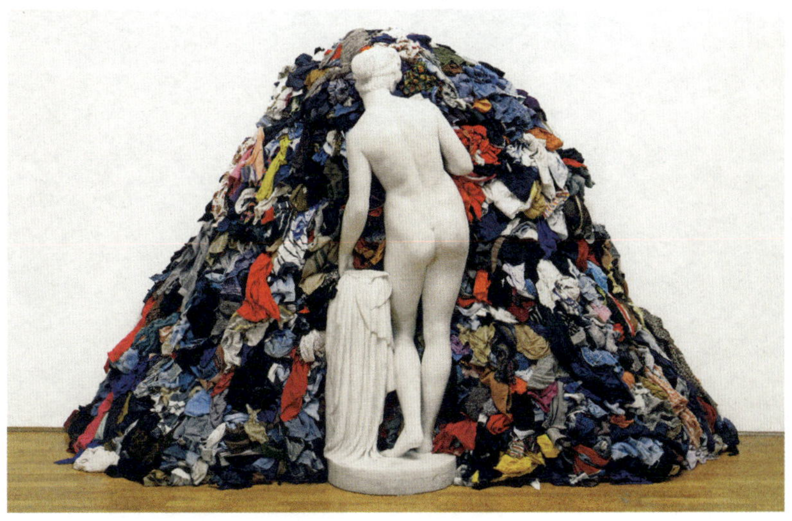

Michelangelo Pistoletto, *Venus of the Rags*, 1967/1974

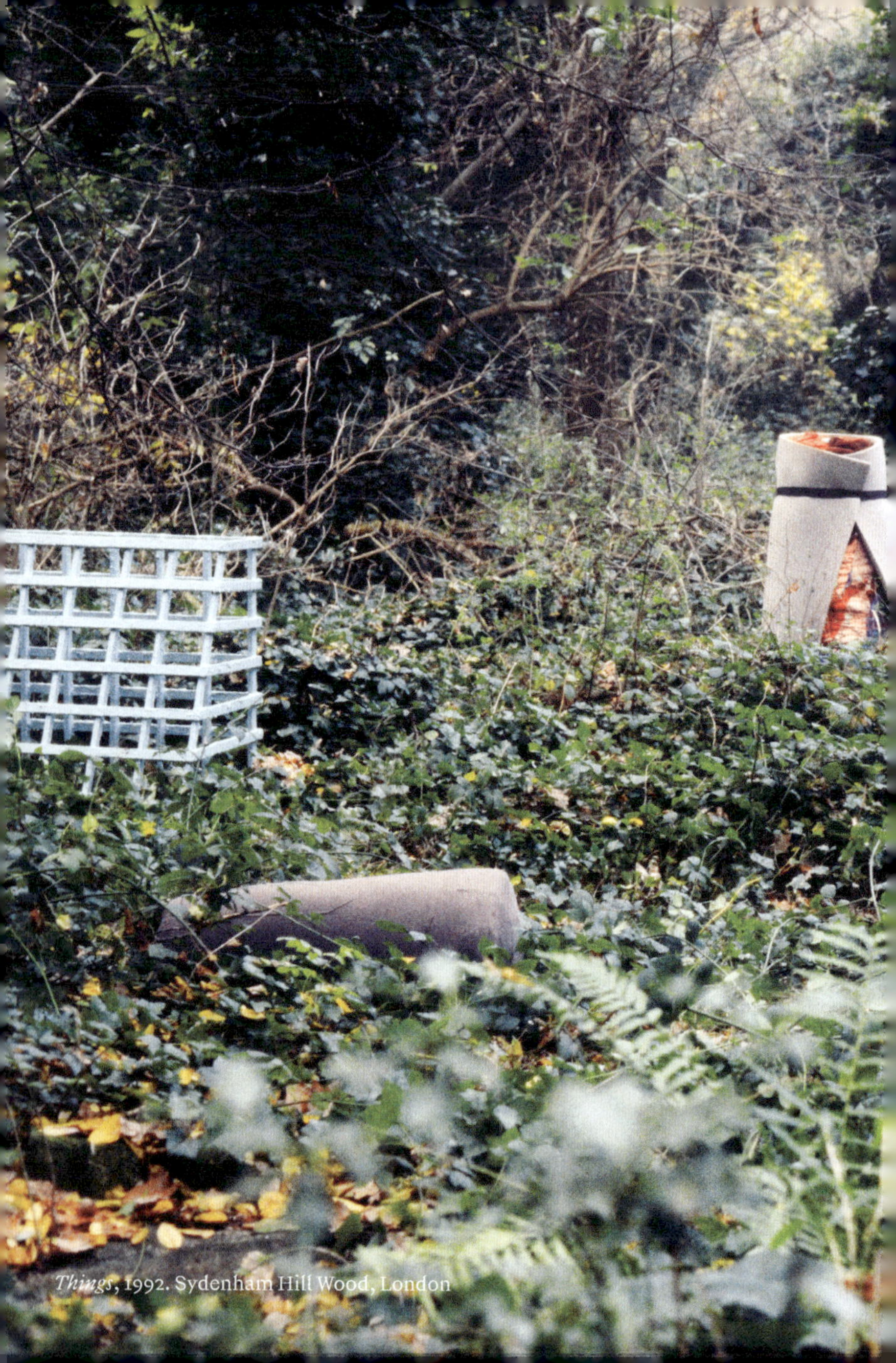

Things, 1992. Sydenham Hill Wood, London

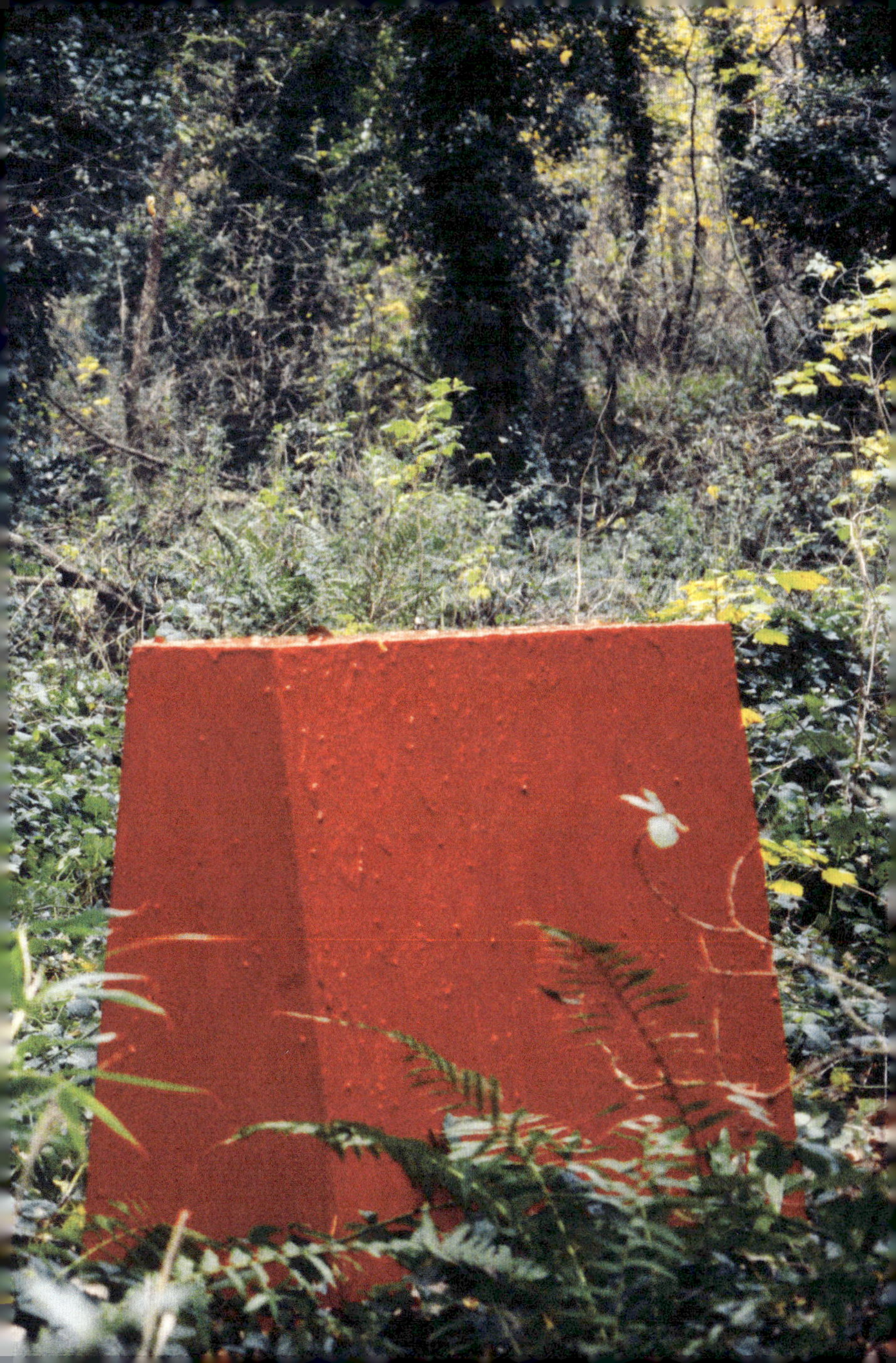

Hearsay, Rumours, Bedsit Dreamers, and Art Begins Today

From a paper Barlow wrote in 2002, looking back
at the 1965 sculpture exhibition *The New Generation*

The increasingly tedious debates about sculpture [in the
mid-1960s]: to plinth or not to plinth, the value of the
laborious grind of making, truth to materials, etc., etc.,
paled into more art-school academicism as new rumours
and hearsay of what was going on elsewhere began to filter
through. And what was it that was being talked about and
rumoured? Stories of works in deserts and excavations in
derelict warehouses employing a different kind of labour:
straight manual labour as seen on the street and building
site, diggers and excavators were being appropriated to
make sculpture, whilst at the opposite end of the scale,
resin and a new material, latex, were being used like
paint, not as a substitute for bronze, but as stuff in its own
right, to be dunked into, painted on cloth to make it rigid,
moulded off rigid forms to make them soft, poured, spilt,
and thrown. Weight, mass, scale, and size were all being
usurped by gesture, touch, and the here and now. And
artists were taking to the streets, like so many others at that
time, and foregoing the studio; anywhere and everywhere
was a site, and anything and everything could be made
into art. Excitement and imagination had arrived. By 1968,
the New Generation exhibitions were dead history.

… As the hearsay and rumours increased from the US and
Europe, the more academic and institutionalised the British
art scene seemed to become. The hearsay and rumours
offered an entirely different experience, an experience
rooted in the forbidden and despised notion of theatricality.

The Artist's Voice

No more the need for permanency, weightiness, handicraft, the learnt, and to be taught restraints of what was and what was not sculpture. Instead, in with impermanency, temporariness, dematerialisation, the fugitive, the ephemeral, the here and now. Out with the welding shop and the learnable techniques and in with experimentation with anything and everything: materials and physicality were opened up for anything, everything, everywhere. And the artist him or herself could be anyone, and as such they could be subject and object of the work. …

So for me the legacy of the 1965 exhibition was not in the show itself but in what it spawned as an opposition to it. Sculpture continued to be made in studios but there was a burgeoning feminising of the processes, and a different take on labour intensivity was beginning to emerge. The studio could look beyond itself for inspiration. The kitchen, the dressmaker's, the garage, agriculture, roadworks, building sites, and, of course, the bedsit, the home of most art students, could all provide processes to be plundered and appropriated as means to an end. Speculation was the game and time was of the essence. … Why devote hours to labour-intensive activities when results could be produced immediately, as was beginning to be seen through the work of Hesse and Bourgeois. Why go to the macho means of production when twiddling your thumbs and putting things together from your immediate environment was all you could afford to do. What about staring at the bedsit ceiling and dreaming up the wild, the wonderful, and the way beyond from the patterns on the ceiling and making it become reality by any means possible? The smoothed-out surfaces of the fibreglass and resin aficionados were becoming clichéd, let alone the fact that resin was carcinogenic, and therefore an unsuitable

material to spend too much time with. All the more reason
for speedy, direct application; all the more reason for hit-
and-run techniques.

Theatricality and time became absorbed into all aspects
of sculpture. … Again, it was and is the camera in all
its guises which provided the evidence, and it is only
evidence, of such work. Therefore, I believe, sculpture as
a fundamentalist activity which could only tell the truth,
the whole truth, and nothing but the truth became tedious
and irrelevant. Released from its history of permanency
and absolute materiality, sculpture could fragment space,
could be cinematic in its relationship to how to occupy
space, and could fib and lie itself into its own reality.
Objects could connect and interrelate over spaces that
they would charge with atmospheric and moody resonances,
and time had to be taken to experience the whole encounter:
objects, space, time.

And so hearsay, rumours, bedsit dreams, and "art-begins-
today" attitudes came to stay and have stayed. Sculpture,
for myself, still resides in the experience of unreality:
the walking around of things that have no use in the world
and which defy absolute categorisation and definition. …

… The future of sculpture always lies in the unexpected.
Therefore, this most awkward, recalcitrant, and
unmanageable of art forms can be relied upon to make
believable the imagination. Imagination has to be what is
inherently new and surprising, and essential to sculpture,
its past, its present, and its future.

 The Artist's Voice

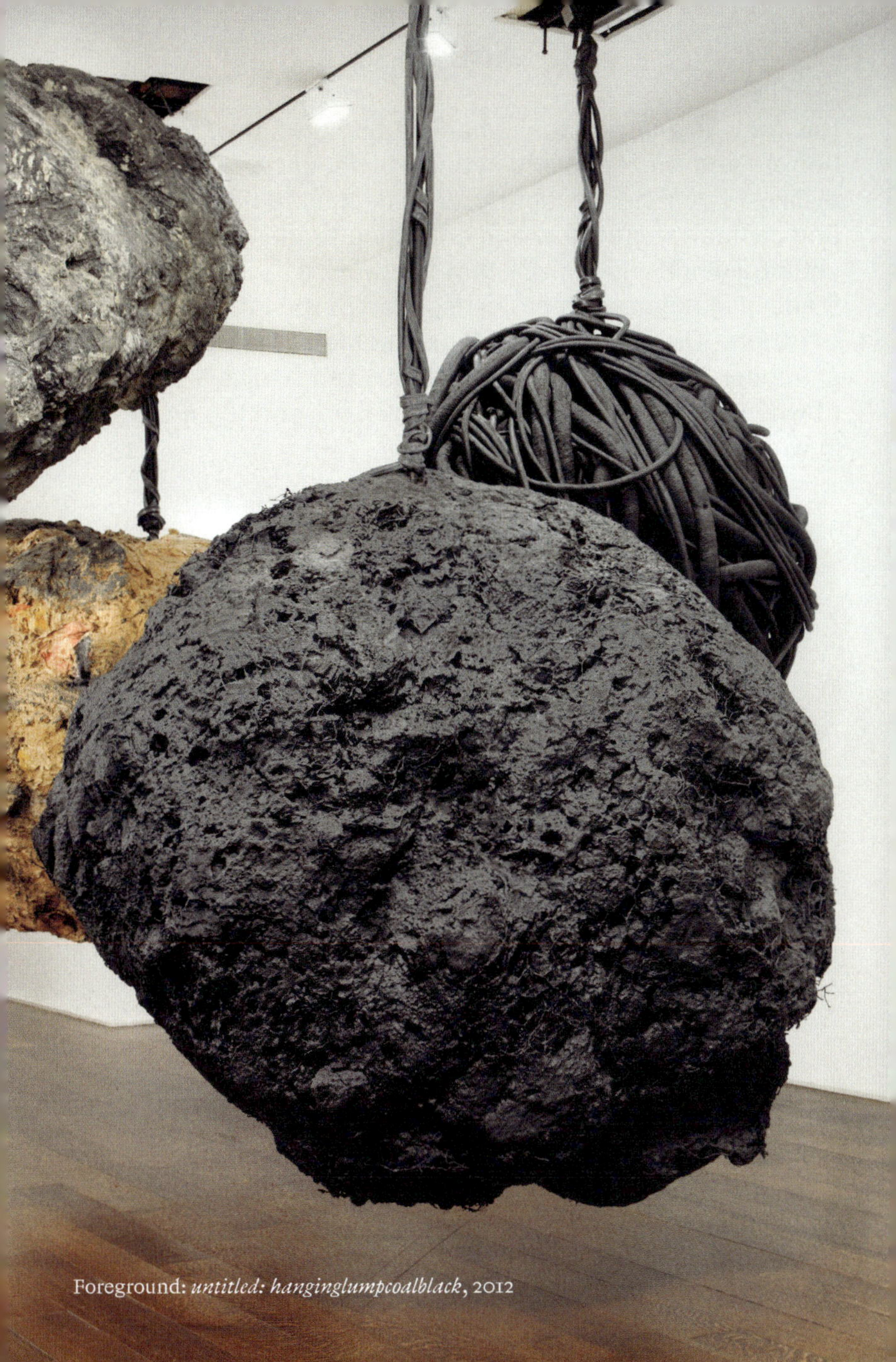

Foreground: *untitled: hanginglumpcoalblack*, 2012

Barlow was an avid "consumer" of artworks throughout her life and was open and articulate about her likes and dislikes. From her student years she maintained a keen and critical eye for new and emerging tendencies in sculpture and recognized that her work was inescapably made in dialogue with or in response to the influence of others. On the following pages, some key works by a number of these artists are illustrated to give a sense of where Barlow's own work comes from and the context in which she understood it.

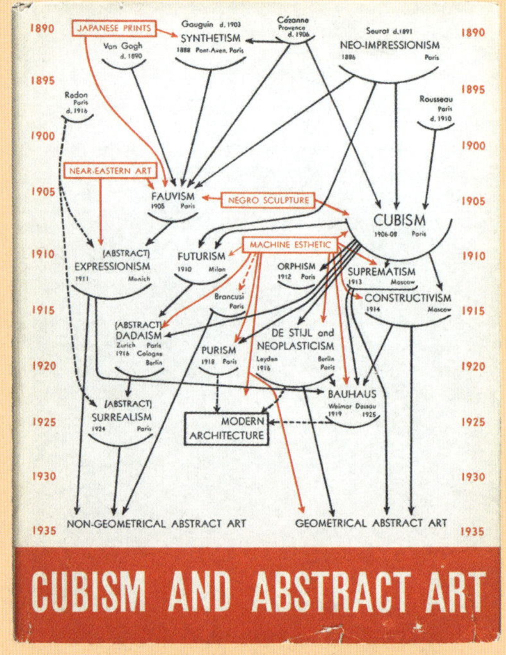

Cover of the catalogue for the 1936 exhibition
Cubism and Abstract Art at the Museum of Modern
Art, New York, featuring a diagram by the
institution's director, Alfred H. Barr Jr.

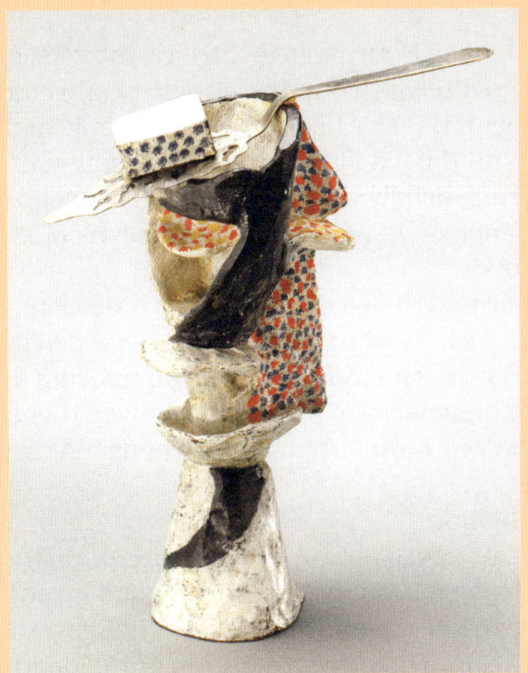

Pablo Picasso, *Glass of Absinthe*, 1914

Pablo Picasso

Barlow considered Picasso, Marcel Duchamp, and Piet Mondrian to be artists whose work shaped the principal narratives of modern art. It was Picasso's work in collage, his assemblage works composed of discarded remnants of materials in his studio or found on the streets, that stimulated her own move away from modeling in clay and plaster and her incorporation of waste materials. Barlow was also influenced by the way Picasso combined painting with sculpture. His *Glass of Absinthe* (1914) was, for Barlow, an especially important work, and she relished its "deceitful" combination of real shadows alongside painted shadows.

Eva Hesse

Alongside Louise Bourgeois (p. 56), Hesse offered Barlow
a compelling alternative to the austerity and reductionism
of Minimalism. Hesse's use of modern tactile and malleable
materials and the fragility of her anti-monumental works
resonated powerfully with Barlow, who recognized that
the experience of viewing a work by Hesse could not be
put into words.

She described Hesse's *Contingent* (1969) as
"a wonderful work" whose parts, half dipped in latex
and half in resin, she found "utterly compelling and
completely mesmerising in how they hover there in
space." She was captivated by their apparent simplicity.

Eduardo Chillida

In Barlow's words: "Chillida's *Modulation of Space I* [1963]
is a hybrid fusing both the readymade and invented form.
The solid iron bars from which it is forged are themselves
readymades. … The transformation of the dead weight
of the bars into the interlocking series of raised loops …
has to be achieved so quickly in the forging that a moment
in time is forever captured within the folds and coils of
the sculpture. Similarly, the heat is somehow retained.
It is as if it is still darkly smouldering, emanating an
inherent sense of danger. …

"Gravity, as well as time, heat, and forged iron, are its
materials. The effortless loops, arching upwards as well
as folding on top of each other, defy their own weight.
The visceral piling-up of these apparently weightless
curves begins to beg questions. How did Chillida know
when to stop wrestling with the hot iron, to not add
another curve or angle? When was enough enough?"

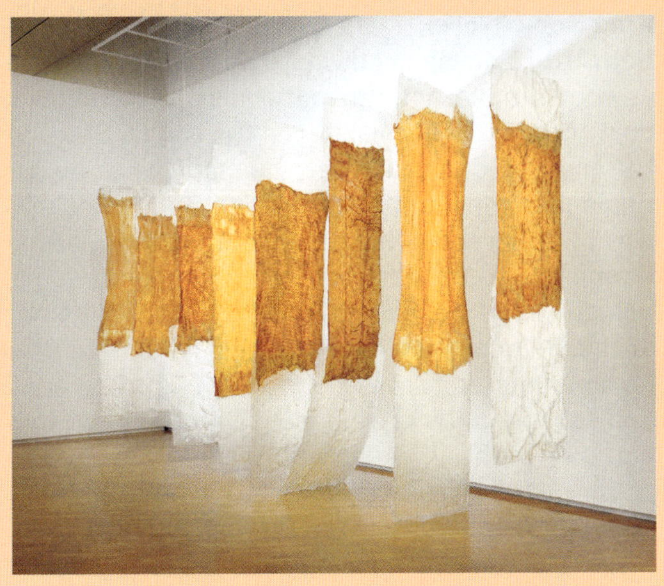

Eva Hesse, *Contingent*, 1969

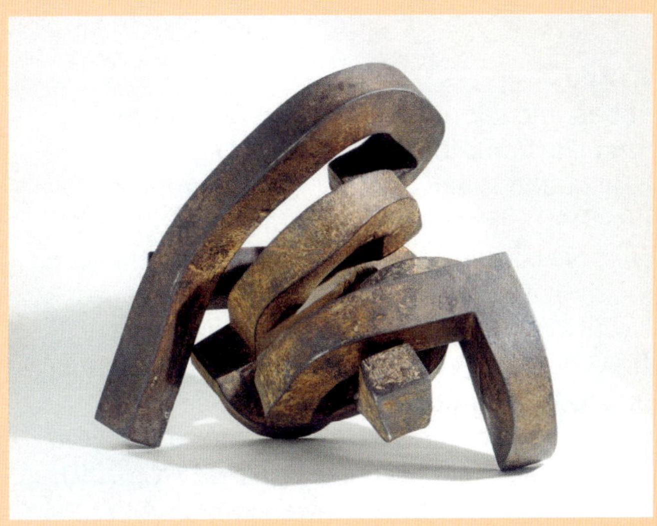

Eduardo Chillida, *Modulation of Space I*, 1963

Kurt Schwitters

Schwitters considered waste as having the same value
as conventional artistic materials and for many years
he worked, like Barlow, under the radar. She admired
the small object/sculptures he made when he came to
England in the late 1940s, putting things—including plastic,
wire, feathers, bus tickets, bits of newspapers, and candy
wrappers—together in inventive ways and seeing what
transpired. It was, however, Schwitters's lifelong project
of the *Merzbau*—the ever-evolving room-size environments
he constructed first in Hannover from 1923 onward,
and subsequently in exile from Nazi Germany in Norway
and then in the UK—that was an enduring reference
point for Barlow's later installations. She recognized
Schwitters, alongside Luis Buñuel, Salvador Dalí, and
Meret Oppenheim, as one of the great artists of the
twentieth century, an artist who has not been celebrated
sufficiently within the canon, but whose relevance and
importance continue to be felt.

Jean (Hans) Arp

Barlow first became acquainted with Arp's work as
a student, and she continued to look at and respond
to his work throughout her career. A work such as
Pagoda Fruit (1949)—in the collection of the Tate, which
Barlow regularly visited—provided her with a continuous
reference point in its visceral and spontaneous sense
of formal invention. Arp was a pioneer of biomorphic
form, and his influence is visibly present in the sensuous
and erotic sculptural language present in Barlow's
earliest recorded sculpture. Arp's influence reasserted
itself many years later, spectacularly, in *PRANK* (p. 20),
whose seven comedic characters owe much to Arp's
elastic formal inventory.

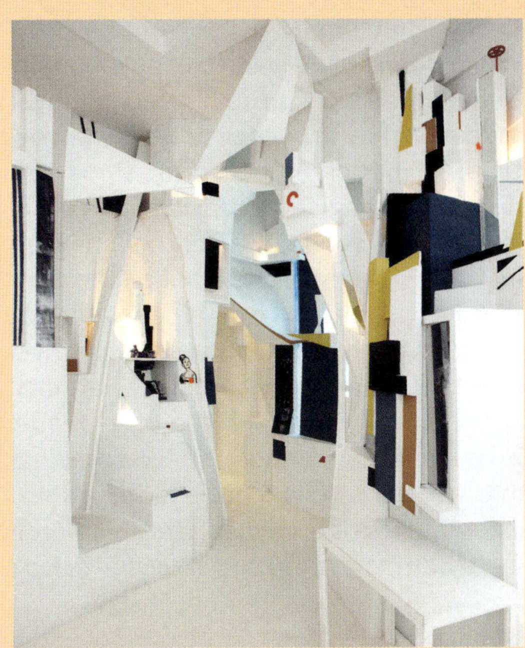

Kurt Schwitters, *Merzbau*, 1933, reconstruction in the Sprengel Museum Hannover, 1980–83

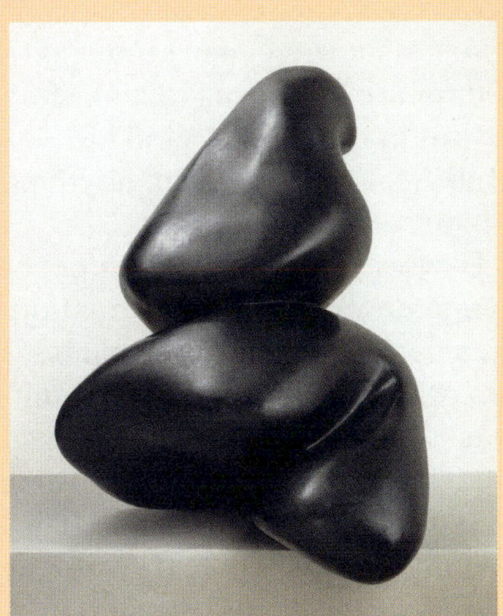

Jean (Hans) Arp, *Pagoda Fruit*, 1949

Louise Bourgeois

While not interested in the psychoanalytic side of
Bourgeois's work or in her biography, Barlow was
fascinated by the elder artist's approach to and
transformation of materials. One work she was repeatedly
drawn to was *Avenza Revisited II* (1968–69), which,
in Barlow's words, "is a kind of spewing up, a welling-over
of stuff. … It is fearless about the non-beautiful but it does
give beauty to the monstrous, endowing the fat, full, and
overflowing forms with sensuality. *Avenza Revisited II* shows
how her subjectivity and her relationship with herself can
be manifested through the most traditional of sculptural
forms and techniques. 'I have complete confidence
in the inner self; the outer one is of no concern to me.'
This sculpture is raw and hot. … *Avenza Revisited II* is wild
in its confrontation and fearless in its nameless identity."

George Fullard

Fullard's work and his outlook were important to Barlow.
Thinking back to when he became head of sculpture
at Chelsea School of Art in her last year studying there,
Barlow recalled his admonition that "all talking should
take place in the pub, not in the studio," and his claim
that artists "should talk a lot because then anything
that can't be talked about will get made."

Thanks to Fullard, Barlow wrote, "worn-out processes
were revitalised through new descriptions: casting was
magical because, like a conjuring trick, an object is made
to disappear and then reappear in a completely different
material; … metal was like paper and could be treated
like fabric for dressmaking; and clay was mud. On and on
it went, and the maxim of Picasso, 'Before you use a nail,
you must reinvent it,' became the motto by which we all
began to exist."

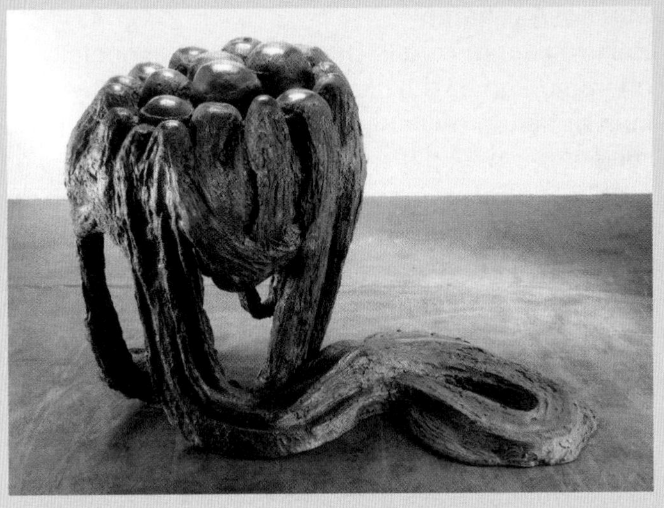

Louise Bourgeois, *Avenza Revisited II*, 1968–69

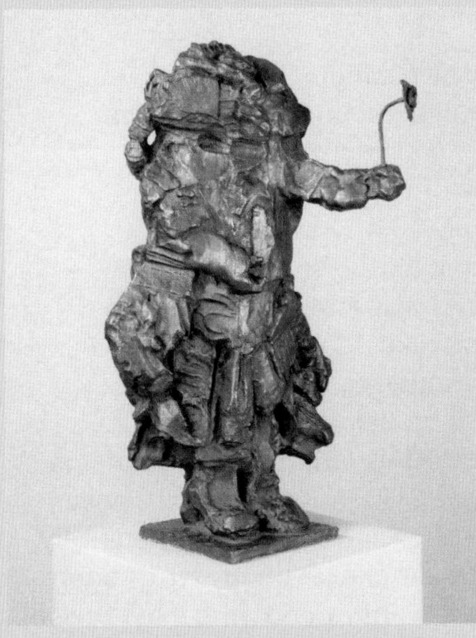

George Fullard, *Infant with Flower*, 1958–60

Marcel Duchamp

Barlow recognized in Duchamp, and especially in his championing of the readymade, a major threat to the kind of hands-on sculptural processes through which she forged her own personal artistic voice, but his provocative stance was also important in encouraging the self-reflection and rigor she brought to her own work.

She exclaimed in 2019, with a slide of work shown behind her: "Marcel Duchamp, my enemy! He is an extraordinary artist. There's no doubt about it. … This is a remarkable work, a very sexually charged work called *Why Not Sneeze Rose Sélavy?* [1921/1964]. It's filled with these marble cubes that look just like sugar cubes and it has this cuttlefish bone in it, and a thermometer. It's just got this sense of waiting. And the sneeze as [an] idea of sexual thrill is obviously something that I think Duchamp played around with a lot."

Jean Fautrier and Germaine Richier

Barlow retained a high regard for European postwar sculpture from her days as a student, referring—affectionately—to the work of Fautrier and Richier, among others, as "ugly sculpture." As she recalled: "I took against British art, violently, seeing it as moral and corrective, [and] I was looking very much at European art. And artists like Jean Fautrier and Germaine Richier, I've continued to love the whole time, because they seem to be doing something with materials that gave the materials a different kind of voice. They weren't just rooted in skill and craft. There were things going on in the surface that were absolutely alive. Richier always said about clay, 'You mustn't touch it too much. It knows what it wants to do. It is a hysterical medium.' I love that idea."

Influences

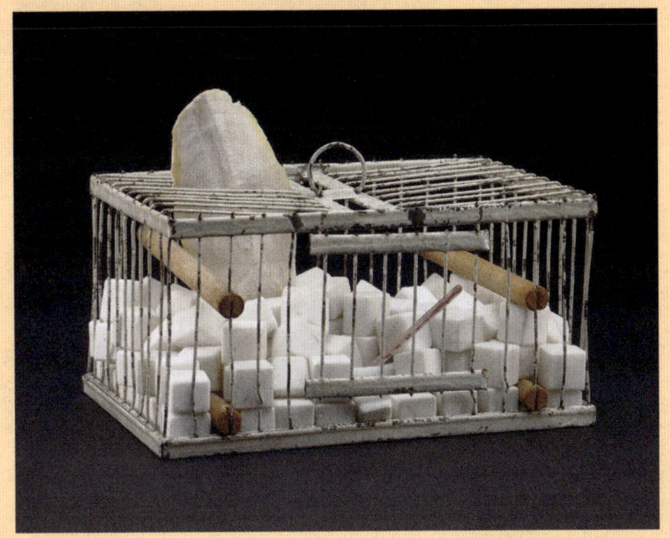

Marcel Duchamp, *Why Not Sneeze Rose Sélavy?*, 1921/1964

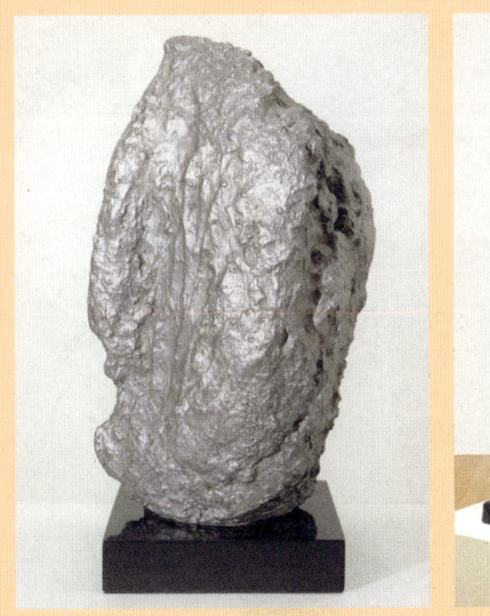

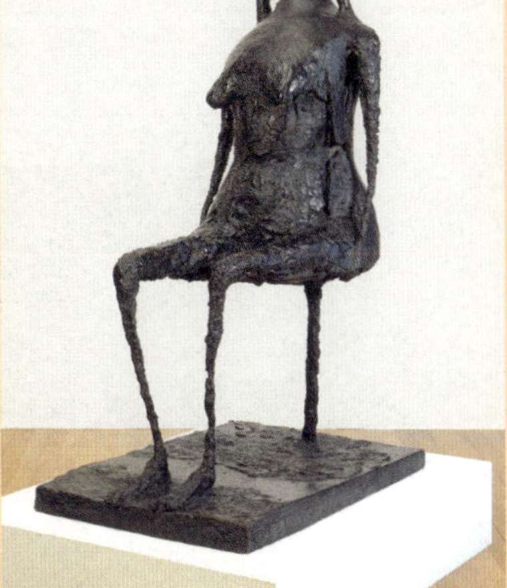

Jean Fautrier, *Head of a Hostage*, 1943–44   Germaine Richier, *Water*, 1953–54

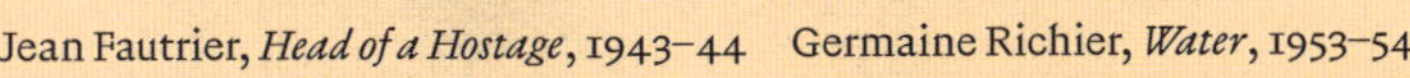

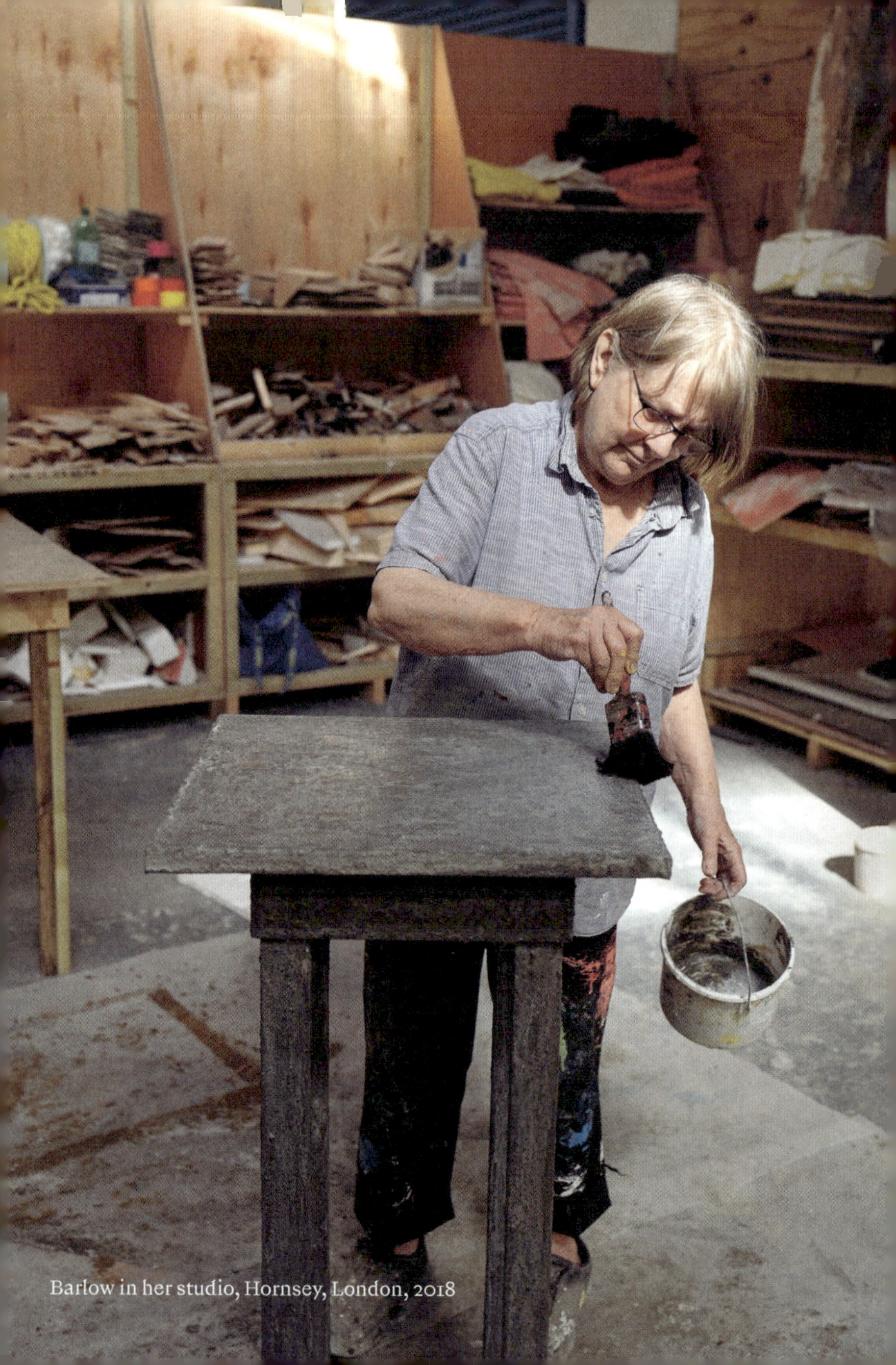

Barlow in her studio, Hornsey, London, 2018

Sculpture

Barlow liked nothing more than to head downstairs to her basement studio, pick up a handful of stuff—discarded elements of something made earlier, most likely—and start, without a particular plan in mind, to "feel" her way into a work; she found a kind of "anarchic pleasure" in the tactile process itself, and in negotiating the shifting boundaries between what felt "right" and "wrong" in the emerging form. When her children were very young she necessarily and largely confined her sculpting activities to the nighttime hours. Among the projects she began during this time is the series *Touchpieces*, which is made up of objects created in the dark by touch alone (p. 62). Occasionally she would find time to explore a single material—such as a roll of sticky tape, which she wrapped repeatedly around her forearm—to generate a form. Working with many materials or just one, without anticipating an outcome, involved continuous interaction between hand, brain, and material. Barlow used the term *approximate* to refer to the moment, for her, when a work was sufficiently right (rather than conclusively perfect) to warrant—in fact to necessitate—moving on to the next. Her entire career progressed in a similar manner, as an unfolding, circular economy of action and response.

By the 1980s Barlow was sourcing her materials from the vast quantities of light-industrial and domestic waste so readily available in the days before recycling became customary. An inventory drawn from works of that decade would include the following items: plastic sheets, trash bags, rags, foam rubber, polystyrene, Formica, and Sellotape. These are for the most part cheap, synthetic, flexible, utilitarian materials so ubiquitous and banal as to be practically overlooked, with almost no distinguishing

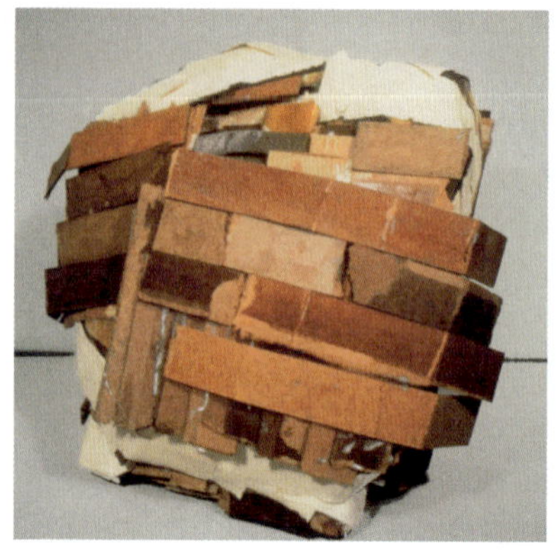

Touchpiece, 1982–83

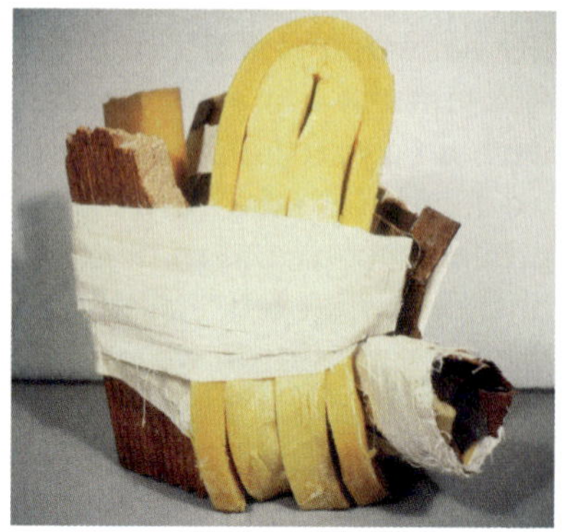

Touchpiece, 1982–83

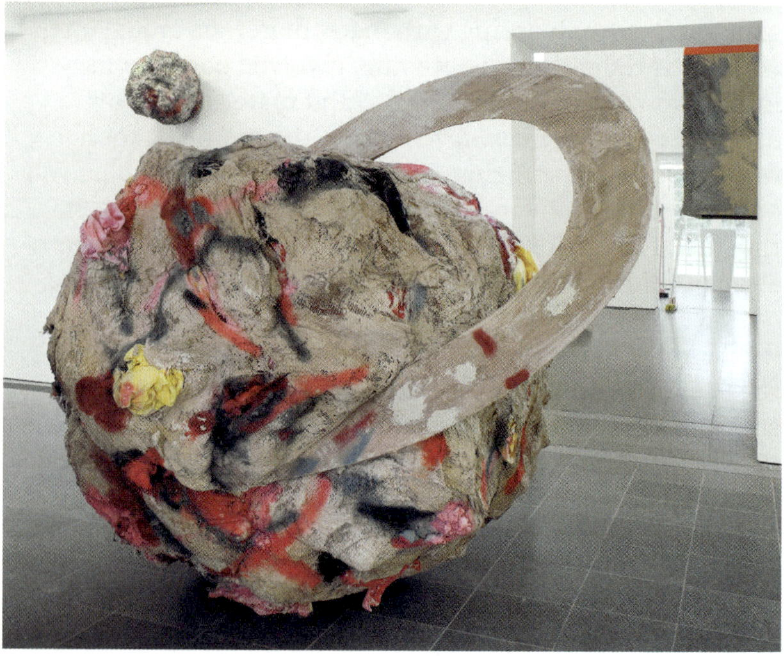

One of the two parts of *untitled: double act*, 2010, at the Serpentine Gallery, London

characteristics of their own beyond their functional roles in relation to objects, including people. They are materials to tie up or bind, wrap around, drape over or to stuff. To Barlow they were "recalcitrant" materials that presented the sculptor with interesting problems. Because there is no obvious or established way of working with them, they lend themselves to experimentation, contingency, and spontaneity: all key characteristics of Barlow's artistic procedure.

Many of Barlow's favorite materials are formless in themselves, without structural integrity or load-bearing capacity, with a tendency to slump, sag, slip, or spill when left to their own devices. And yet they can be given form when manipulated in certain ways, rolled up, folded, twisted, or brought into contact with contrasting structural elements such as factory-milled plywood or machine-cut timber, materials that she favored as neutral structural devices, free of historical weight or overt symbolic resonance.

Interaction between material and process is central to the business of art. Barlow's art-school training had furnished her with an arsenal of technical knowledge and an ample respect for skill, and she had gained, via George Fullard, a fondness for Picasso's maxim "Before you use a nail, you must reinvent it." Playing fast and loose with categories of style and medium, and parodying the aesthetic tautology of "truth to materials," Barlow subjected materials to handmade, repetitive gestures, relishing marks left by the hand in the finished objects and installations. She evidently enjoyed reflecting the action of making in the titles of her works, which often refer directly to the process through which a material had been transformed.

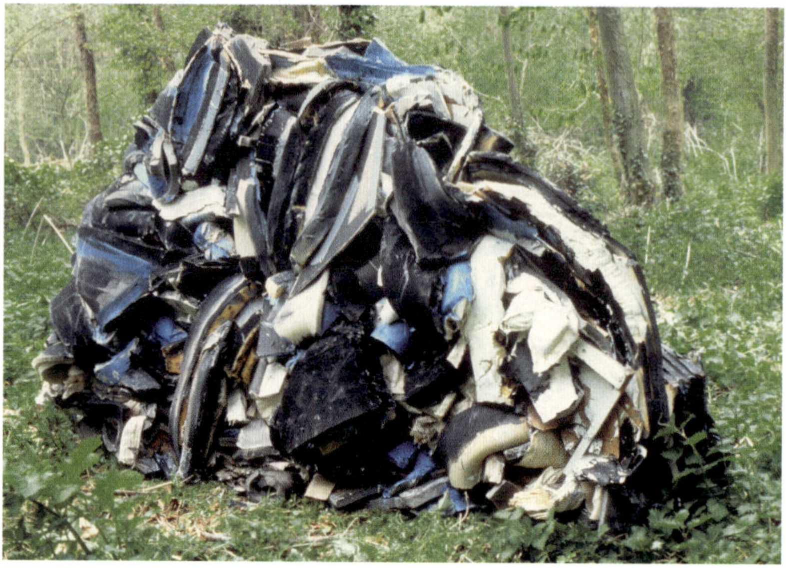

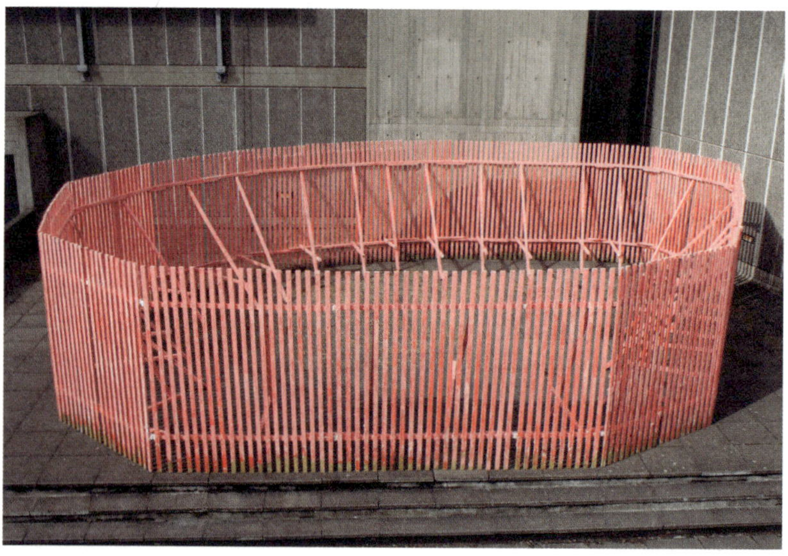

Wrecks, 1984. Bayfield, Norfolk

FENCE, 2008, at the Southbank Centre, London

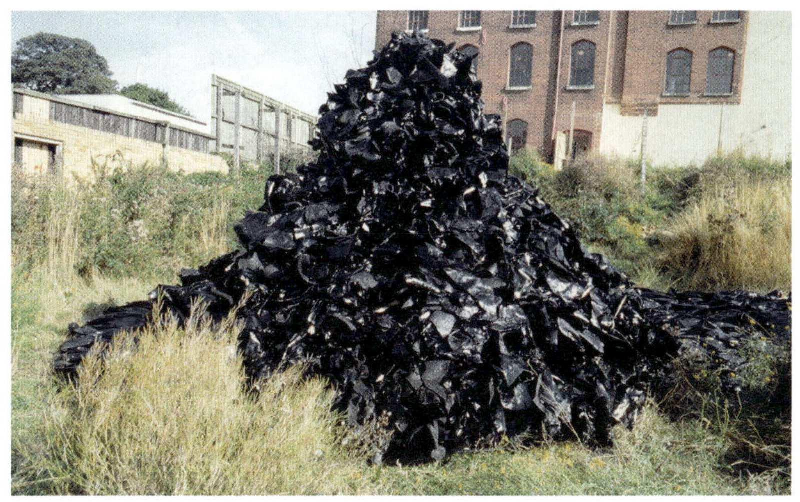

Threat, 1986, at the Canterbury Festival

She used vivid nouns/verbs such as *stack*, *fill*, *fold*, *wrap*, or *crush*, *break*, *spill*. But Barlow was just as likely to move in the opposite direction and make works that challenged this kind of material self-reflection: she had a fondness for dropping a work in progress on the floor to see what suggested itself from the wreckage (p. 75). She strove to transform her materials into objects that would resist easy classification, and she allowed them to behave in contrary ways. She relished jarring combinations—dissonance, contradiction, and deception (she habitually hid forms under drapes, for example, or concealed them in cardboard boxes)—as well as camouflage and disguise. With the deft addition of paint and liquid plaster, she made scrim look like cement and polystyrene exude the weight of steel.

Over time, and as her external exhibition commitments escalated, Barlow began to make a distinction between the works she made for installation "out there in the world" and those she made as part of her ongoing private practice and not always with an intended end in mind.

In 2019–20 she made a number of notable solo works, including *hostage ii; 2019* and *untitled: girl ii; 2019* (p. 68), both of which are bound up with deeply personal experiences. During the months of lockdown following the onset of Covid, Barlow generated dozens of fascinating small works, in an outpouring of new ideas. Among them were objects, no bigger than a hand, that would trigger a run of incredible stand-alone sculptures created in the aftermath of the pandemic, among them *untitled: modernsculpture; 2022* (opposite) and *untitled: hollow; 2022* (p. 69). Barlow appreciated how in the studio each work could be autonomous, free from any ideology of context, containing a history of its own while remaining fundamentally embedded in a history of art and traditions of sculpture such as modeling and construction.

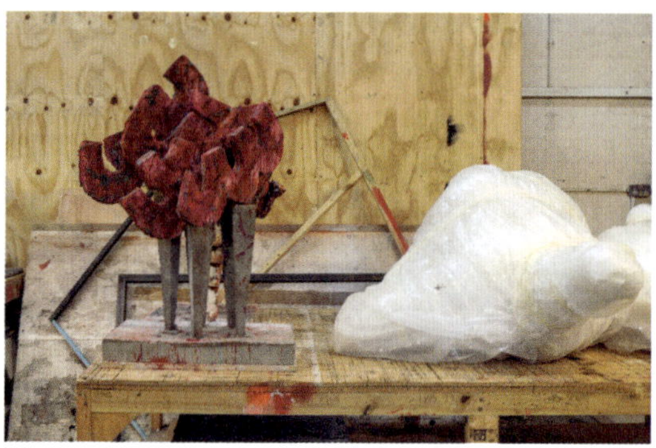

View of Barlow's studio, Camberwell, London, 2023

Making work to command a major public venue was different. Working in public for an audience and in real time is performative; an exhibition is a temporary staging

Materials and Making

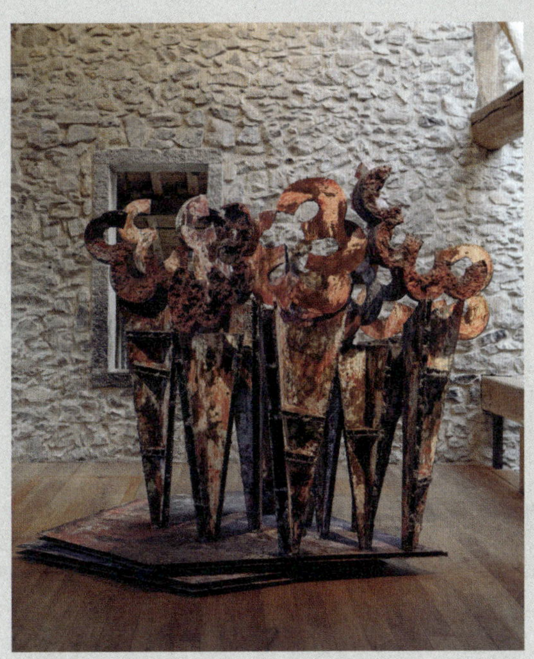

untitled: modernsculpture; 2022
Made from plywood and painted red, black, brown,
and pink, with a rare attention to finish, this sculpture
was included in Barlow's first posthumous exhibition,
which took place in 2023 at Chillida Leku, a museum in
the Basque country that occupies the former home of
Spanish sculptor Eduardo Chillida. Mounted on a steel
base and with a canopy of sharply curved elements,
the sculpture is unlike anything Barlow had made before.
Elements of the composition, especially the curving
loops of the finials, seem to reference Chillida's formal
vocabulary, suggesting, along with the work's title, that
it is related to *smallmodernart*, a 2020–21 series of tiny
works exploring Barlow's roots in postwar European
art that she made during the Covid-induced lockdown.

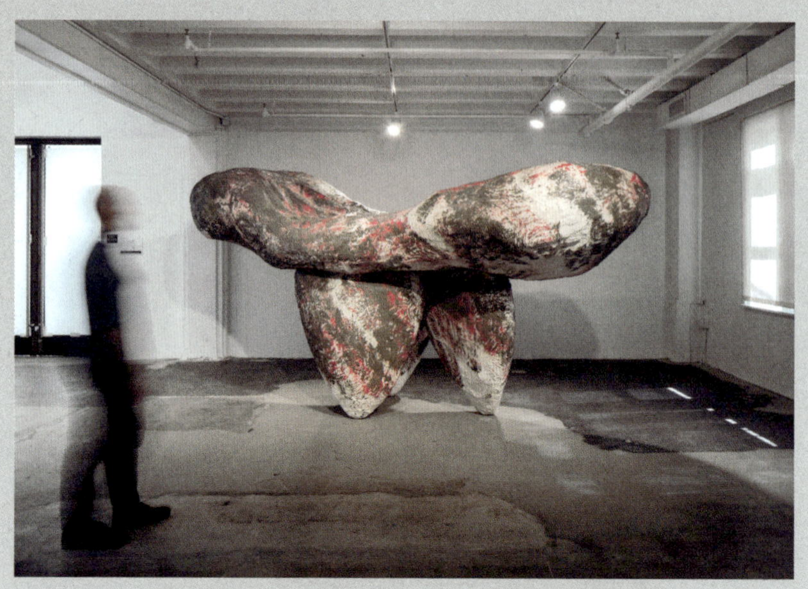

Untitled: girl ii; 2019 (2019–20)

Although Barlow acknowledged personal experience
as foundational in the conceptualizing of an artist's work,
she preferred not to explore, in public, her own private
biography as a source. This work is an exception to that
rule. It relates to a persistent memory of the notable
occasion when her childhood au pair stood on a kitchen
chair, revealing her stout (and hairy) thighs. The au pair
attributed their ample proportions to the exertions of
a long journey escaping her native Poland on foot from
the Nazis. Intriguingly, the bulbous pink-hued forms that
we read as "legs" and "skirt" in this work appear—when
inverted—strikingly similar to the rabbit-ears Barlow
first created in 1994 for *Object for the television* (p. 23).
This signature motif resurfaced in 2019 and recurs
in a number of related works before its final staging
in *PRANK* (2023; p. 20).

in a specific place. Museums and galleries embody their own histories and traditions: their spaces are charged with the energy of each location, shaped by particular issues of culture, economy, ideology, and global affairs. Working on large-scale international shows and on space-invading installations necessitated a huge shift in gear for Barlow and involved teams of assistants, considerable technological support, and laborious planning and preparatory work. These were high-risk projects, and the drama of realizing the finished installation in an unfamiliar space was as challenging as it was exhilarating.

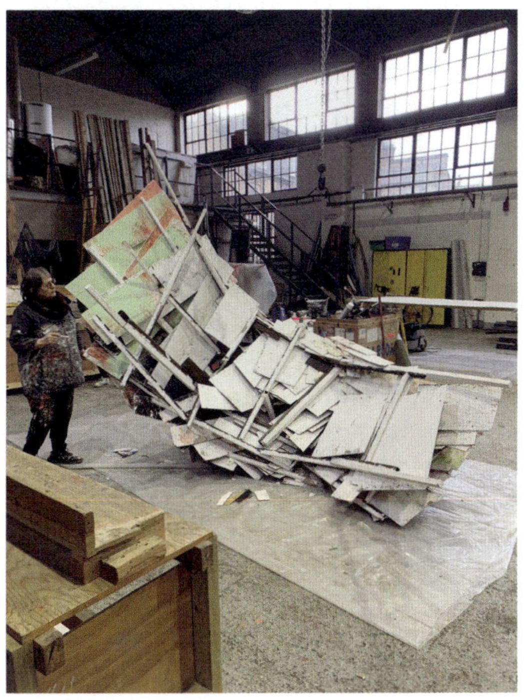

Barlow working on *untitled: hollow; 2022* in her studio in Camberwell, London

The Hatred of the Object

In this text from 1995, Barlow sets up a contrast between "two kinds of traditional studios: the enlightened studio and the grim studio." While the latter was the kind she experienced during her own education, "the grim abode of the punitive, the repressive, and the backward-looking," in the former—the ideal for her own studio—"the artist is at the centre of this self-created world, ... in control of the development and eventual showing to the outside world of their individual expression."

The studio in either its enlightened or its grim guise can seem to force a moral attitude to work—passing on an inheritance of a kind of Protestant work ethic in which is entrenched a strong sense of struggle out of which good must surely come. ... My proposition of the hatred of the object hinges on the perception of the traditional studio as an inheritance loaded with morality and stringent work ethics enforced for no good reason. Furthermore, where such a domain is thought to abide by rigid hierarchies of good and bad, right and wrong, these judgements seem to be passed according to the extent to which the artist can deposit evidence of struggle on their sculpture-object through the act of making.

Craft, and the hands-on/hands-off debate emerges. Again, the spectre of the grim studio rises, claiming the high moral ground with its demand for the handmade, with the added insistence that maximum evidence of the mark of the artist be left on the work. Thus the essential need for the studio is justified—as the place where the object is processed through private and personal rituals of making. In this blinkered

environment Duchamp has never existed, nor any attempt
to acknowledge the wealth of iconoclastic gestures erupting
out of twentieth-century art which have kept the processes
of sculpture awake and contentious.

Understandably a revulsion can set in. The object—
the hot object—that is, the object loaded with the all-too-
visible signs of the act of making, can repulse through its
somewhat desperate need to attract. It becomes an object
of emotional blackmail, persuading us to feel for it because
it shows us so clearly the marks, wounds perhaps, caused
through its struggle to come into existence. For those who
are questioning the necessity for such agonised creativity,
these objects arouse suspicion and eventually a kind of
loathing because they rely on predictable mannerisms
with which to generate a reaction.

Similarly, our culture abounds with objects demanding
to be loved—but produced in a totally different way—
that is, industrially designed and manufactured products.
These are cool objects, hands-off maybe, but objects
which impose a similar emotional blackmail to their
opposite numbers, demanding to be bought, to be owned.
These product-objects which saturate our daily lives
infiltrate our emotions, often seductively and pleasurably.

But on closer analysis they can also generate loathing
as their true destructive or pollutant identities are revealed
behind their fabulous disguise of, for example, rounded
forms and glossy surface. The car is, of course, the
supreme example.

Therefore my notion of the hatred of the object is born out
of what I perceive to be a conflict between opposing species

of sculptures: one hot and the other cold. However, their supposed differences can, paradoxically, produce similar responses: both demand to be loved and needed, albeit in different ways, and yet both are infinitely capable of invoking the opposite response to the one intended—instead of love, hatred.

… The hatred of the object is manifested through the mistrust and abdication of the studio. The demise of the studio equates with a shunning of and a hatred of the object.

… Perhaps in the end the hatred of the object has had its day, and maybe the tremendous acclaim awarded to [Louise] Bourgeois's sculpture is part of the hated object's demise. I would certainly welcome this as I do consider that [the] ancient processes [of traditional sculpture practice] … provide independence and an inappropriate, expedient, and human antidote to the worlds of the virtual and the removed, the sanitised and the hands-off.

The Artist's Voice

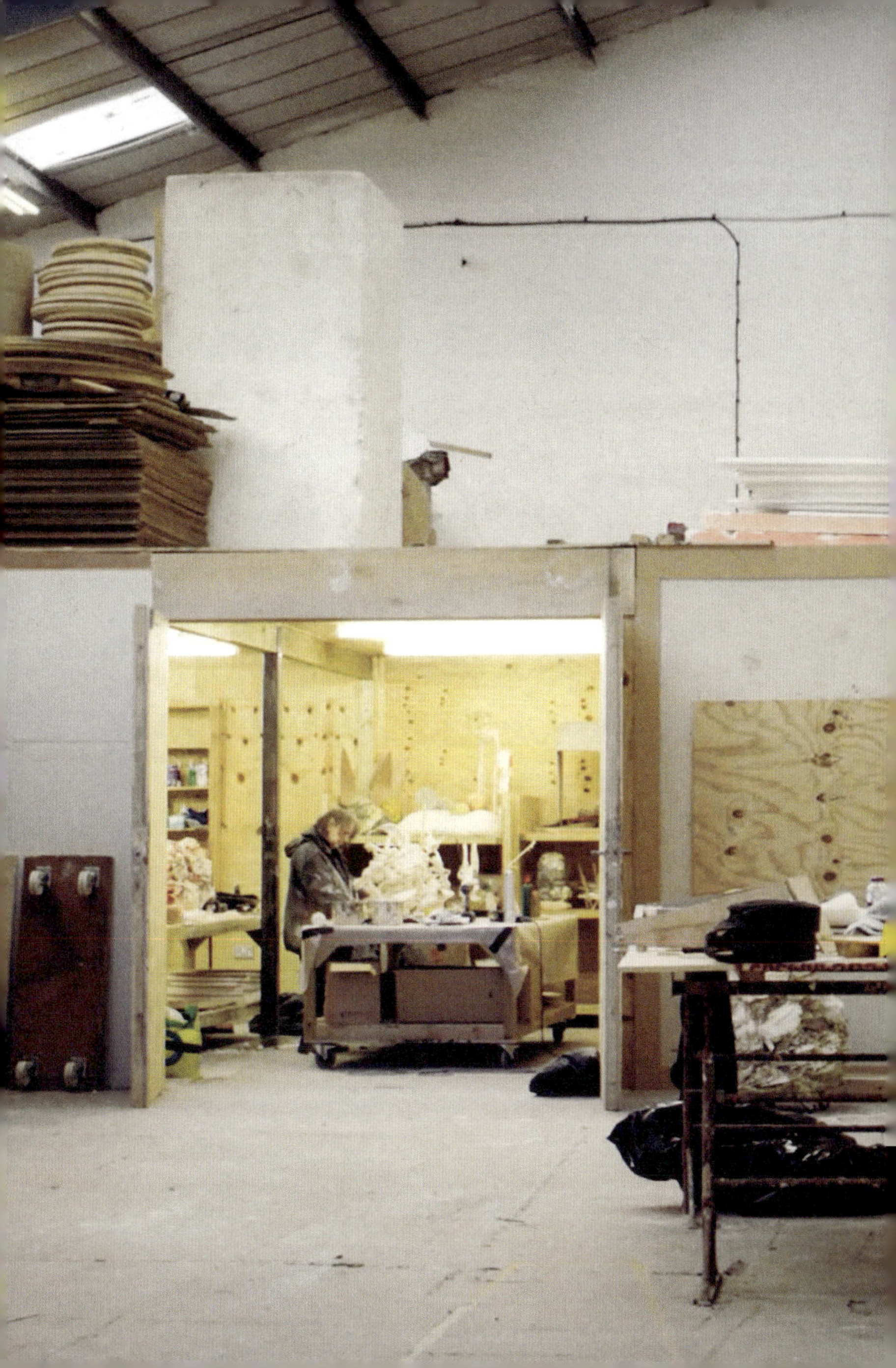

PHYLLIDA

In the run-up to Barlow's 2019 exhibition *cul-de-sac* at the Royal Academy of Arts, London, Cosima Spender directed *PHYLLIDA*, an intimate documentary portrait exploring the artist's practice and outlook.

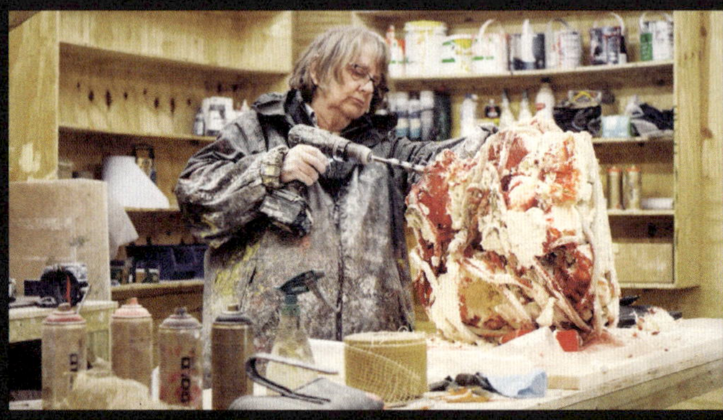

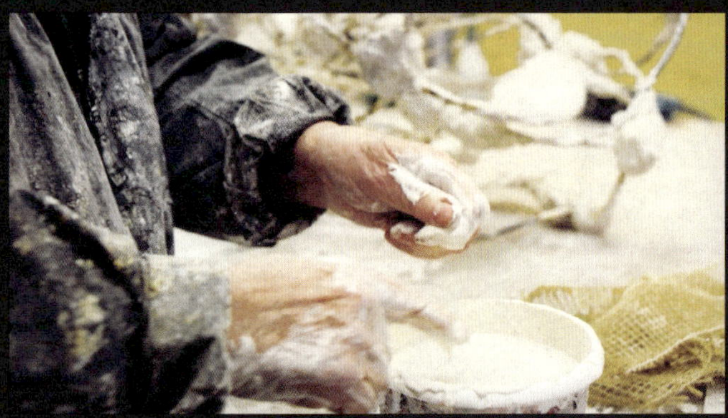

Stills from *PHYLLIDA*, 2019

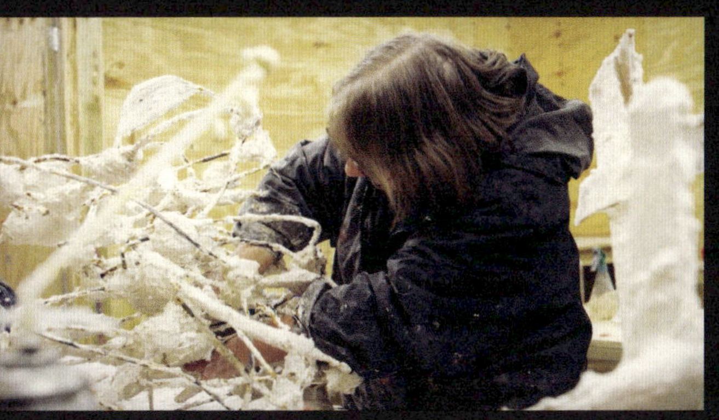

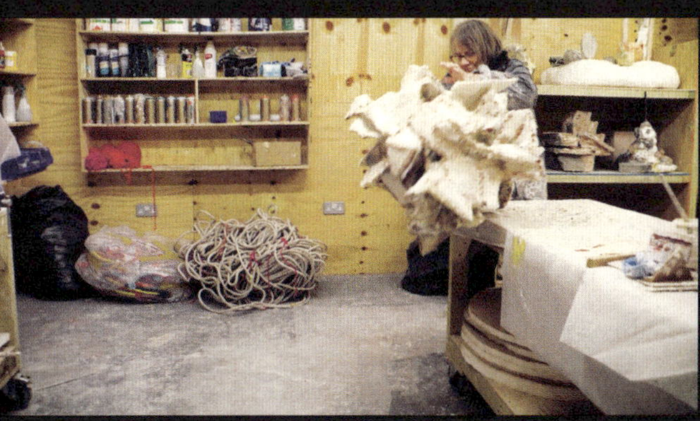

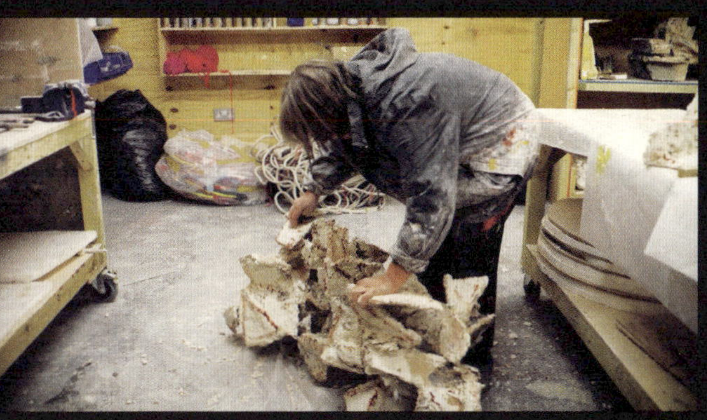

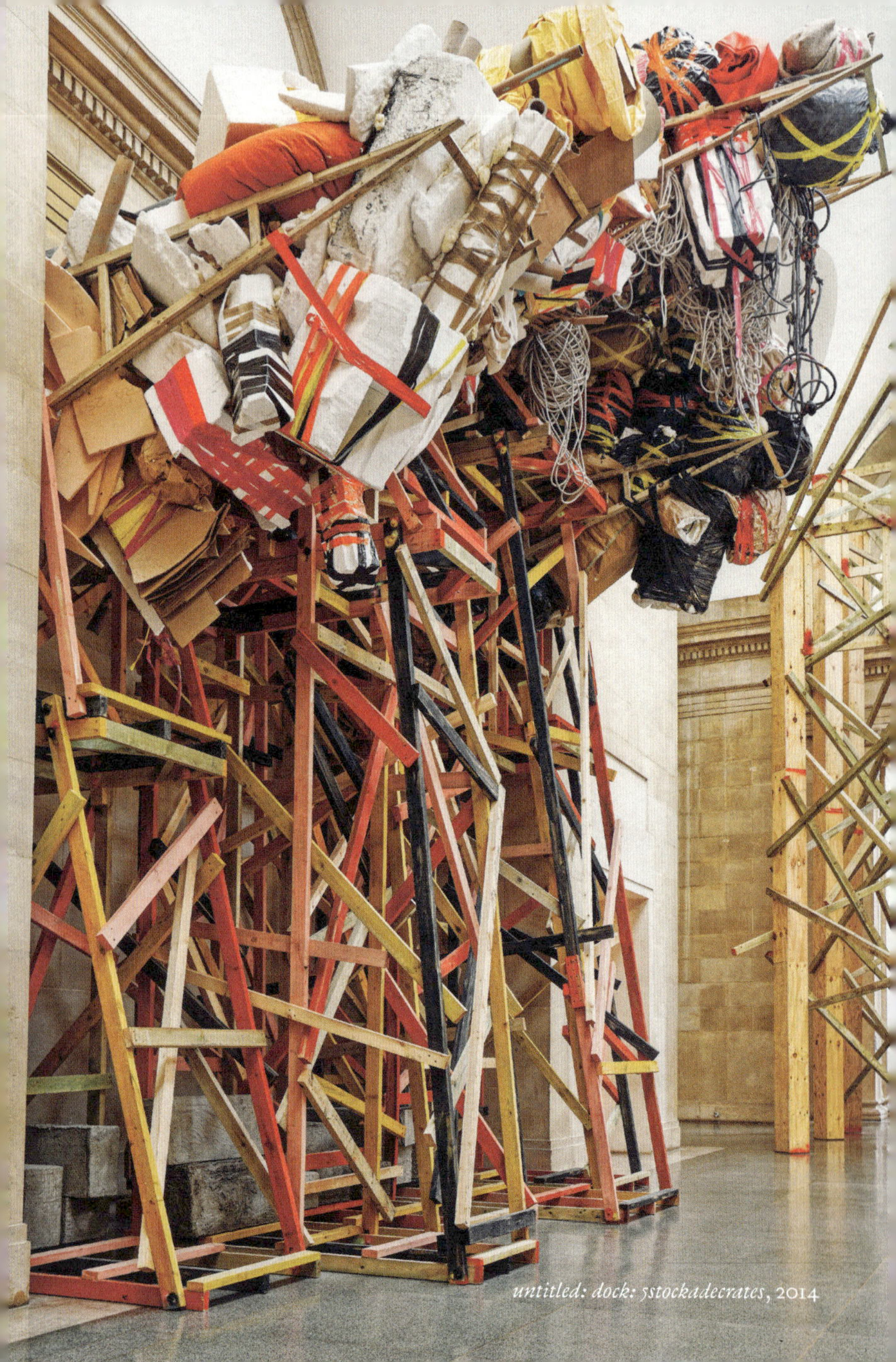

untitled: dock: 5stockadecrates, 2014

Culture and Chaos: *dock* at Tate Britain

Before the 2010s Barlow's career had been taken up principally with teaching. Upon her retirement from academia, she had little to show by way of an exhibition history, almost no work available for sale and therefore to collect, and no gallery representation. It was at this moment, however, that she began to receive offers of exhibitions in galleries outside London and then at independent spaces in the city, as well as abroad, all of which began to generate serious interest in her work. Gallery representation led to her standout show *RIG* at Hauser & Wirth London in 2011 (p. 79), which took the art world by storm. Over the next few years, major museum shows in America and Germany gave her—finally—the opportunity to work on a large scale in an international context.

Her work until this point had tended to be shown in group exhibitions of emerging "British art" alongside that of artists half her age. When she was approached for a project at Tate Britain in 2013 it was not for a retrospective, as one might have expected, but to present the annual Duveen commission the following year. The prestigious commission is a kind of rite of passage into the establishment of British art, and in taking it on Barlow was following on from a succession of younger artists.

The Duveen Galleries were built in the 1930s specifically for the display of sculpture. With their Ionic columns, towering Portland stone walls, and sweeping floors, they provide a central spine to Tate Britain's building. Designed to inspire awe and respect, the galleries are best approached

via the grand staircase ascending to the museum's
riverfront entrance. Barlow's *dock*, as her installation
was titled, countered the galleries' vast scale with a dense
assemblage of sculptural elements. In what she called an
"argument with the space," *dock* took over and crushed the
air out of the hall, filling its length and much of its height.
Vertiginous towers made of brown paper and belted with
colorful tape teetered unnervingly in comic parody of the
"phallocentrism" (her word) of the Duveen's neoclassical
columns. Near the ceiling, objects and materials hung,
or were slung, on shambolic timber frames, and beams
cantilevered precariously into the void. Bundles of black
plastic, sweepings of foam, tape, wood, and other materials
left over from the process of construction were packed onto
a kind of storage shelf, like an upended landfill. At ground
level, two huge encumbrances blocked viewers' pathway and
line of sight. One was a makeshift gantry from which Barlow
had suspended two large, black, container-like objects; the
other was a rickety framework staircase splattered in paint,
one side of which was fronted by a huge hoarding, a collage
of panels painted in Barlow's signature colors of red, pink,
and mint green, turned forty-five degrees to the orthogonal,
one corner pointing into the roof.

Thrown together in gimcrack fashion from her go-to list
of DIY materials, the work was, of course, more than a
forest of stuff. It bristled with references to projects that
had previously occupied the same space, and to works by
other artists in Tate's collection, which found echoes in
the formal elements of Barlow's installation. The two forged
steel blocks of incredible weight in Richard Serra's powerful
Weight and Measure (the 1992 Duveen commission) were
the "trigger objects" for her suspended containers, flimsy
approximations fabricated in polystyrene and cardboard.

                            Life and Work

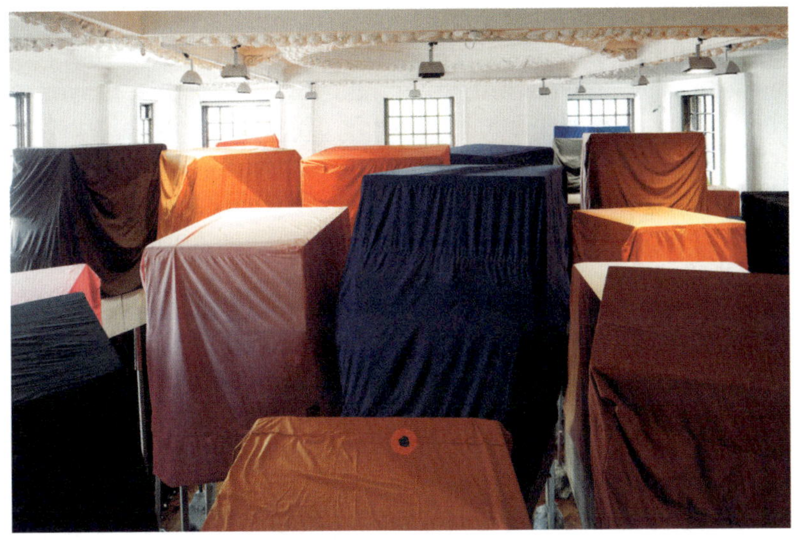

RIG: untitled; blocks, 2011, at Hauser & Wirth London

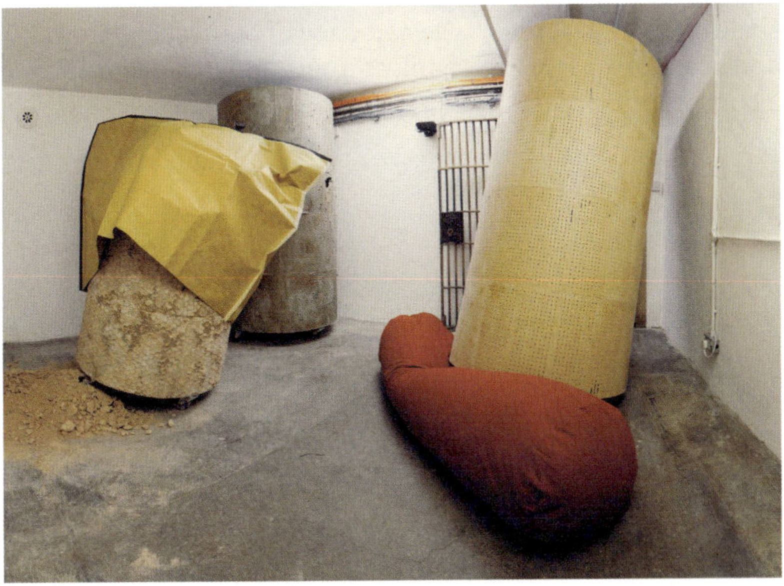

RIG: untitled; containers; leaningcoveredholed, 2011, at Hauser & Wirth London

Meanwhile, visitors to *dock* could spot Anthony Caro's
elegant, red-painted *Early One Morning* (1962) through
a doorway in an adjacent gallery. Barlow especially enjoyed
the opportunity to place her messy, ungainly, and painterly
work in full view of the artist she had directed so much
of her energy against as a student.

dock was not so much an homage to Barlow's art world
as it was a manifesto for breaking the rules, an assertion
of sculpture's freedom to associate with pretty much
anything at all, in art and in life. Beyond the references
to art history, the installation resembled a construction
site or a demolition yard, deliberately evoking the hugely
aggressive urban regeneration project rising rapidly on the
south bank of the Thames, across the river from the gallery.
Barlow recoiled at the crude inelegance of the ersatz tower
blocks rising from the dust and railed at the lost opportunity
for architecture, even as she was enthralled by the sheer
scale of chaotic activity: the carapace of cranes, core towers,
and scaffolding, the riverbank at night transformed into
a constellation of lights flickering over the rising blocks.

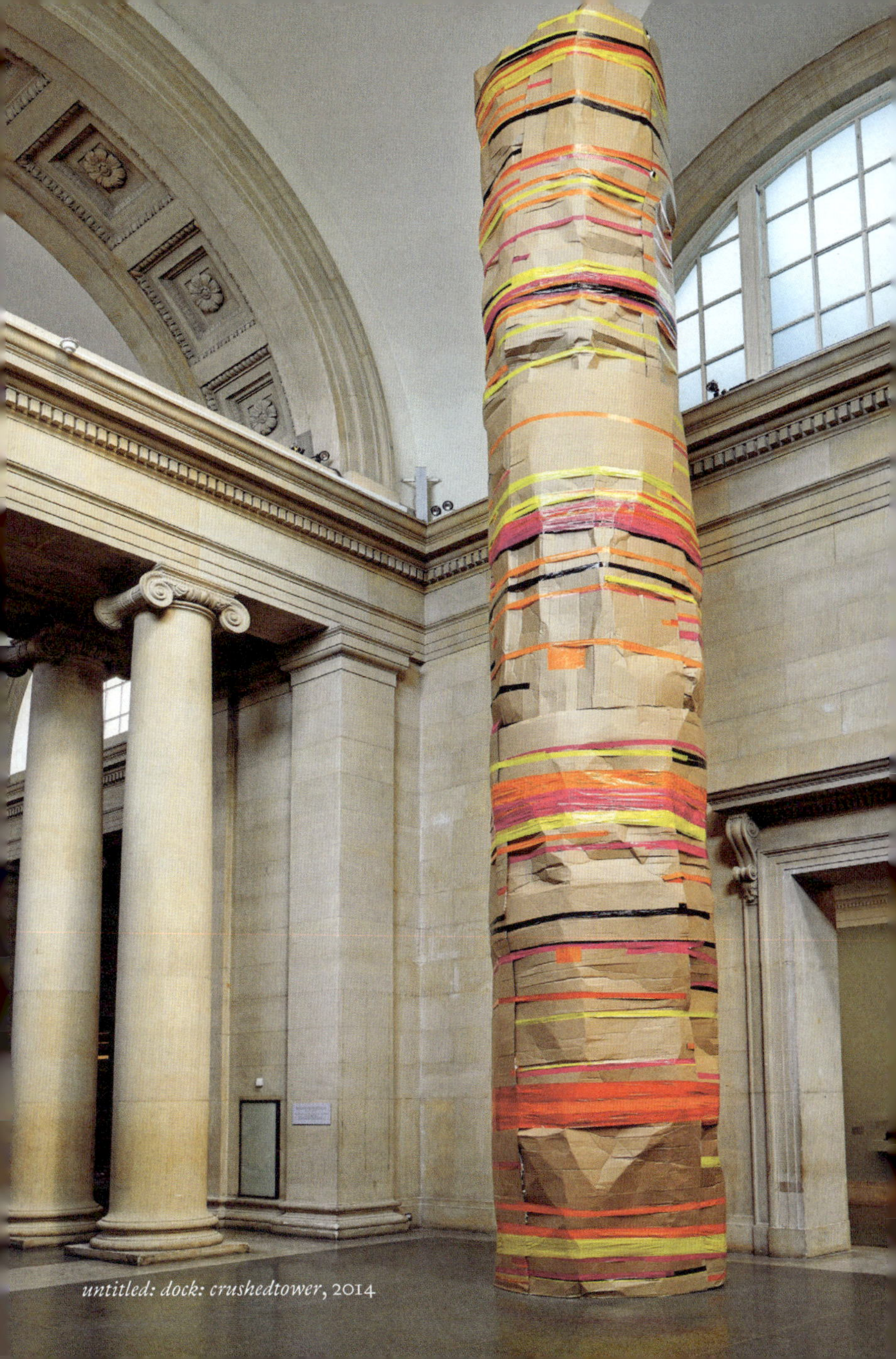

untitled: dock: crushedtower, 2014

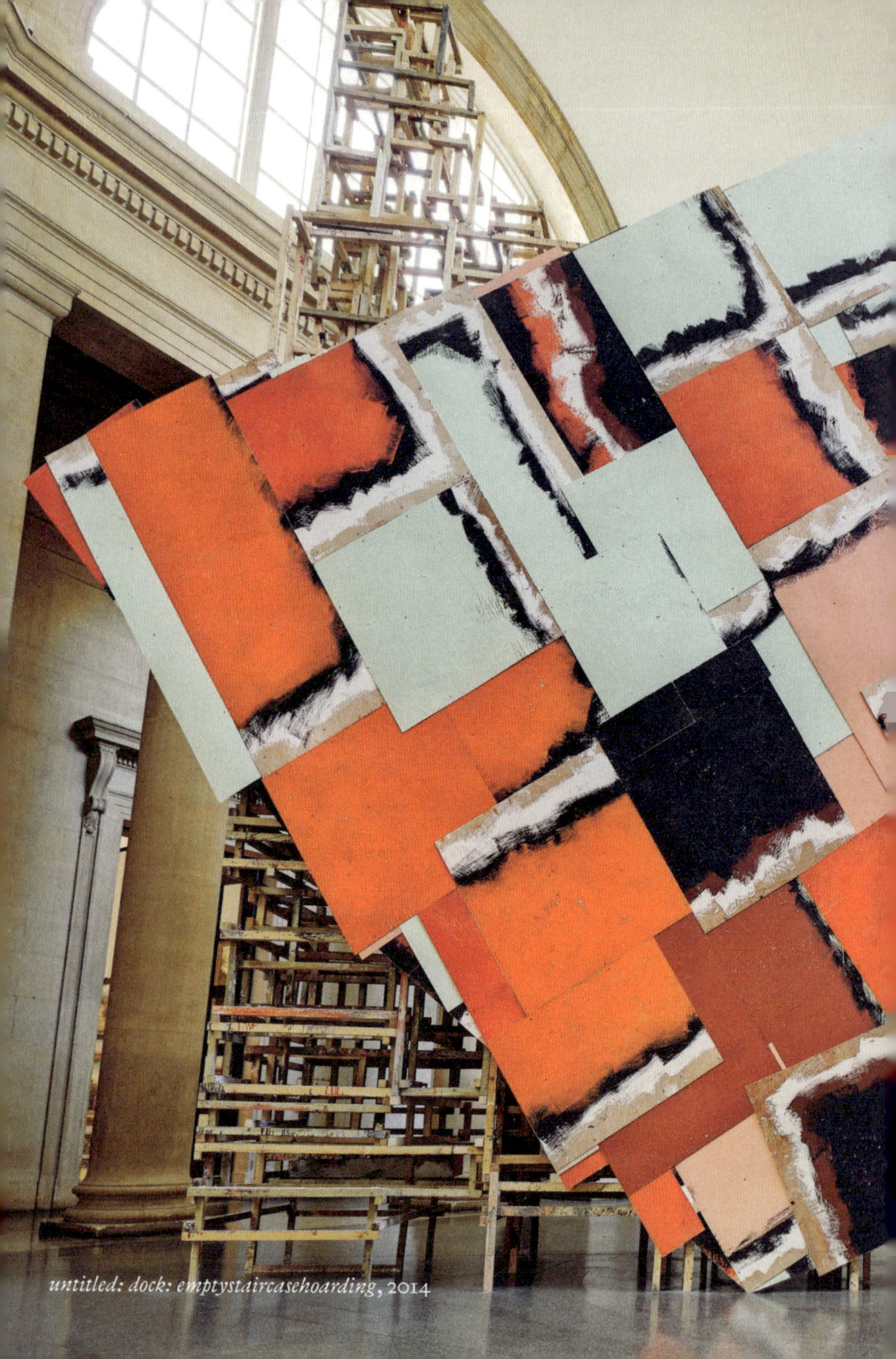

untitled: dock: emptystaircasehoarding, 2014

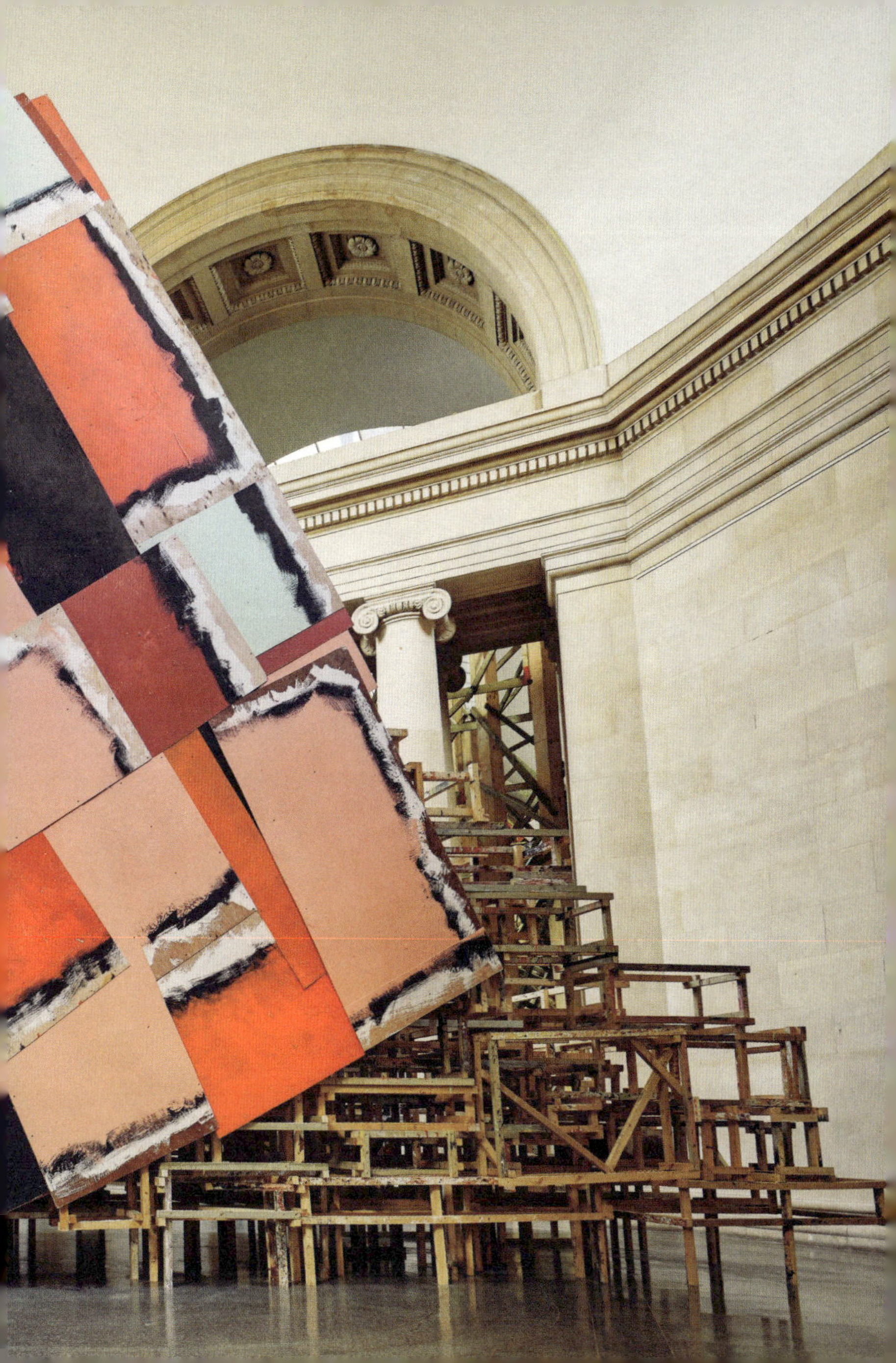

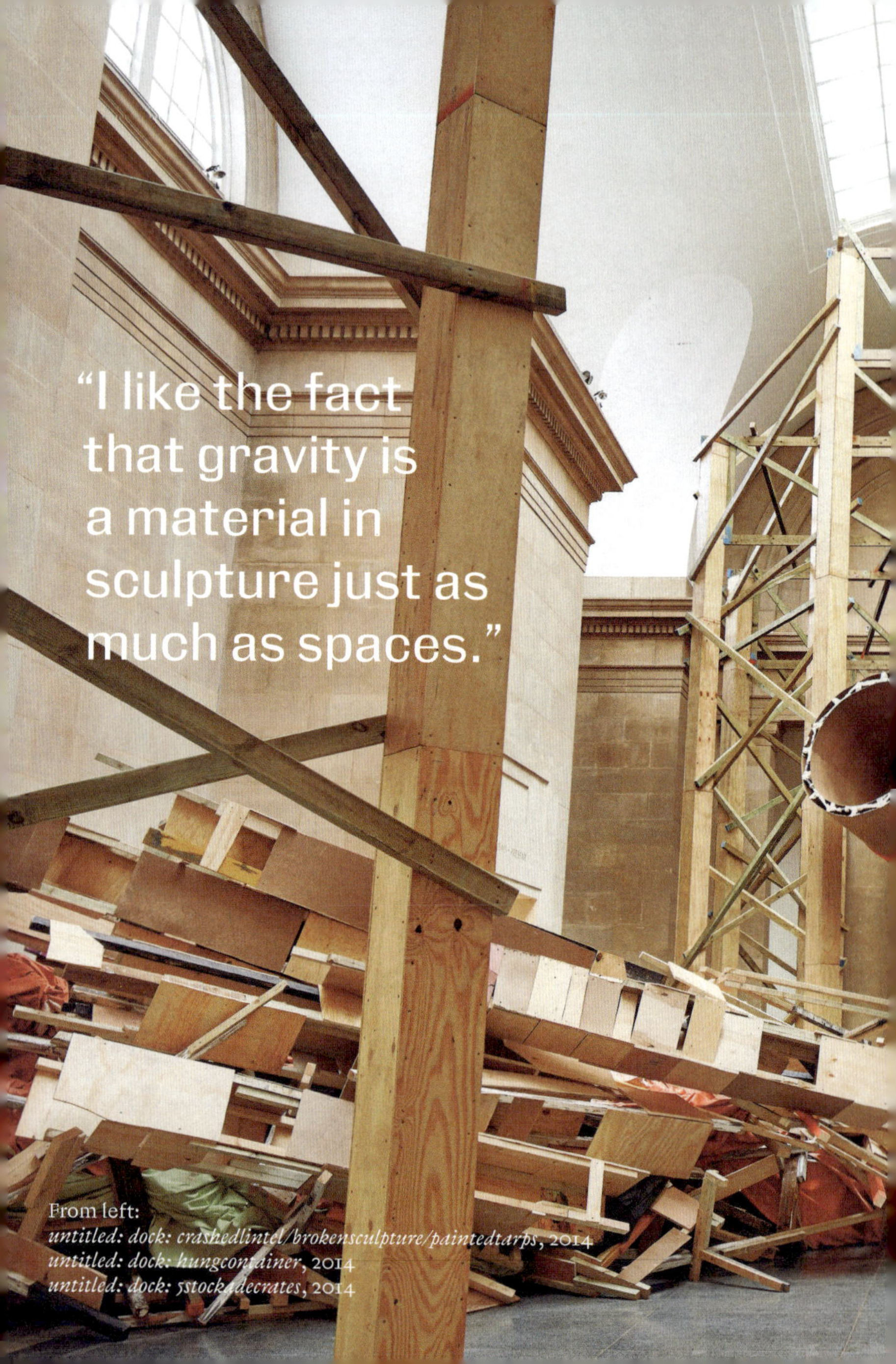

From left:
untitled: dock: crashedlintel/brokensculpture/paintedtarps, 2014
untitled: dock: hungcontainer, 2014
untitled: dock: 5stockadecrates, 2014

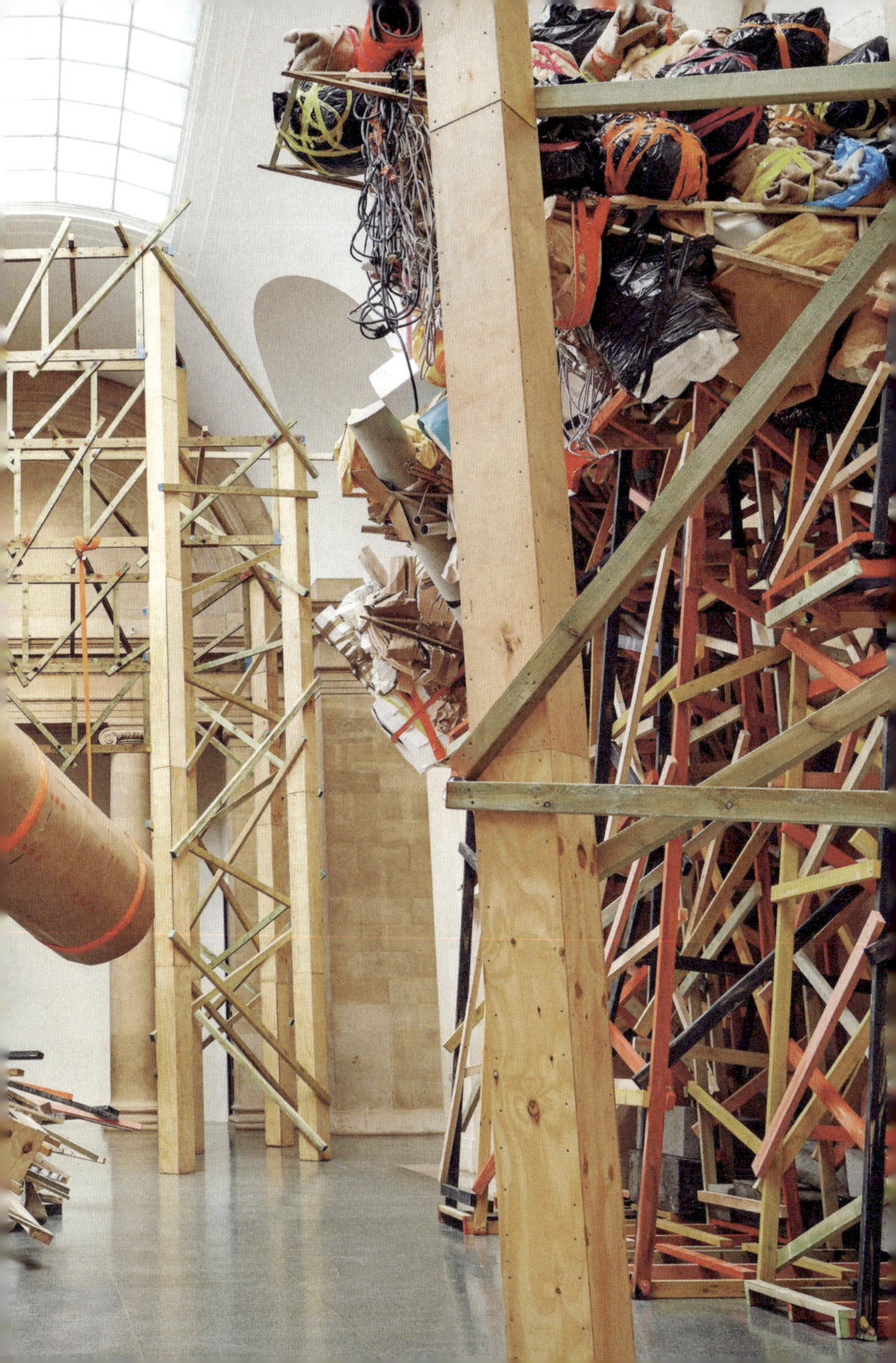

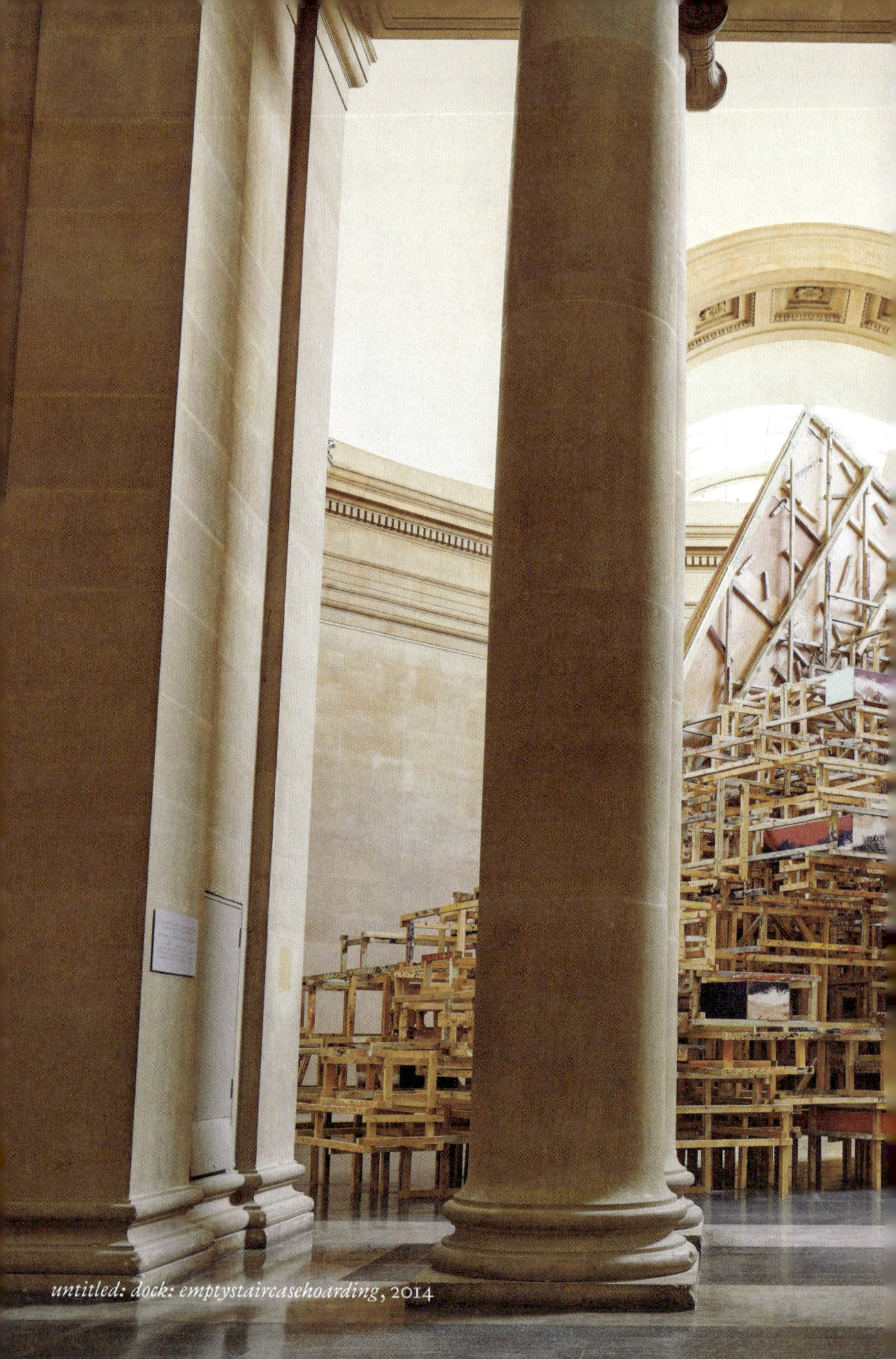

untitled: dock: emptystaircasehoarding, 2014

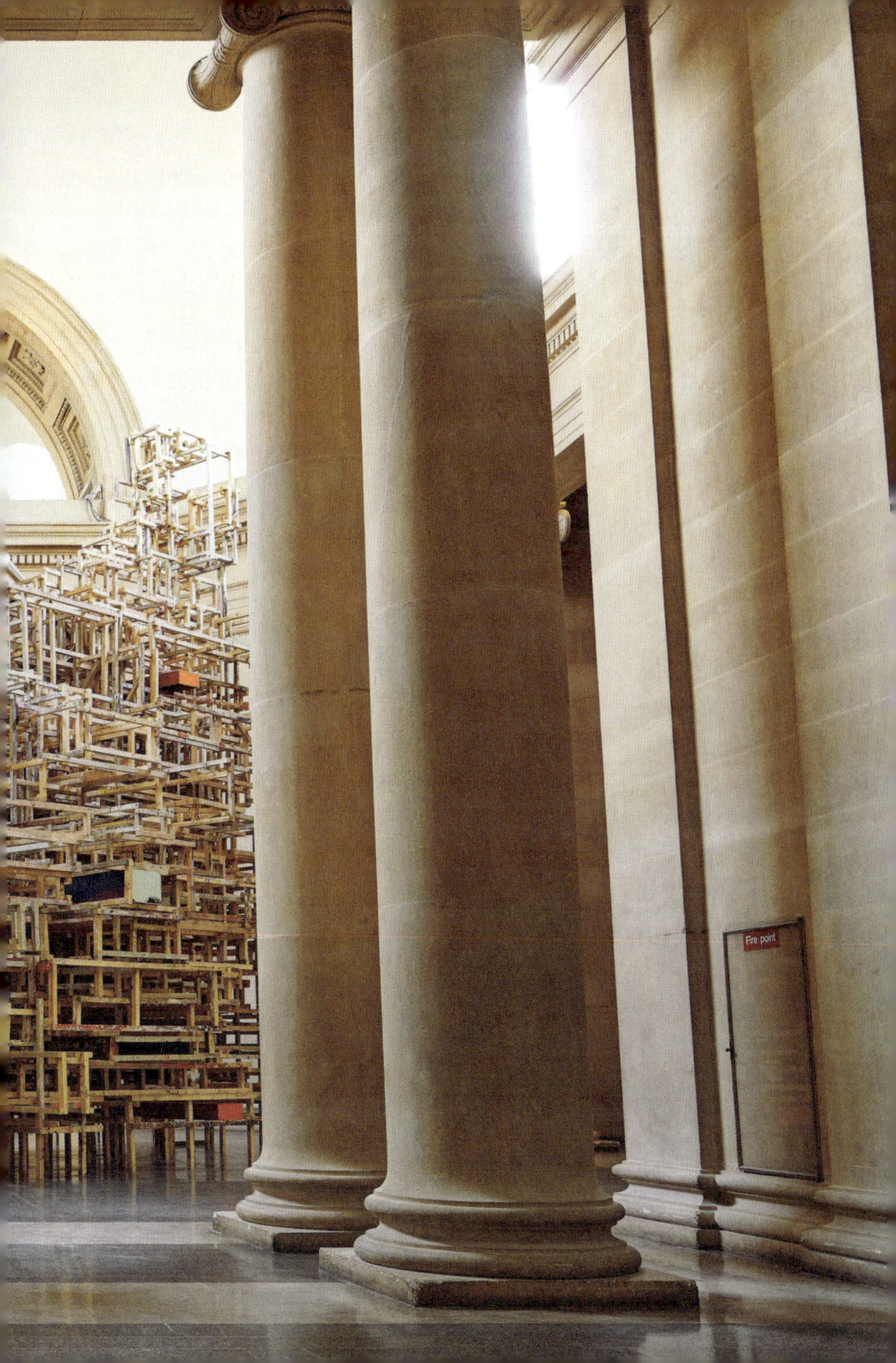
Fire point

A House of Cards
and Other Maquettes

These maquettes were not exhibited during Barlow's
life and reflect the more private aspects of her practice.
Some but not all of them were realized in larger versions;
others can be seen as a kinds of "open" experimentation
around questions of structure, precarity, and form,
offering ways to explore the sculptural and compositional
strategies that were of enduring interest to Barlow
without necessarily leading to a finished work.

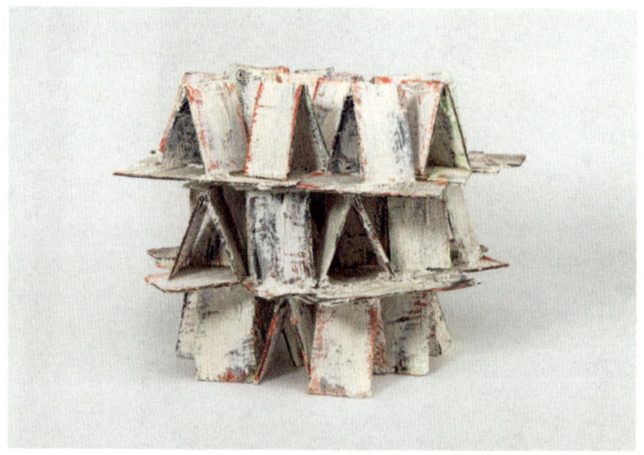

untitled: parkhousemodel; 70, 2015–23

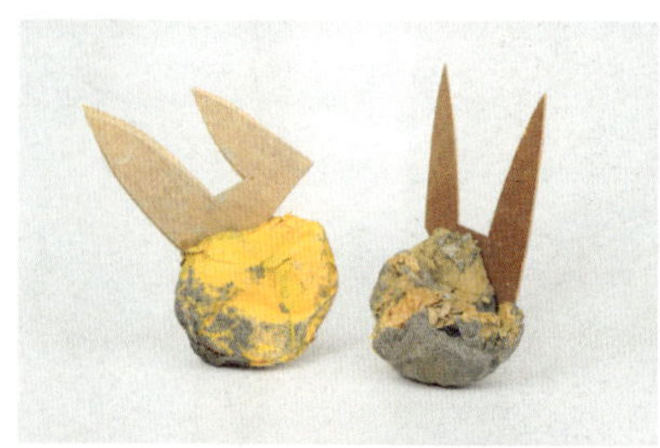

untitled: parkhousemodel; 57, 2015–23

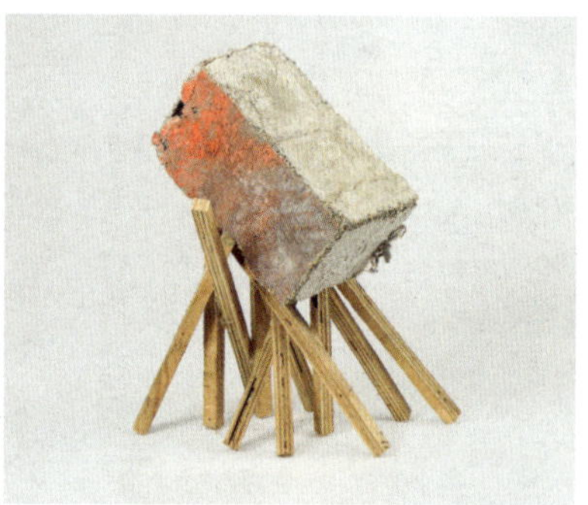

untitled: parkhousemodel; 49, 2015–23

In Pictures

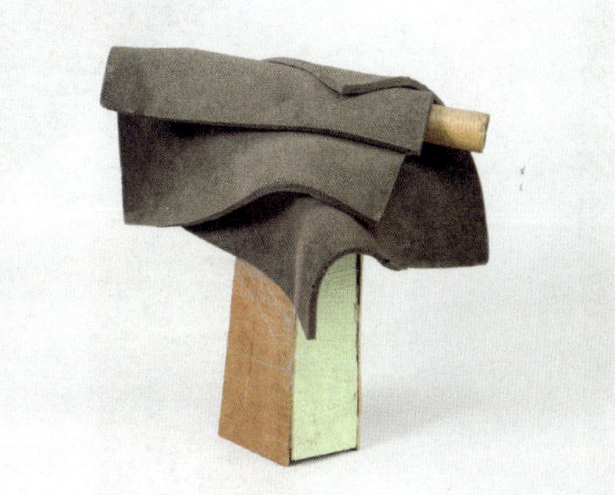

untitled: parkhousemodel; 35, 2015–23

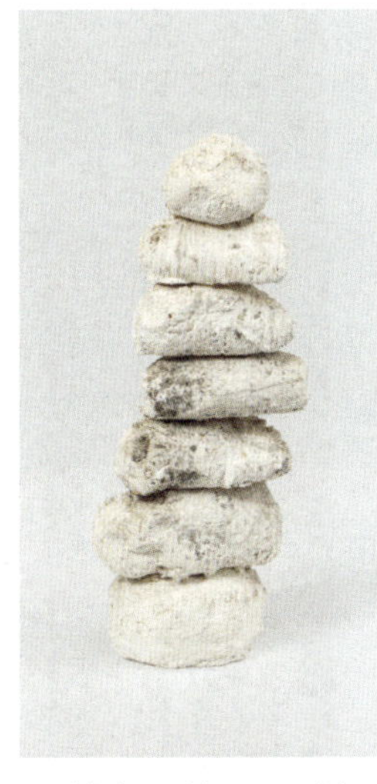

untitled: parkhousemodel; 21, 2015–23

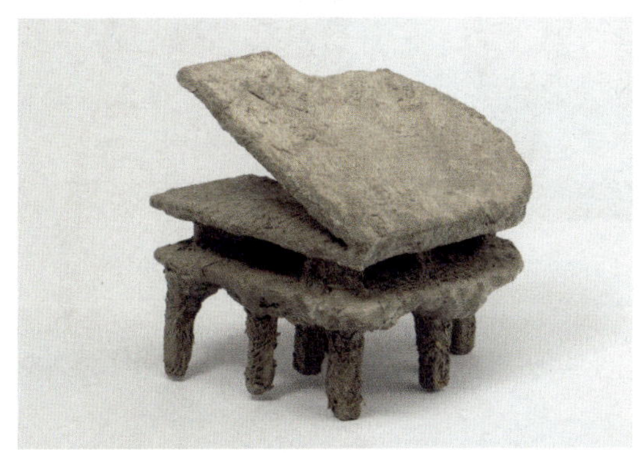

untitled: parkhousemodel; 48, 2015–23

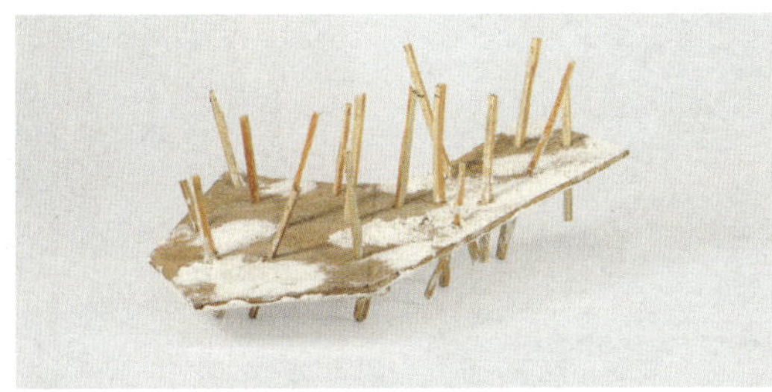

untitled: parkhousemodel; 44, 2015–23

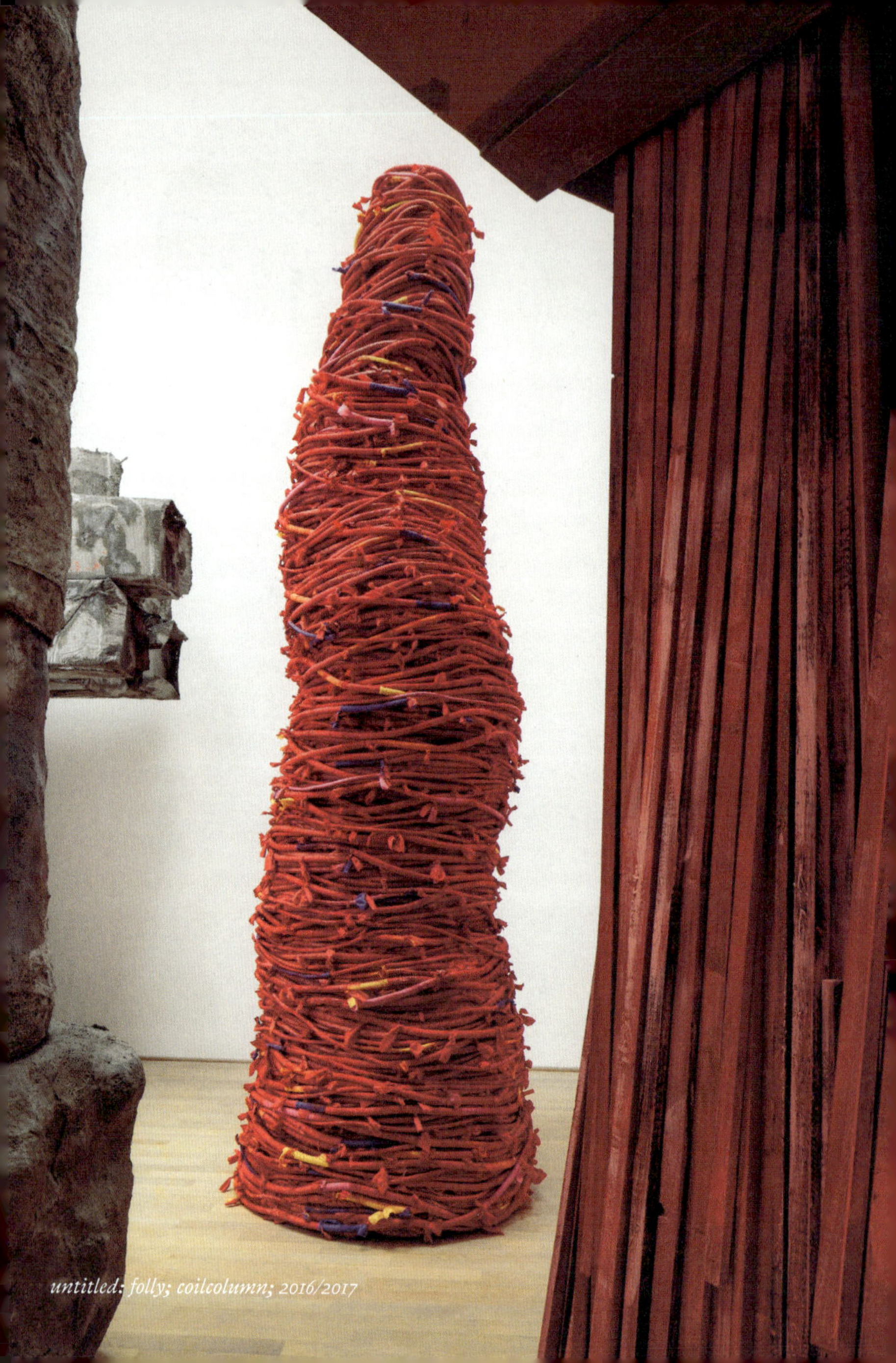

untitled: folly; coilcolumn; 2016/2017

Frivolity and Forewarning:
folly in Venice

Only two years after *dock* at Tate Britain, with a cluster
of game-changing projects, in Dallas, Edinburgh, Zurich,
and St. Gallen, Switzerland, under her belt, Barlow was
invited to represent Britain at the 2017 Venice Biennale,
to join a roll call of distinguished predecessors deemed
worthy of representing the nation at the premier event
on the international art-world calendar. The British
Pavilion in the Giardini in Venice, a somewhat pompous
little Neoclassical building, its galleries fronted by a
raised portico reached by a flight of stairs, was an ideal
foil for Barlow's passion for taking a proverbial wrecking
ball to outmoded institutions, in this case what she called
the "faded and dejected glory of the British Pavilion."

The passage through her installation was devised not
to facilitate the contemplation of individual works of art
but to accentuate the audience's physical encounter with
the totality of the space: their journey was interrupted
by surprise blockages, with huge walls of painted panels
acting as barriers at significant intervals. The main gallery
was packed with towering columns and fallen boulders,
and elsewhere encounters were to be had with grim, gray,
scrim-clad objects reminiscent (but not representative)
of things in the real world: a piano, an anvil, a megaphone,
and balconies. Occasionally the monotonous gray was
interrupted by flashes of brilliant color, like those bursts
of buddleia amid the bomb sites of postwar London.

Barlow's sculptural objects prompted haunting evocations
of past pleasures. They contained references to Venice's

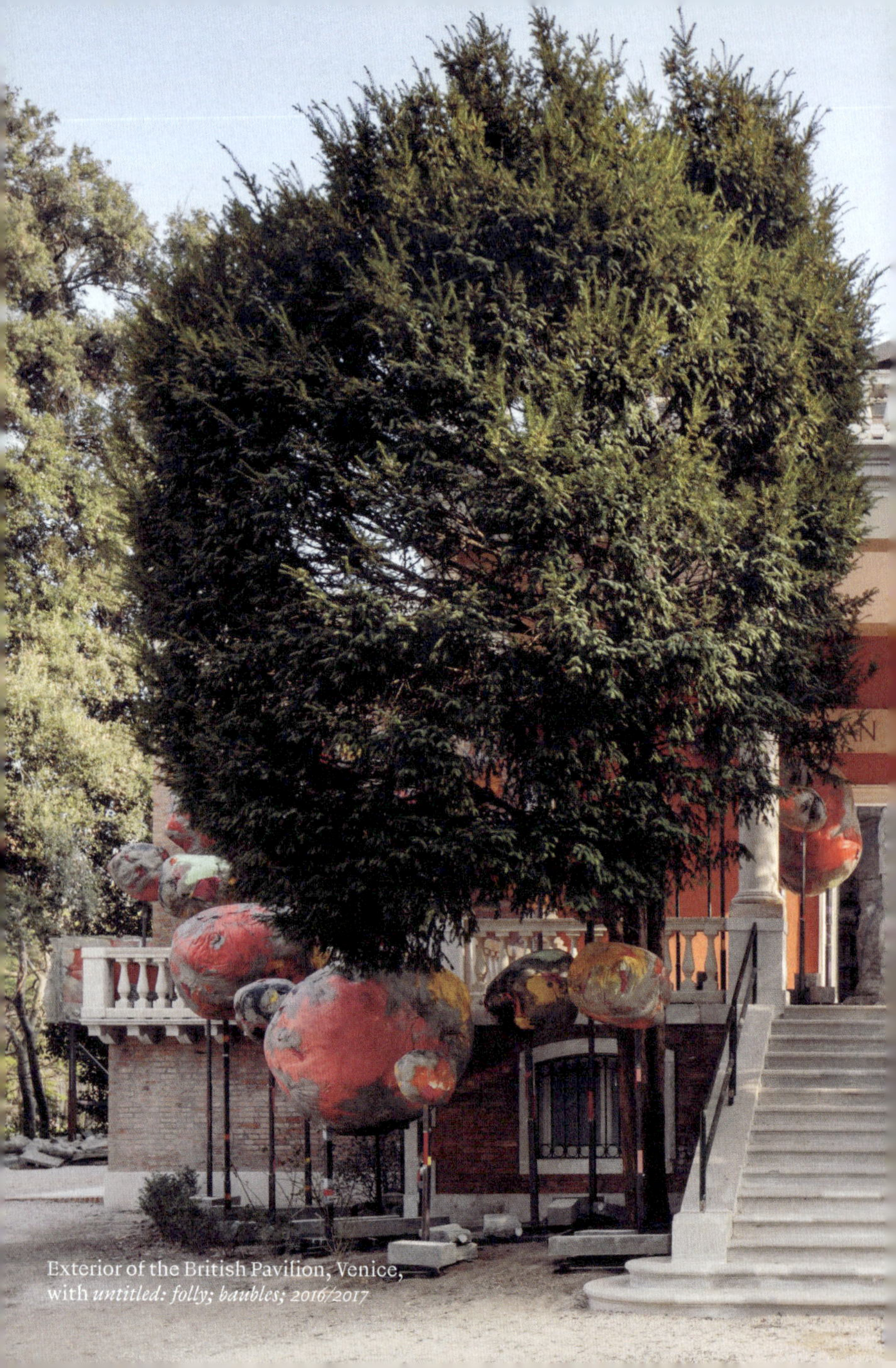

Exterior of the British Pavilion, Venice,
with *untitled: folly; baubles; 2016/2017*

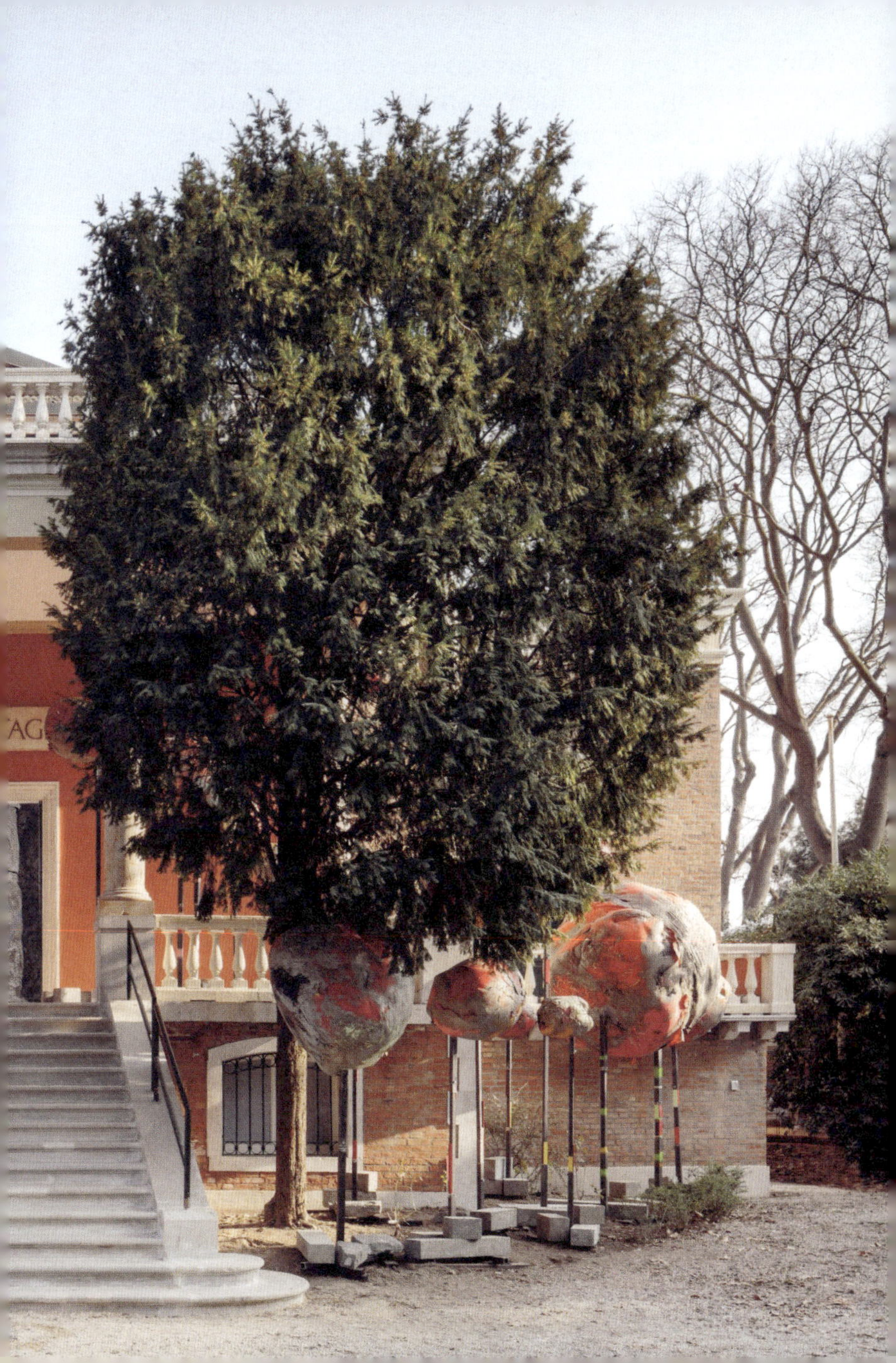

faded architectural elegance as well as premonitions
of a collapsing civilization, warnings of civil disorder.
Outside, a note of mock celebration and frivolity was
struck by clusters of lollipop pom-poms, a mood almost
immediately dampened by juxtaposition with a pile of
debris, and objects evoking a hoarding, placards, and
guns—trace elements of protest and social unrest.

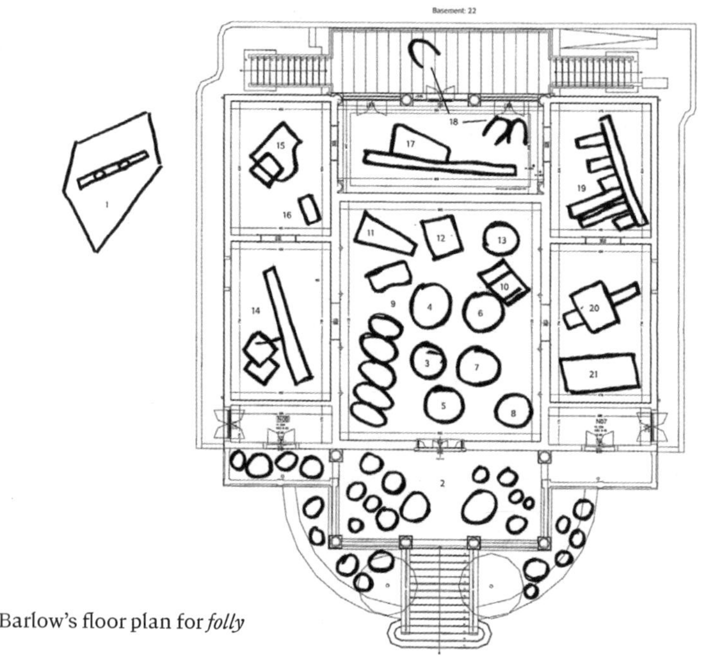

Barlow's floor plan for *folly*

Here, in Venice, was an artist at the height of her powers,
her work a commentary not just on the state of art but
on the state of the world: objects damaged and broken,
impeding our way, choking our space, occluding our
view, weighing on us from above. Part of the impact on
audiences was undoubtedly due to *folly*'s almost cinematic

                     Life and Work

choreography of our experience as viewers. It was not
the objects themselves that were moving as if on film,
but the bodies and eyes of visitors as they ducked and
wove their way through the throng of "stuff." Viewers
became protagonists in an unfolding narrative, one in
which space itself was occupied and transformed via
the command of scale, volume, and light. In these almost
theatrical set pieces, time, too, acted as a material to
be played with and manipulated.

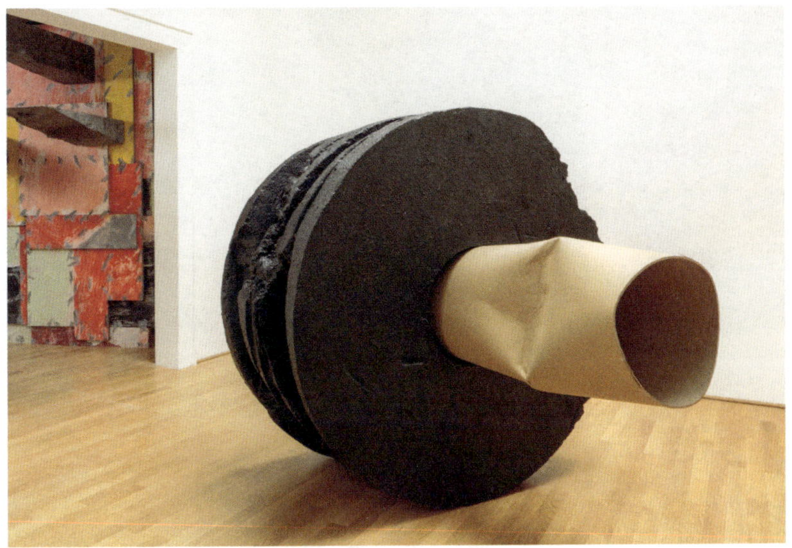

untitled: folly; axle; 2016/2017

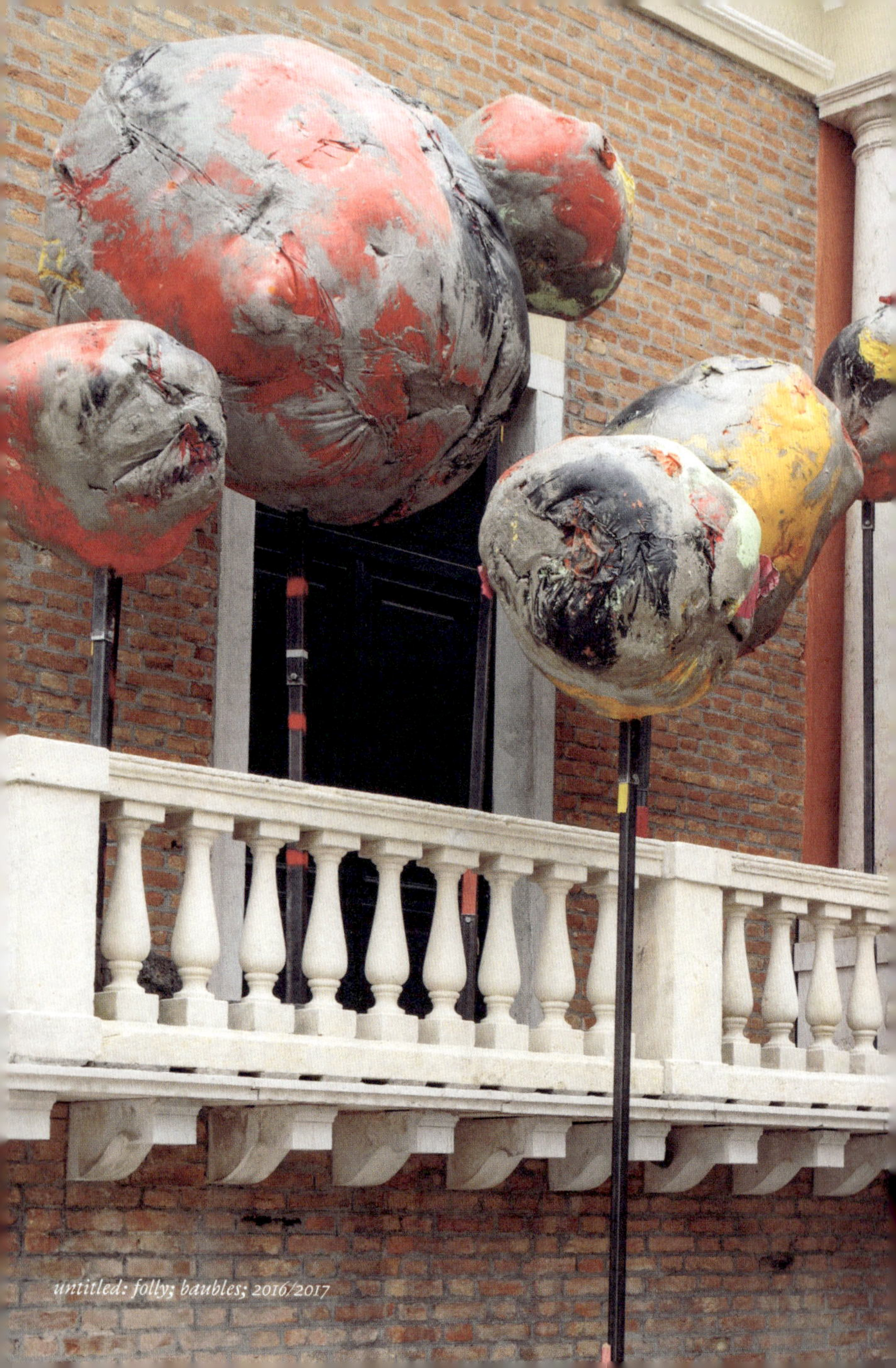

untitled: folly: baubles: 2016/2017

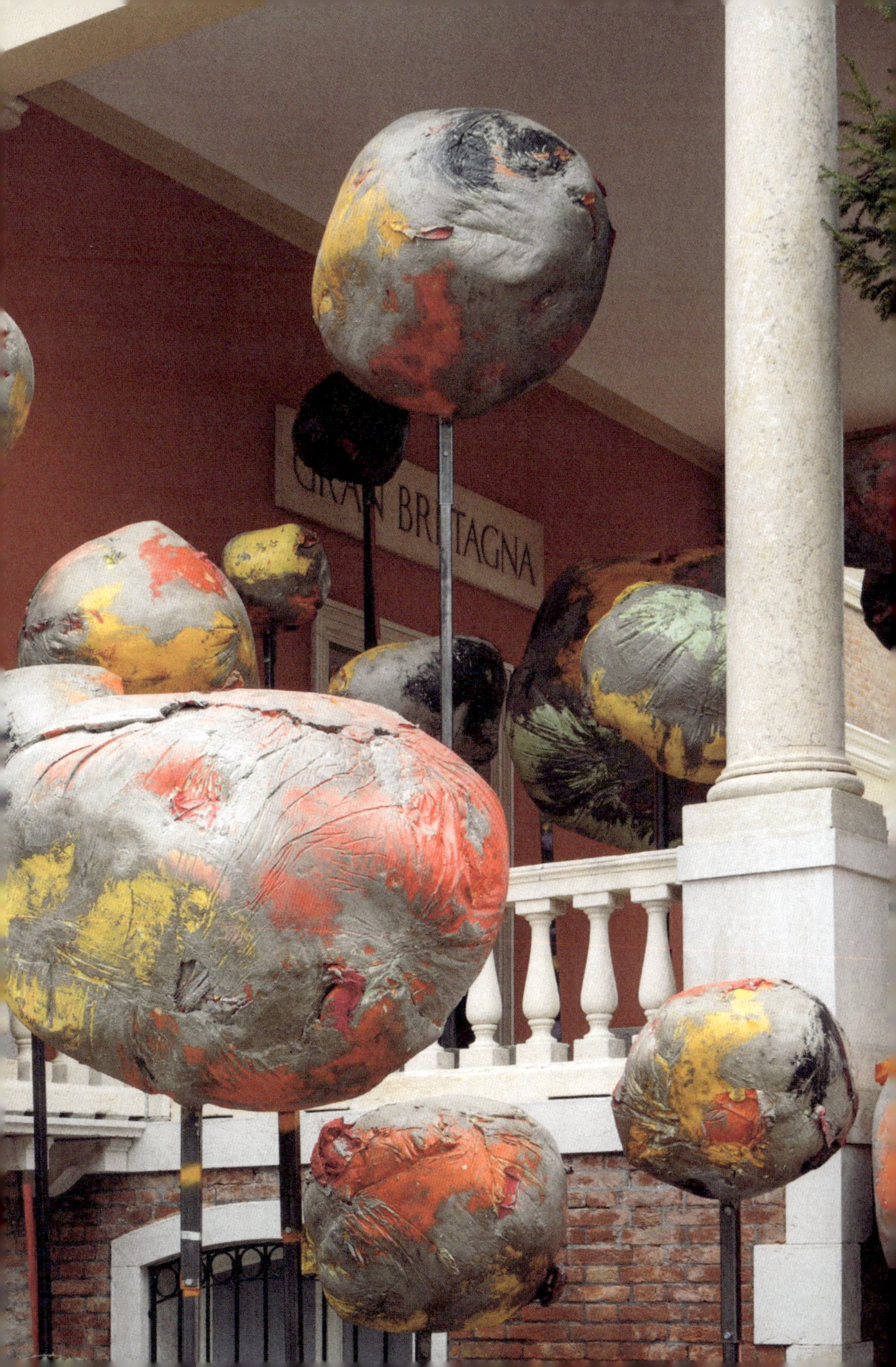
GRAN BRITAGNA

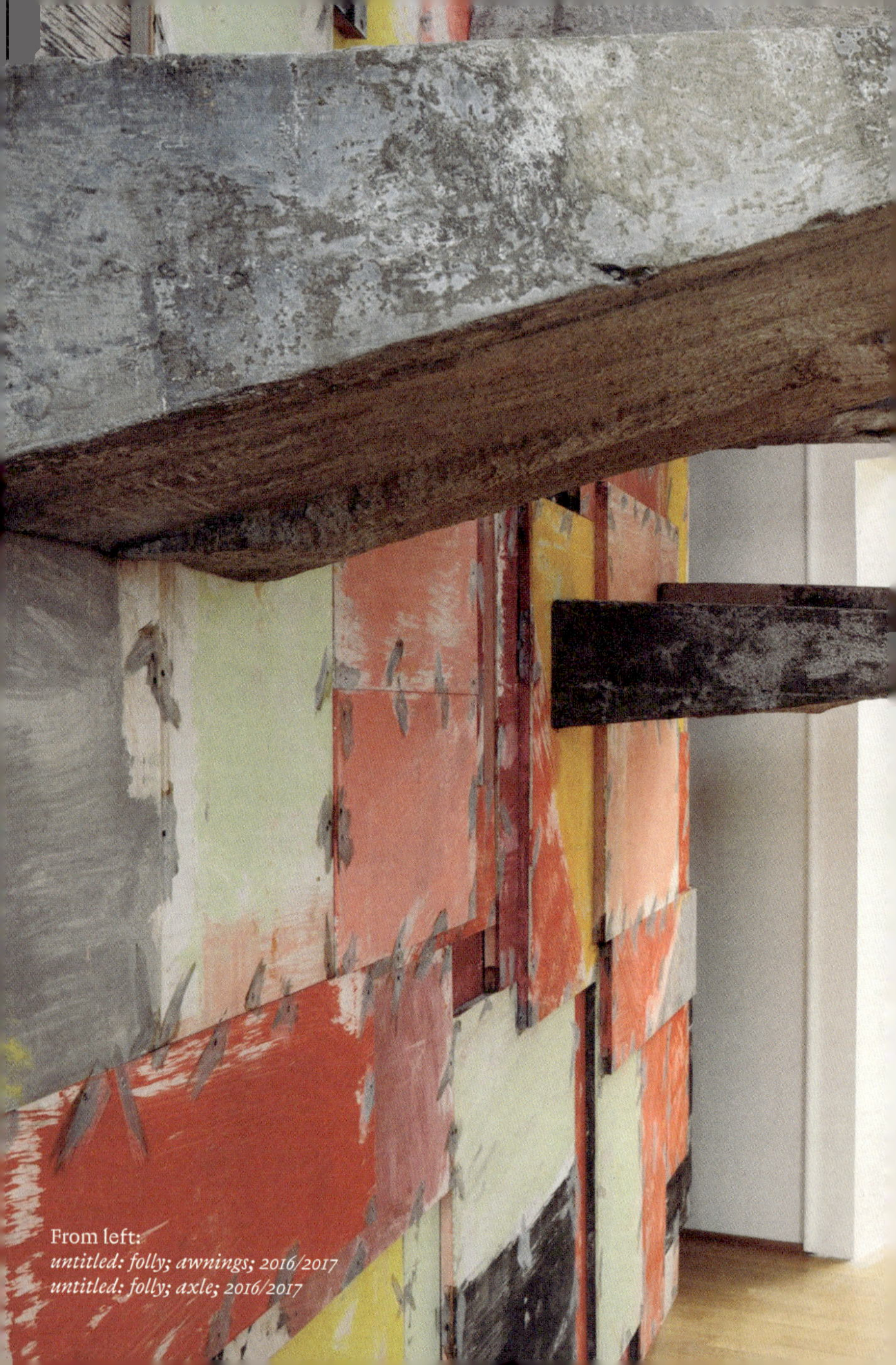

From left:
untitled: folly; awnings; 2016/2017
untitled: folly; axle; 2016/2017

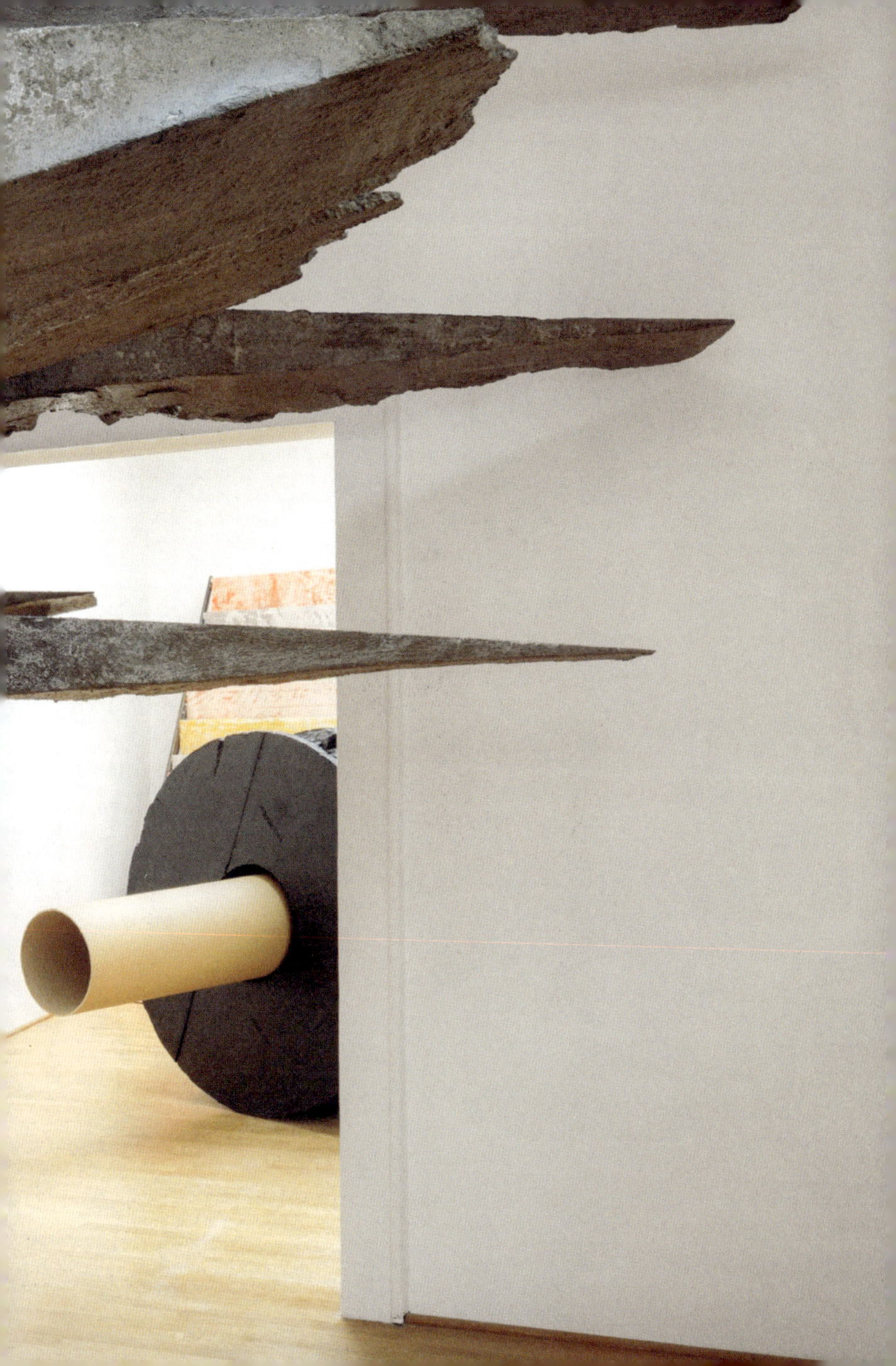

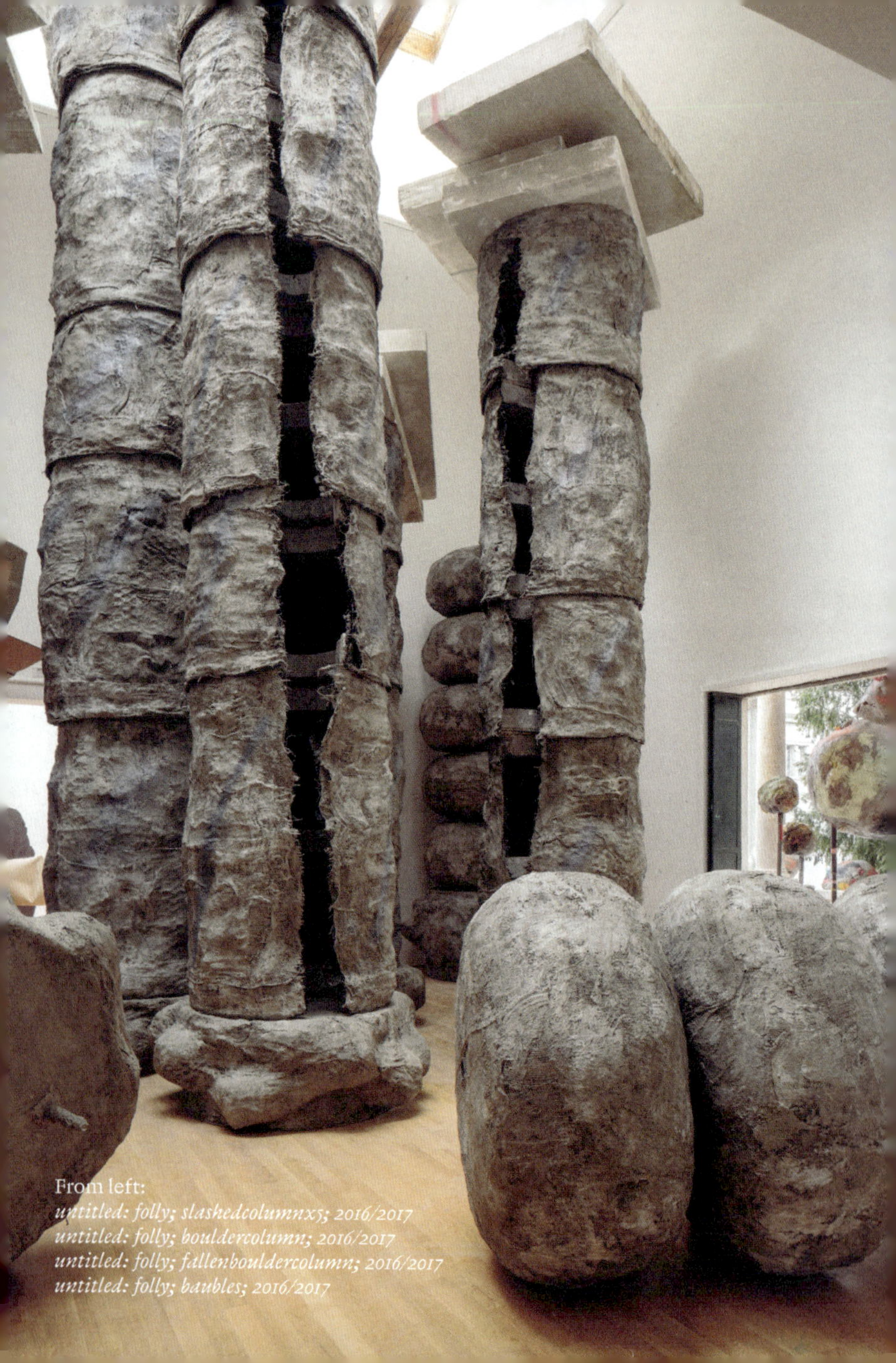

From left:
untitled: folly; slashedcolumnx5; 2016/2017
untitled: folly; bouldercolumn; 2016/2017
untitled: folly; fallenbouldercolumn; 2016/2017
untitled: folly; baubles; 2016/2017

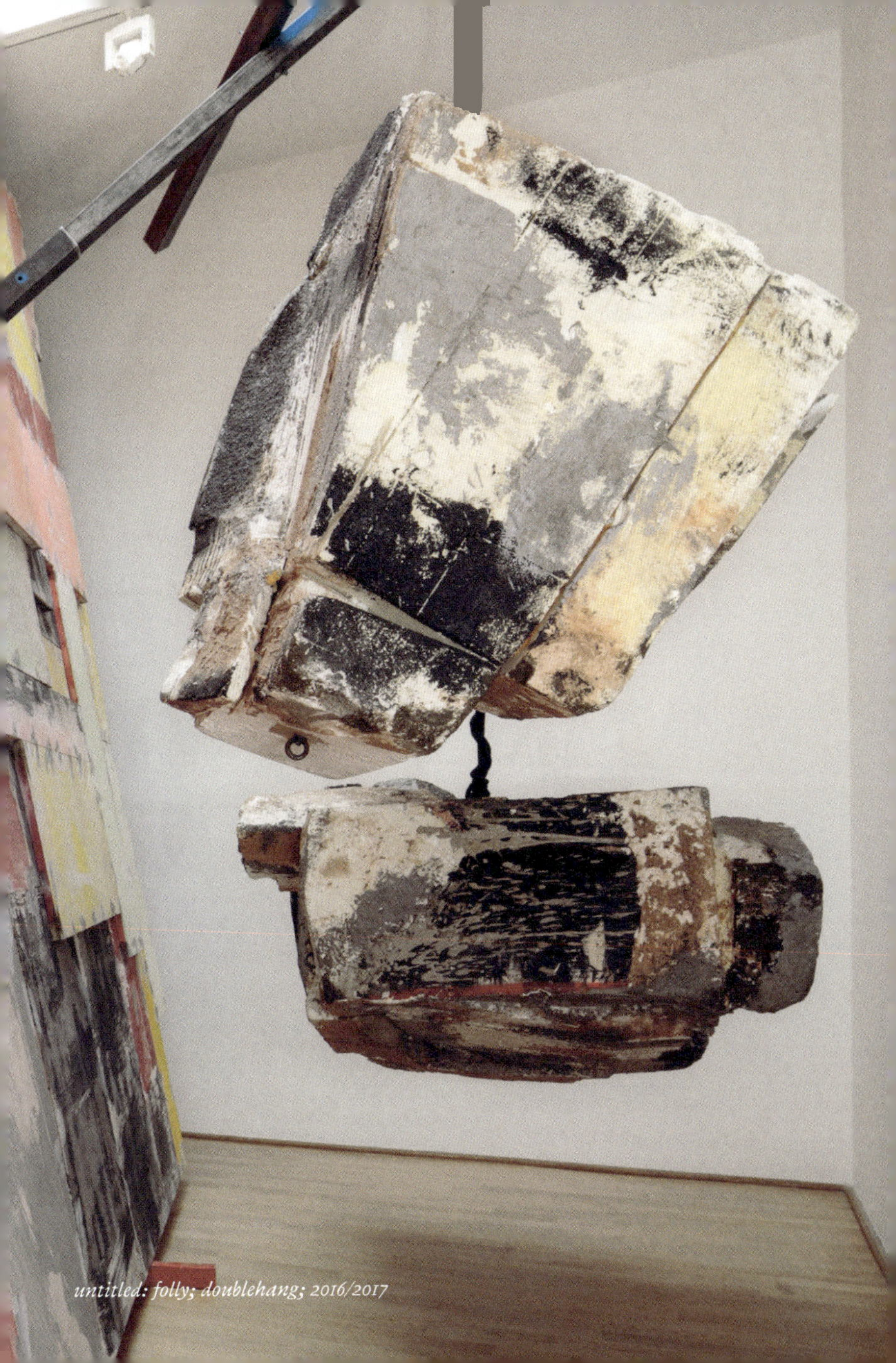

untitled: folly; doublehang; 2016/2017

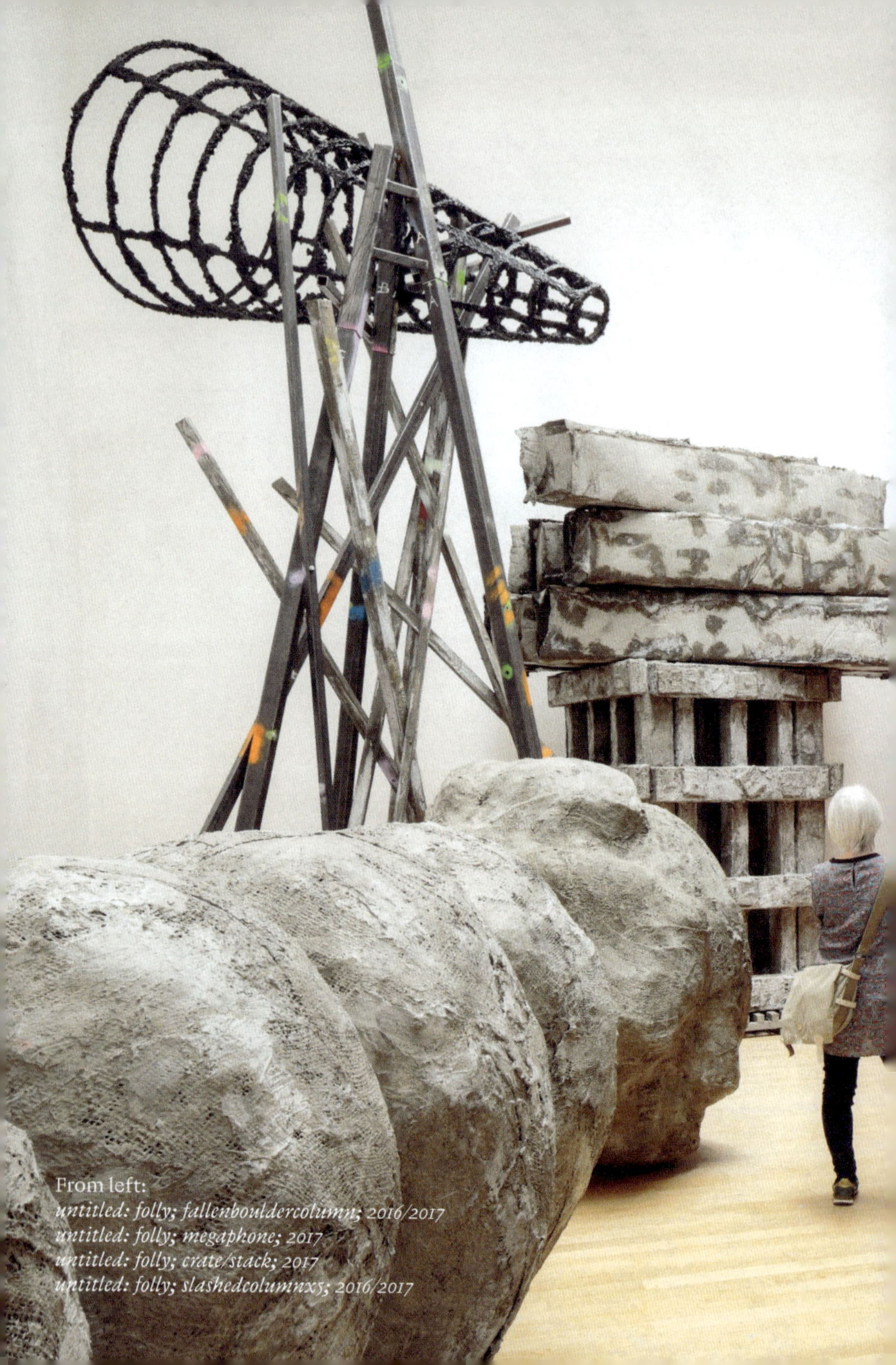

From left:
untitled: folly; fallenbouldercolumn; 2016/2017
untitled: folly; megaphone; 2017
untitled: folly; crate/stack; 2017
untitled: folly; slashedcolumnx5; 2016/2017

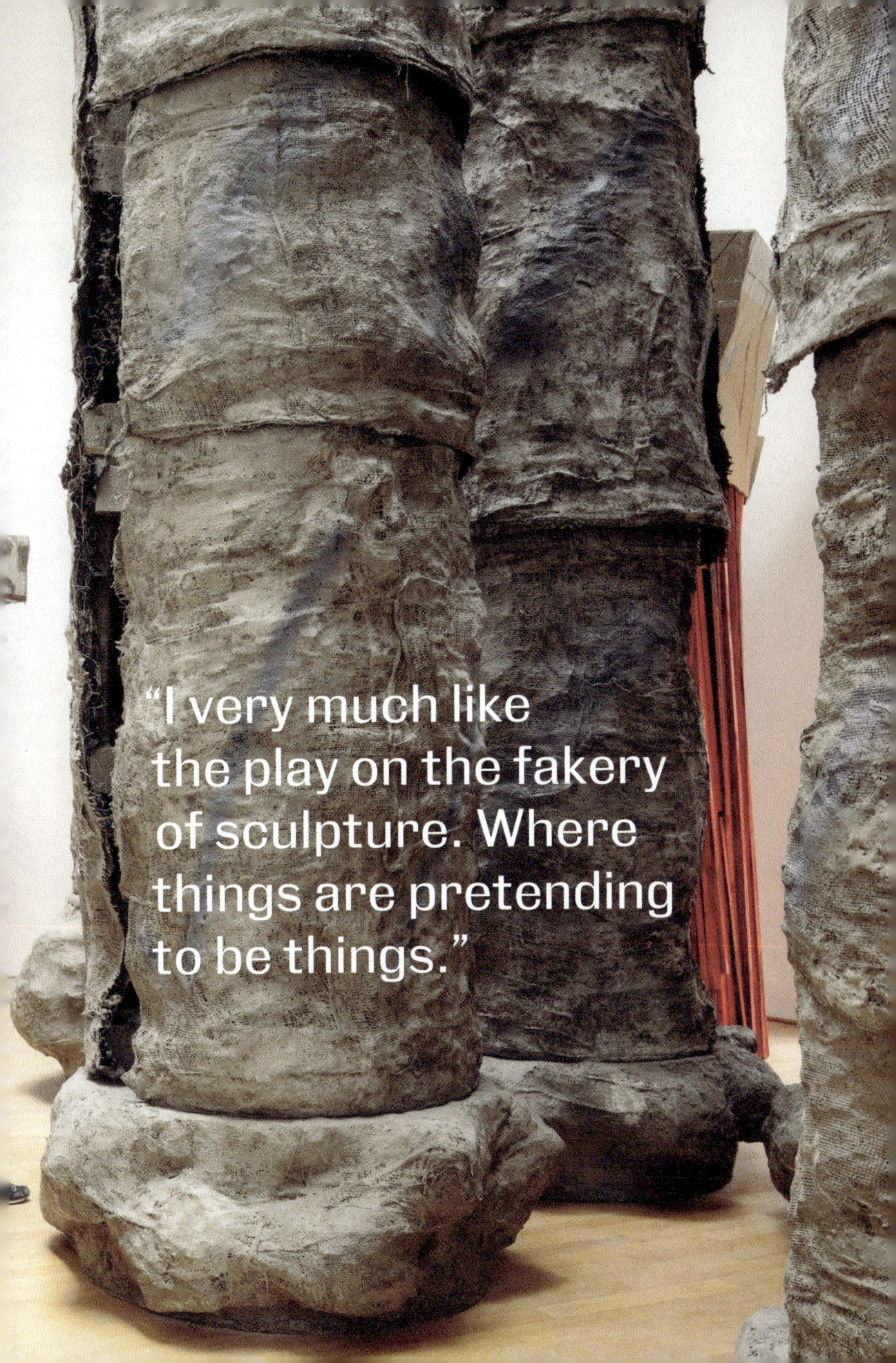
"I very much like
the play on the fakery
of sculpture. Where
things are pretending
to be things."

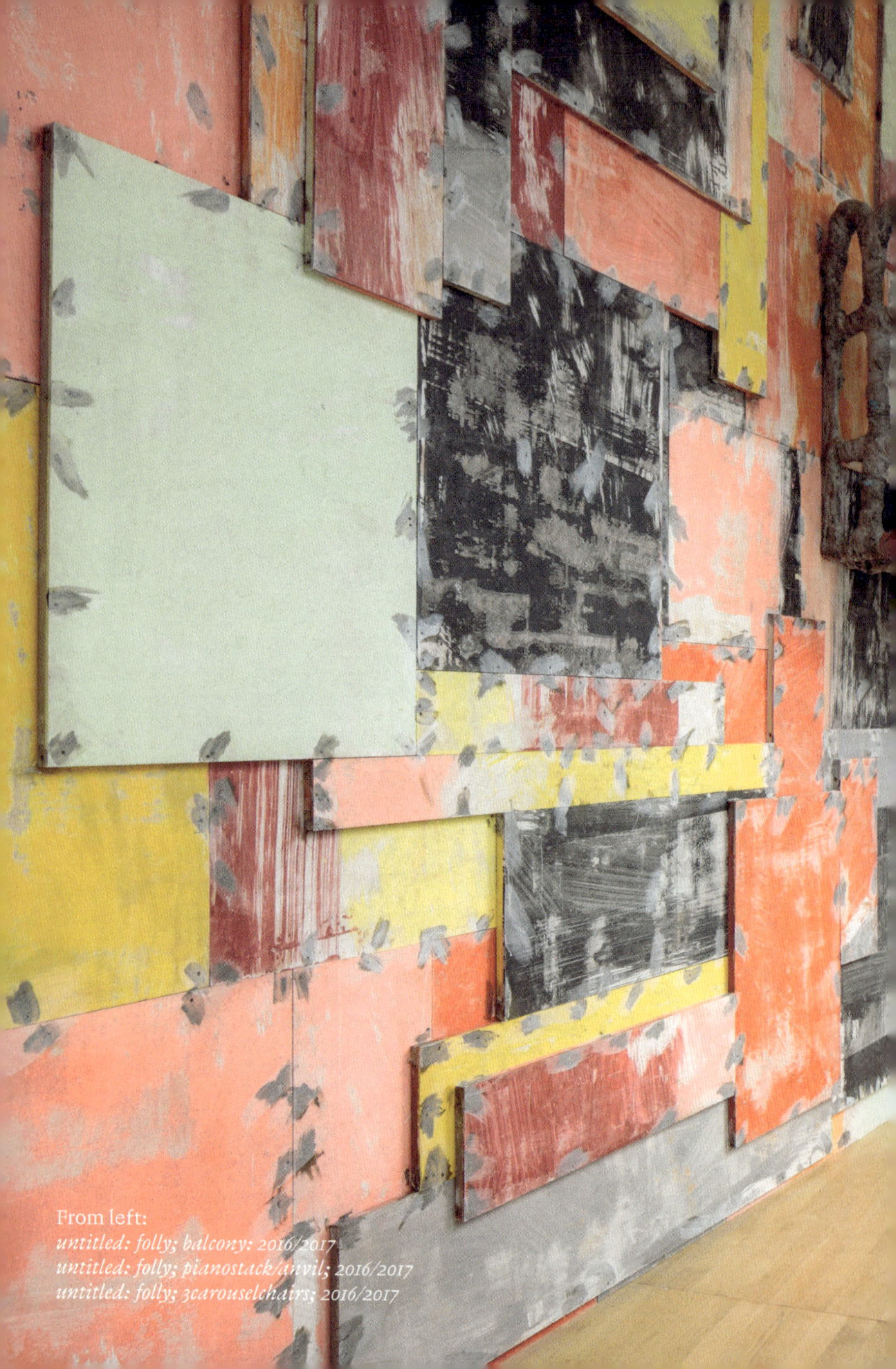

From left:
untitled: folly; balcony; 2016/2017
untitled: folly; pianostack/anvil; 2016/2017
untitled: folly; 3carouselchairs; 2016/2017

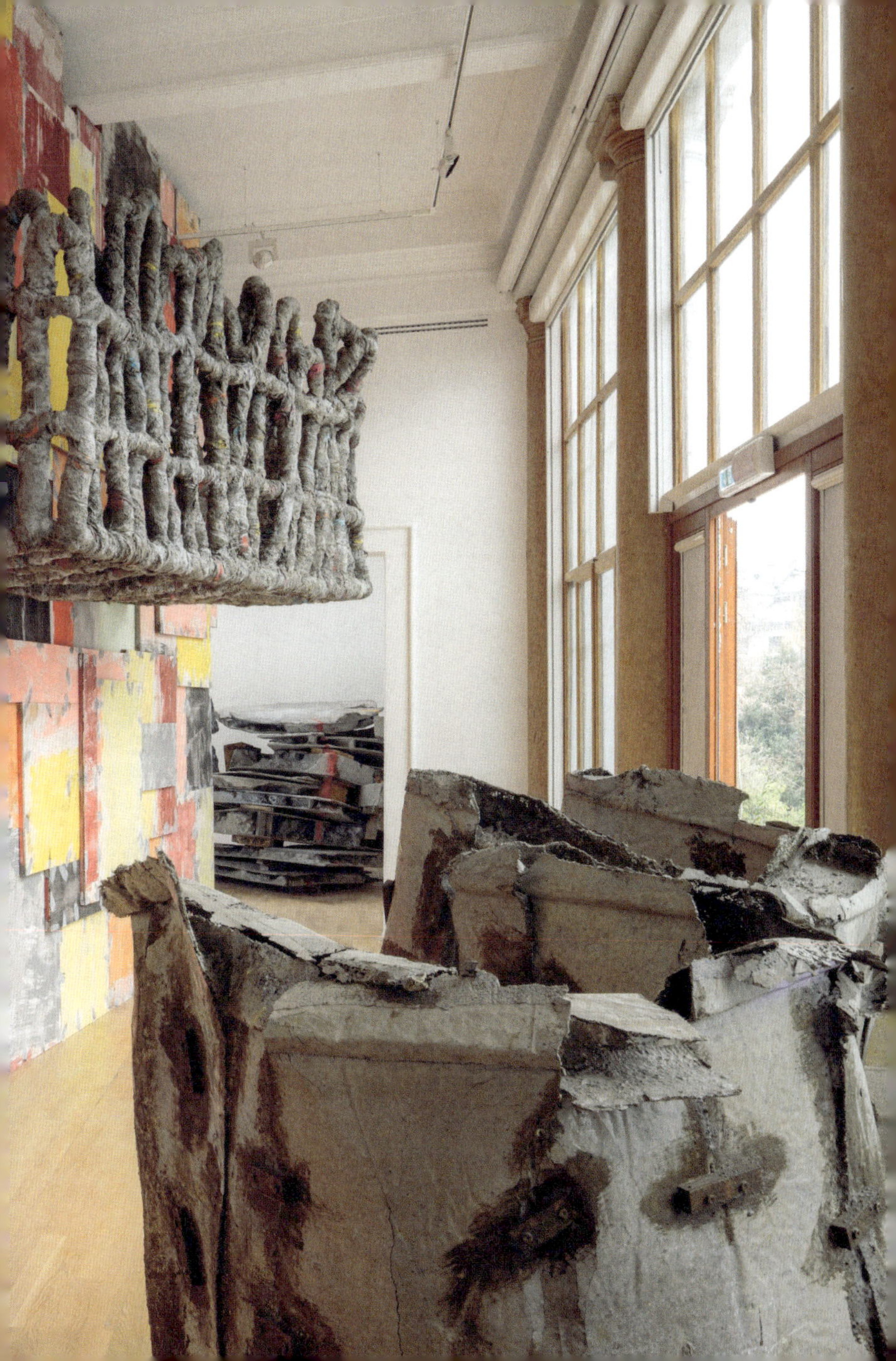

Venice Diary

Barlow kept a diary in the run-up to her exhibition at the British Pavilion. Toward the end of this turbulent and strenuous time, the artist noted her relief that finally "the gloom which the intensity of the work has prompted is beginning to lift." The entry dated February 7, 2017, includes the following, at times self-critical, notes, accompanied here by a selection of the artist's preparatory drawings.

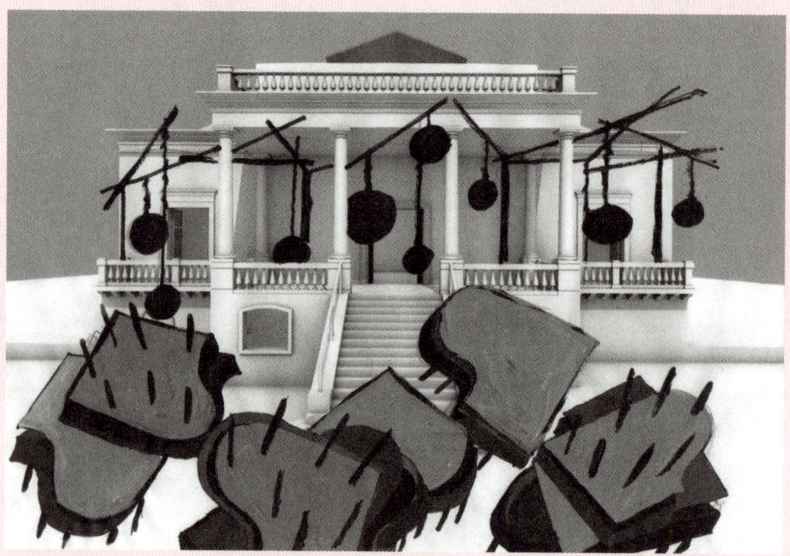

The Artist's Voice

The whole wall structure is tilted towards the entrance,
so there is a lot of anxiety as to how it will work ...

the megaphone has been eviscerated ... stripped of its
skin and is now an open structure where the steel frame
work has been thickly coated and painted thickly ...

it will be located in the far left hand corner of gallery 1—
shouting into nothing

i am surprised by all this symbolism, and it is unnerving—
telling too many stories ...

—the work is reaching its completion, in the studio—it will
all begin again in the space and i will feel i have never seen
it before; and at that moment it will be terrifying, and there
will be this realisation that there are three protagonists:
the space, the works, the audience ...

and the works, this "folly," as it is titled, will be my
anthropology, my evidencing of this time i live in ...

and i have lived with the spaces and the possible works
which will inhabit those spaces (or how the spaces will
inhabit the works) in my head since about this time last
year—and i have yet to grasp its totality ... maybe that's
intentional, to not be too familiar with the work, to keep
me guessing, and to have energy for the install ...

the making of the works is just a rehearsal; the studio
will be taken to the pavilion and stripped of all its protective
defences—and the performance will begin ...

there never was a script, but at that moment, even less so ...

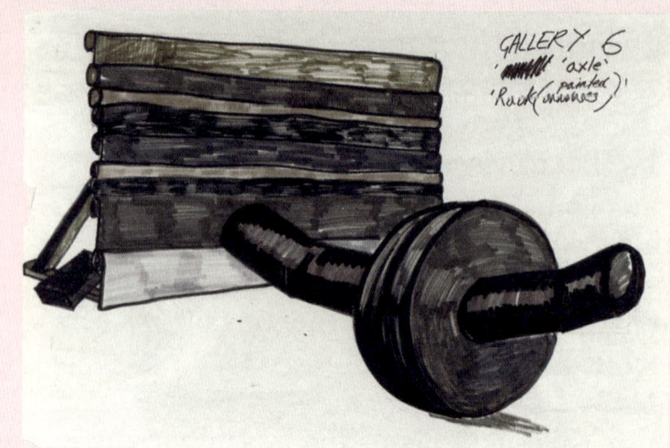

GALLERY 6
'axle'
'Rack (painted)'

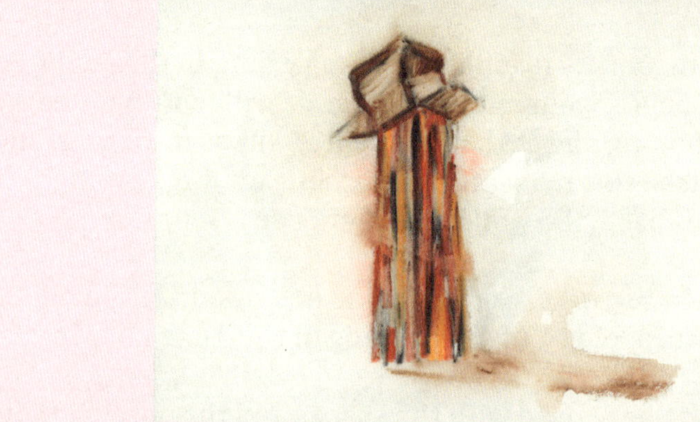

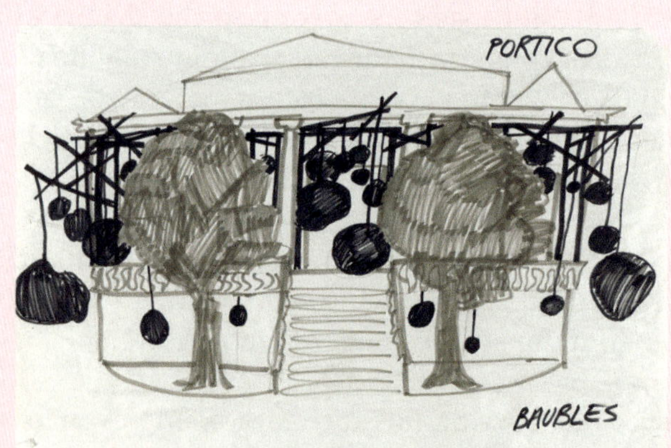

PORTICO
BAUBLES

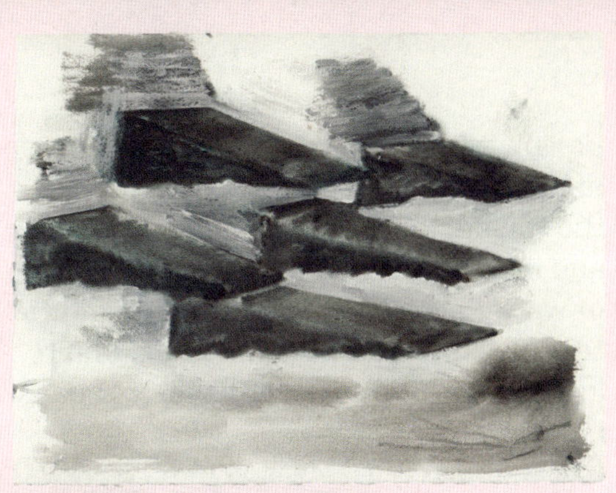

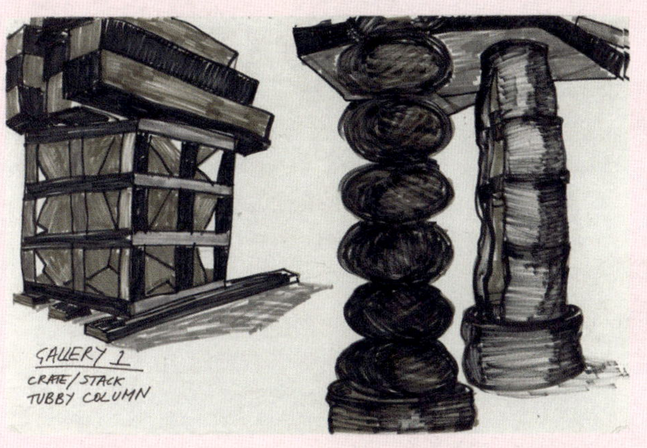
GALLERY 1
CRATE/STACK
TUBBY COLUMN

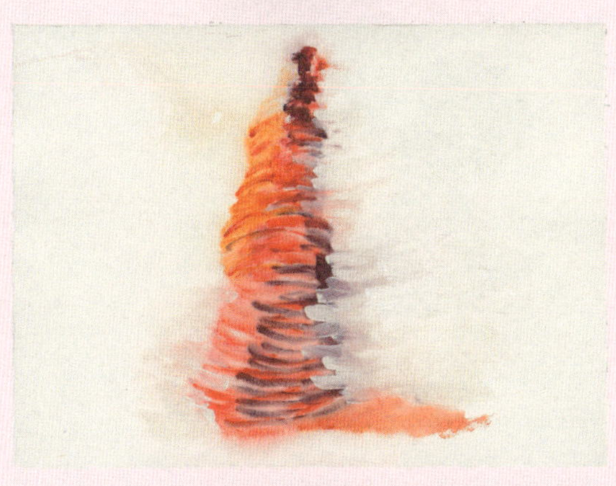

Drawings

Barlow's innumerable drawings capture a changing cast of object-characters. They can be seen as an archive of the forms, ideas, and approaches that recur in her objects and installations. But they are also a significant body of work in their own right, testifying to her willingness to experiment as well as to her affinity for certain shapes and colors and the variousness of possible relationships between them.

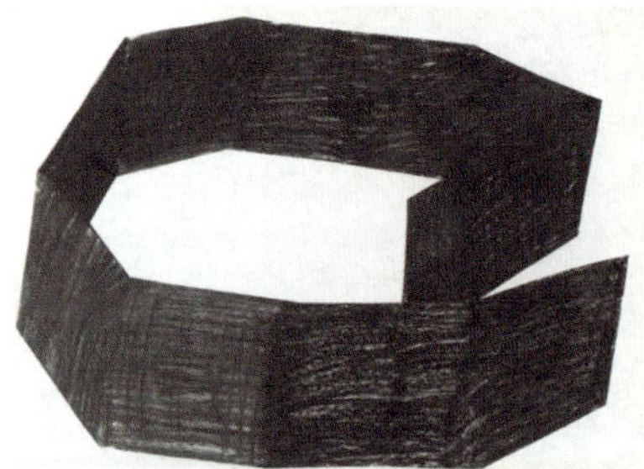

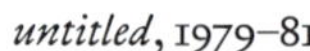

untitled, 1979–81

untitled, 1971

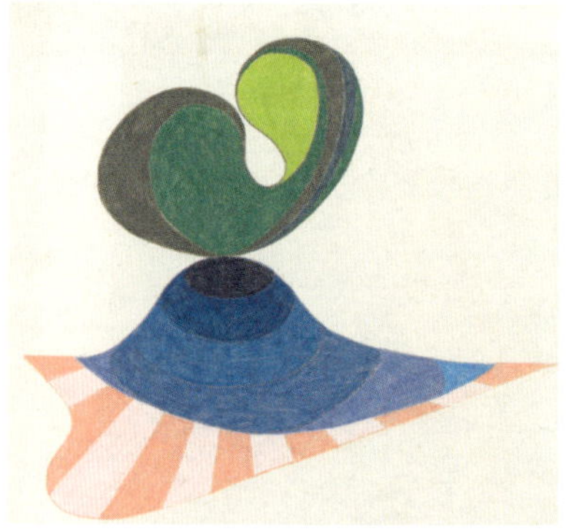

untitled, 1965–66

In Pictures

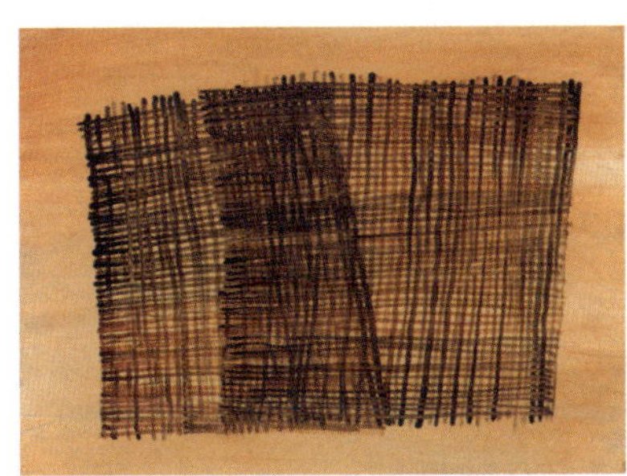

untitled: grids, 2010

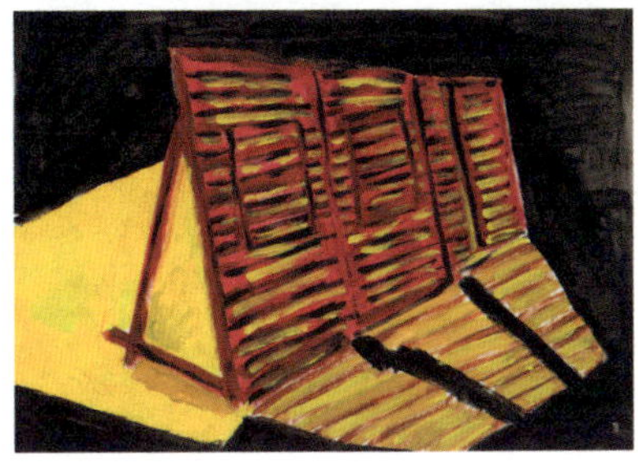

untitled, 2001

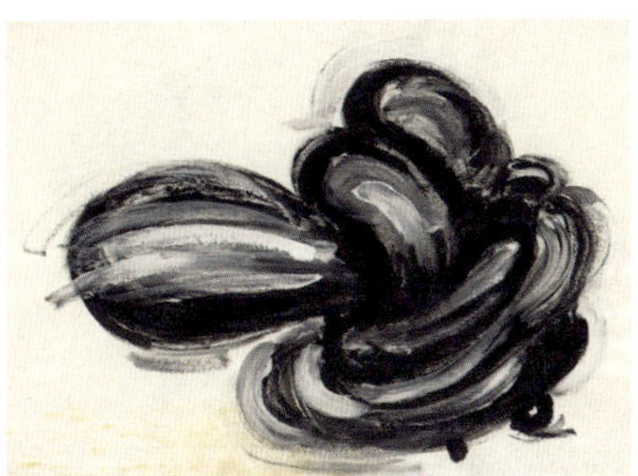

untitled, mid-1990s

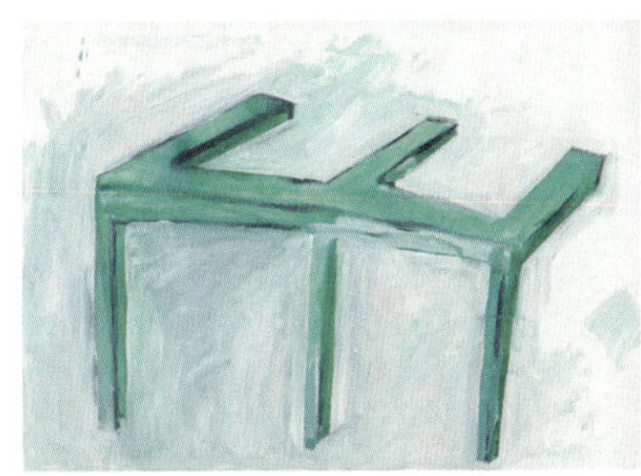

untitled: 3structure, 2015

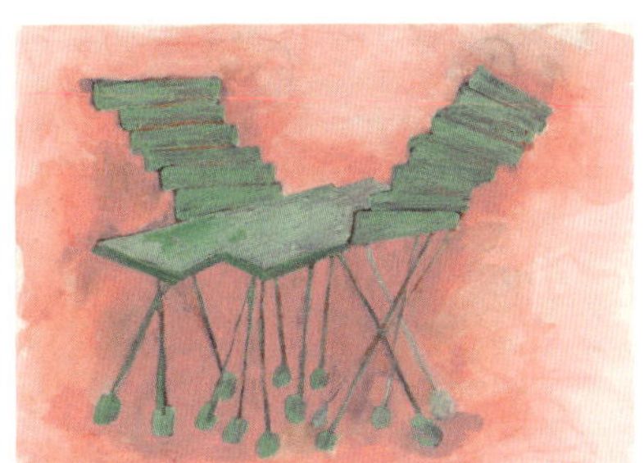

untitled: atticstaircase, green, 2; 2019/2020

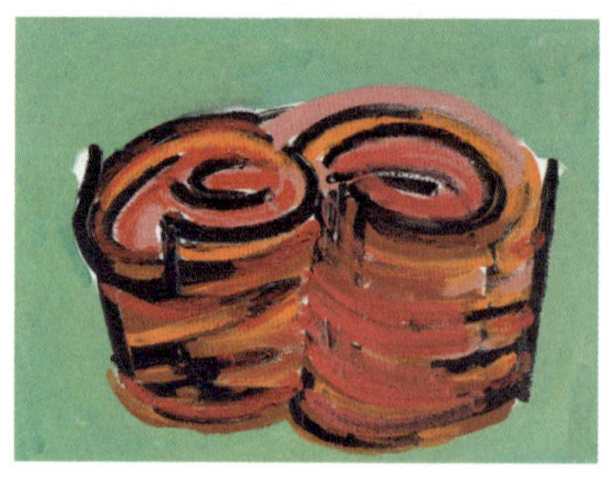

untitled, late 1990s

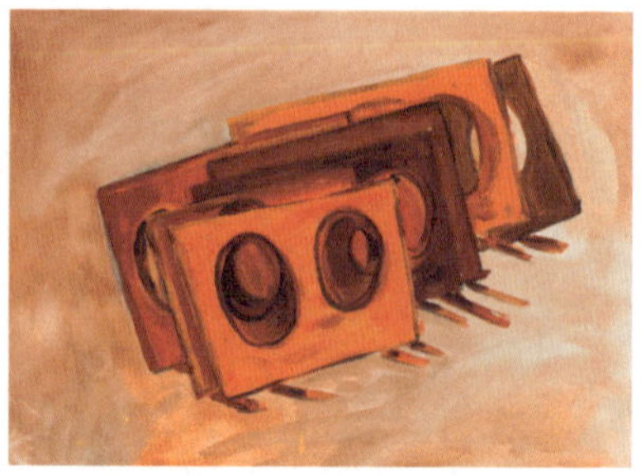

untitled: barricades, 2010

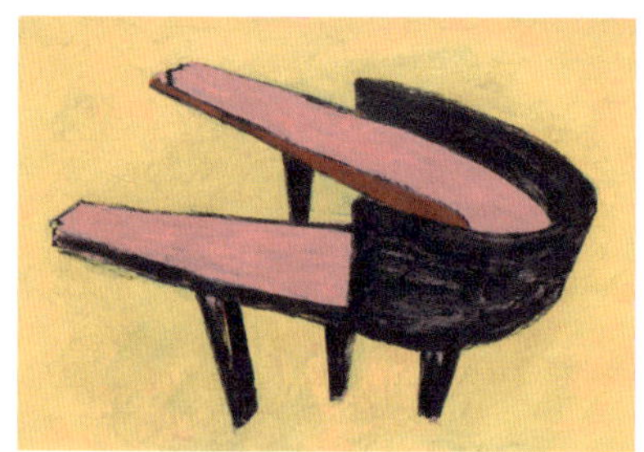

untitled: walledparapet; 2021

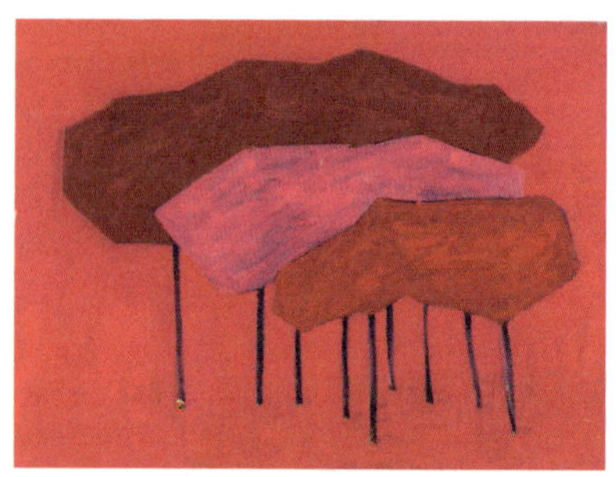

untitled: 3 boulders; idomeneo; 2020

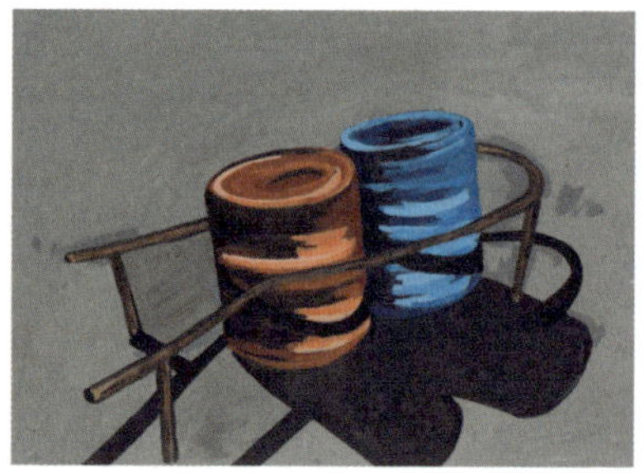

untitled, 2001

In Pictures

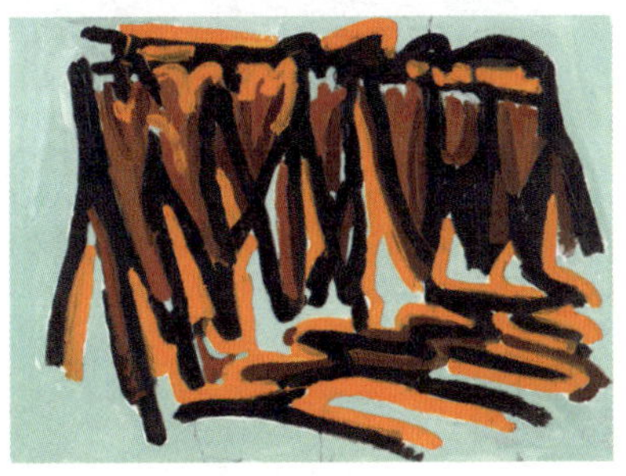

untitled, 1990–2000

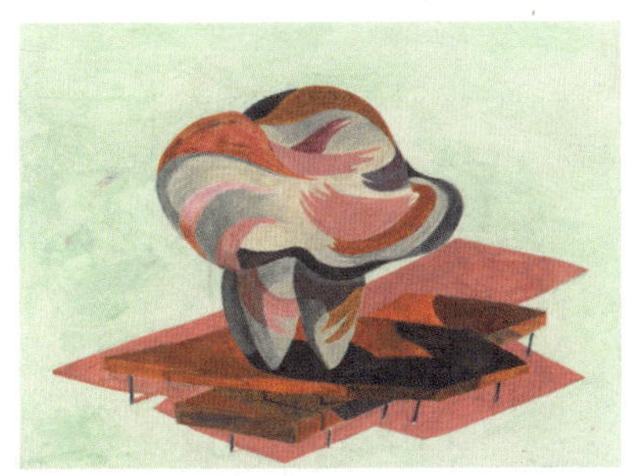

untitled: skirt; 2020

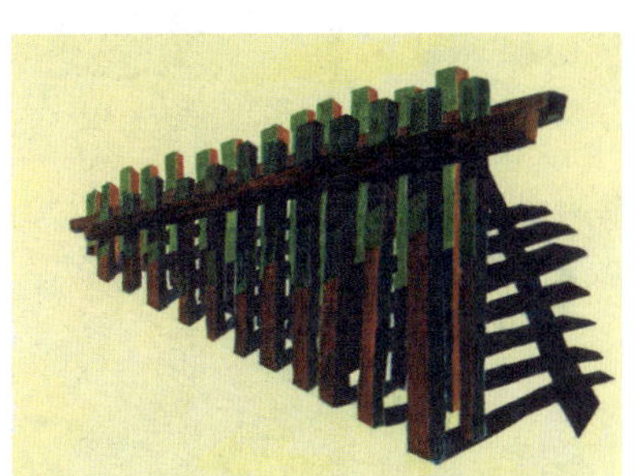

untitled: breakwater; idomeneo; 2020

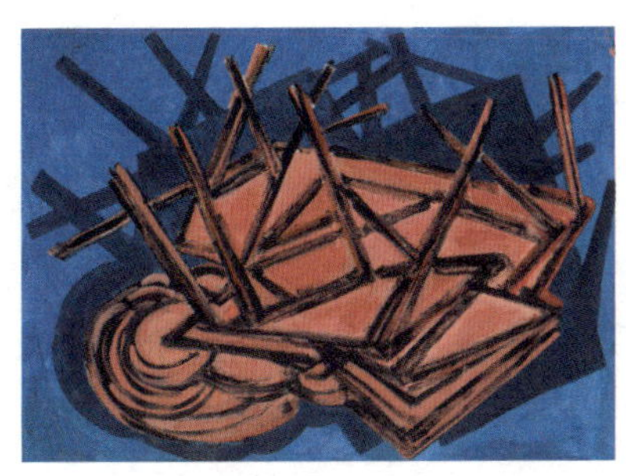

untitled: stacked, 2014

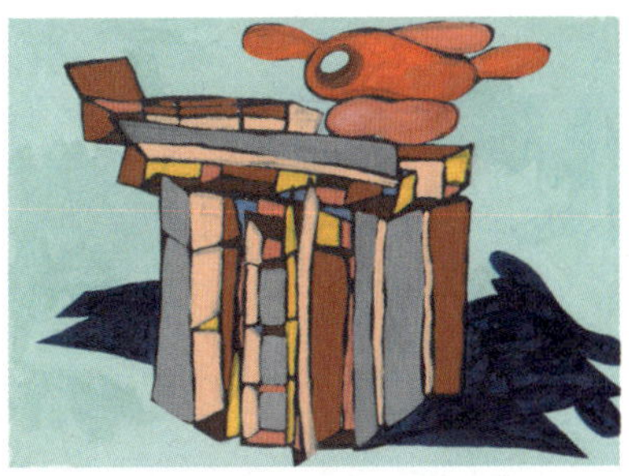

untitled: objectforstudiolockers ii; 2021

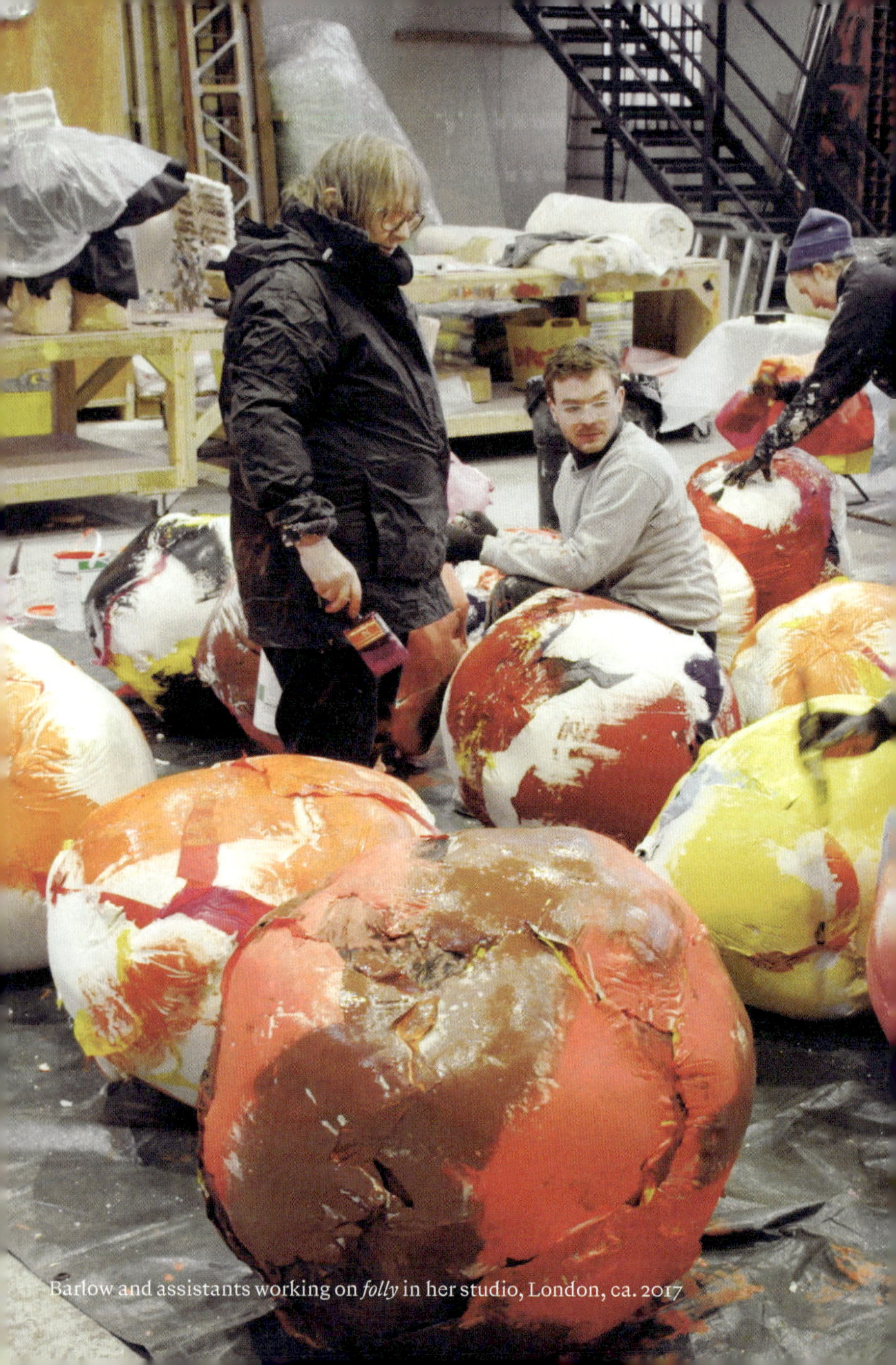

Barlow and assistants working on *folly* in her studio, London, ca. 2017

Drawing and
the Persistence of Painting

Throughout her career, Barlow found in drawing a means of responding to the world that informed and enriched her sculptural practice. She drew, especially, what she saw from her home, mostly from the upstairs window looking out over the railway sidings where the near-constant activity of workers and the movement of vehicles and materials provided her with an endless source of interest throughout the day. She found compelling things associated with storage, including wheelie bins, plastic tubs, and sheds as well as empty wooden reels and lockers. Many of her drawings feature objects related to transportation—trolleys, ramps—as well as traffic barriers and fencing. There are also tarpaulins and gantries, and a multitude of props and wedges and related unnamable kit.

At night the drama continued, slowed down, but vividly illuminated by overhead halogen lighting, and animated by dark shadows and an intensification of the reds, yellows, greens, and blues that pervade urban and industrial locations. In addition to drawing, Barlow would, from time to time, and when sleep eluded her, write vivid and precise prose descriptions of this nocturnal view, noting, for example, how in the middle of the night a streetlamp made "a network of shadows" out of nearby scaffolding and how the workers' own shadows reminded her of "a re-incarnation of early cinema."

Barlow drew, from observation and memory, images that imprinted themselves on her mind as significant. These were always images of things observed, whether in real

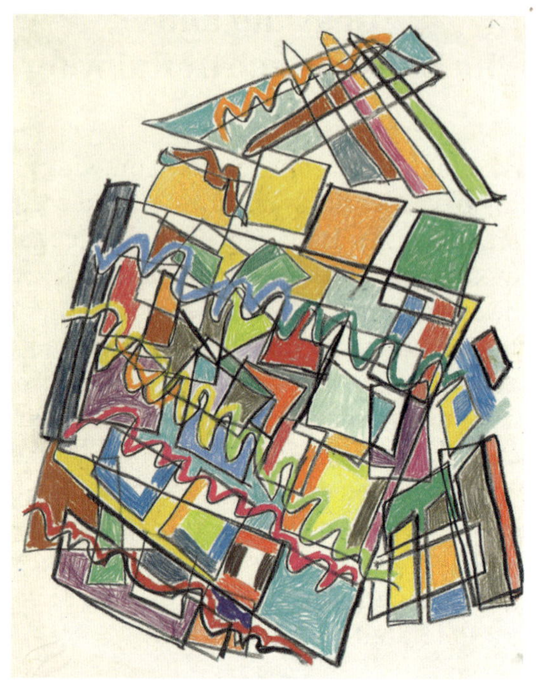

6 Bathing Hut, late 1960s–early 1970s

life or in television footage; once she drew them, she
frequently returned to them, often reinventing them as
sculpture. Brightly colored pencil drawings from the late
1960s or early 1970s include several compositions titled
Bathing Hut. More than fifty years later, in 2015, Barlow was
moved by a news clip of a resident in New Orleans returning
home after the devastation of Hurricane Katrina to find
his house turned upside down. The experience prompted
a sequence of drawings and several large-scale sculptural
representations she called *untitled: upturnedhouse*, which
are clearly indebted, in form and color, to the *Bathing Hut*
works. A similar flow and counterflow can be traced through
many of Barlow's forms: the drawings she made during

Materials and Making

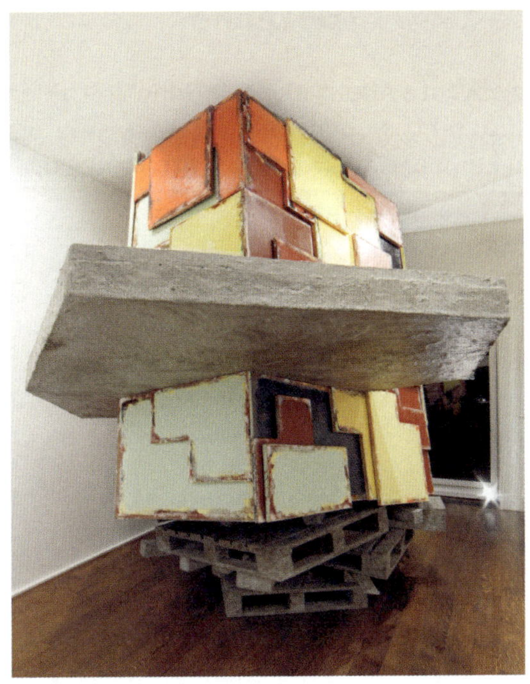

untitled: upturnedhouse, 2012

the 1960s already include recurrent motifs such as window grids, triangles and arches, tables, tubs and fences, blocks and containers. Her preference for bright traffic-light colors was also evident by the end of that decade. As she stated in a 2014 interview, "the colours from the 1950s and the early 1960s have always remained important, as well as colours that you see on the street."

At art school Barlow had been reprimanded for her lack of attention to the model in her life-drawing class. The problem, she later admitted, was that she found the incidental architecture of other students' easels that interrupted her view much more interesting than the model

Cézanne

Barlow wrote about her relationship to Cézanne in 2022, on the occasion of a retrospective of the French artist's work at Tate Modern.

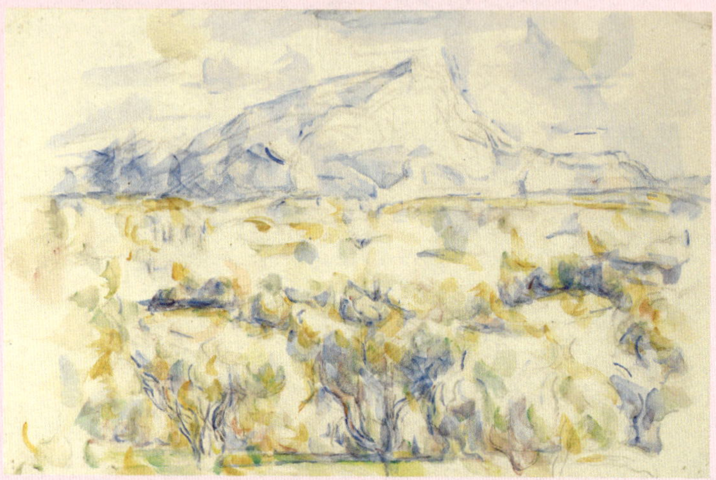

Paul Cézanne, *Montagne Sainte-Victoire*, 1905–6

I recall my first experience of looking at Cézanne's *Montagne Sainte-Victoire*, when I was a student at Chelsea School of Art: it was 1961 and at the Tate Gallery, now Tate Britain, following a tutorial from Michael Andrews: "line is a human invention—there are no lines in nature, or anywhere; go and look at Cézanne's watercolour at the Tate, *Montagne Sainte-Victoire*, and look at how little there is—the economy of colour, line, space, and where an empty space is in fact full." And I have been back to look at *Montagne Sainte-Victoire*, each time a shock, comparable to listening to Beethoven's Opus 133, or being caught in extreme weather—wind, rain, snow, things that disappear, where remembering fails the sentience of the experience.

 The Artist's Voice

itself. Once liberated from compulsory life drawing, she
dropped the human form from her repertoire and began to
focus on the mesmerizing drama of a city continuously in
flux, on the extraordinary things that prop up our modern
lives. When drawing, Barlow would deliberately suspend
knowledge of what things *are* or how they work, and instead
focus on form and color, surface and space, attending often
to the part before the whole. The original function, scale,
or situation of a given subject is not always apparent in
the resulting drawing.

Barlow used different materials to make her drawings:
colored crayons and pencil early on, as well as charcoal and,
increasingly, watercolor and acrylic, arguably bringing the
works closer to painting, albeit on paper. Perhaps on account
of her experiences as a student of painting at Chelsea,
Barlow was always keen to articulate a distance between
her work as a sculptor and the pictorial work of the painter.
For someone committed to making compelling objects to
circumnavigate, or quasi-cinematic installations inviting
exploration, the limitations imposed by the medium of
painting, especially the single frontal viewpoint, were
hugely constricting, or so she maintained. In truth, however,
ever since encountering the work of Cézanne as a teenager,
Barlow had been captivated by painting.

The language, if not the form, of painting is present in much
of Barlow's sculpture, so much so that many works seem to
perform a conversation with painting. Many installations
included painted elements: her *hoarding* and *upturnedhouse*
works and the walls of *folly* are all constructed from
multiple painted boards. Many of her panels are painted
with vivid colors hovering against a dark border, a perhaps
unconscious reference to Mark Rothko, a painter whom

Barlow recognized as essentially a sculptor by other means.
Paint performs multiple roles in Barlow's scenarios. She
had a fondness for painted sticks, gathered in bundles,
and for painted "To Let" signs hanging off walls. Paint was
Barlow's preferred way of adding color to her sculpture,
cutting through the monochrome of her big installations
and adding vivid evocations of flesh and blood to inanimate
objects. Paint could be evidence of action, the means
of leaving a human trace: she often used paint to signify
a work was finished, daubing color onto nail ends and
junctions. The stuff of painting manifests itself also in her
love of canvas. She employed vast rolls of painted canvas,
which she scrunched up as ground cover in her large-scale
installations; she made repeated versions of a rack draped
with painted canvases, and references to stretchers are
evident in her use of grid structures.

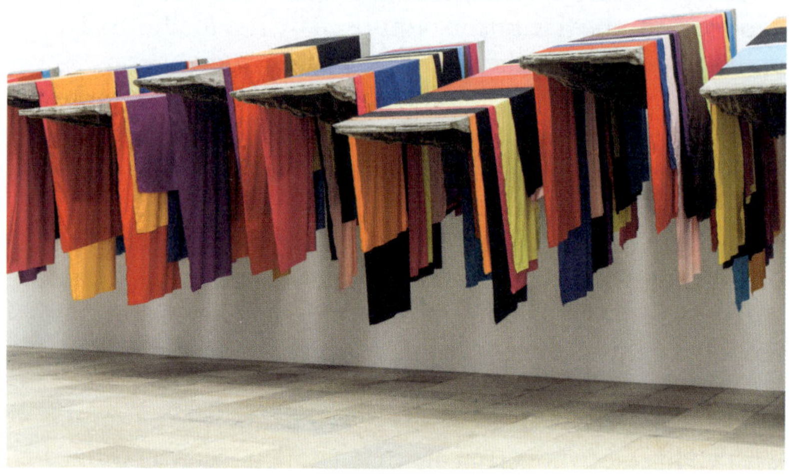

untitled: awnings; 2013, at Haus der Kunst, Munich

                    Materials and Making

After the intensity of the Covid lockdowns and an extended period of drawing afforded by enforced isolation, Barlow confessed that her drawings *were*, in fact, like paintings, or at least closer to painting than to sculpture. Perhaps we should not therefore be surprised to discover that the last new adventure Barlow embarked upon before her unexpected death in 2023 was a series of large-scale paintings intended for an exhibition in Bruton, Somerset. Barlow took her first and only steps in planning this exhibition by painting more than a dozen small canvases. For all their painterliness, their brilliant colors, these little paintings are for the most part paintings of sculpture, and, like her drawings, can be seen as affording another way of thinking about sculpture, itself her primary lens on the world. However, they also represent an unexpected and unprecedented detour from a lifetime spent focusing on three-dimensional objects in space and therefore demand attention.

Barlow did not discuss these ambitious plans for her unrealized exhibition, nor did she live to make the paintings on a larger scale. We are thus left to speculate as to her intentions. Might we not, perhaps, consider these final works as a modest but triumphant riposte to the Chelsea School of Art, as she inserted herself back into the painting school from which she'd felt banished half a century before, refuting—with defiant good humor—the judgments passed upon her by those fusty old tutors? More seriously, however, they evidence Barlow's hardwired determination to take on and challenge her self-imposed disciplinary boundaries. She often described her own artistic development as a continuous cycle of construction and destruction. Barlow's final works, albeit small in scale and neat in execution, are unexpected but typically provocative, showing her forging onward—yet again—into fertile and uncharted ground.

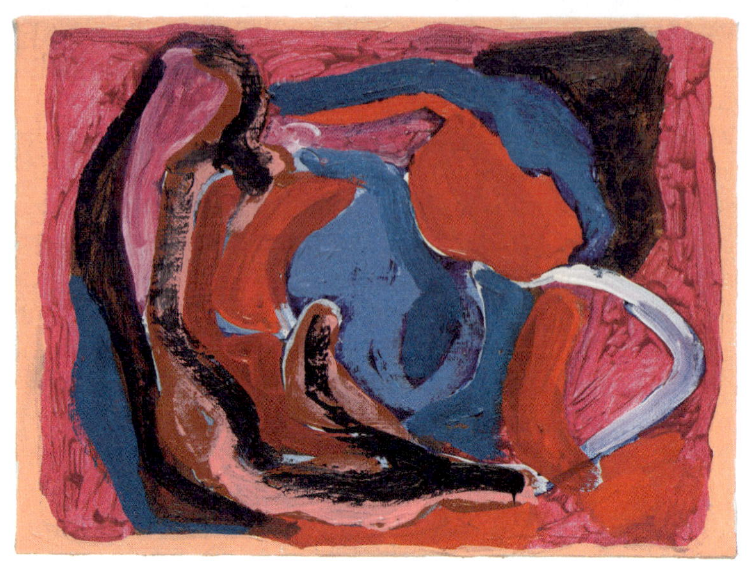

untitled: smallpainting; 17, 2022–23

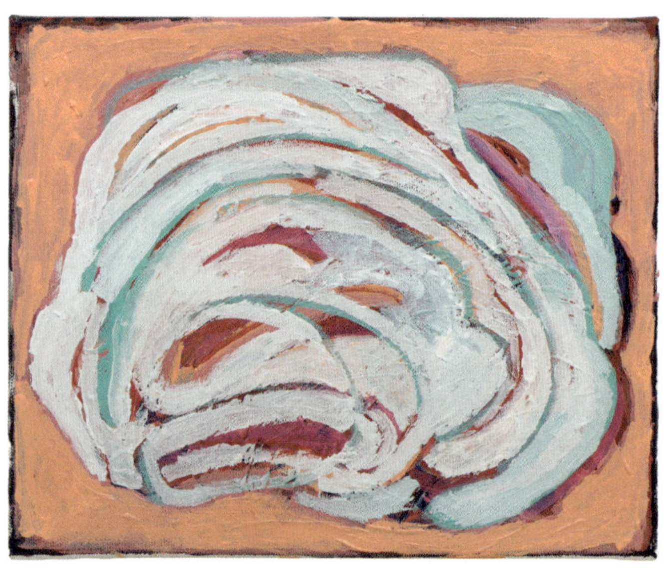

untitled: smallpainting; 1, 2022–23

    Materials and Making

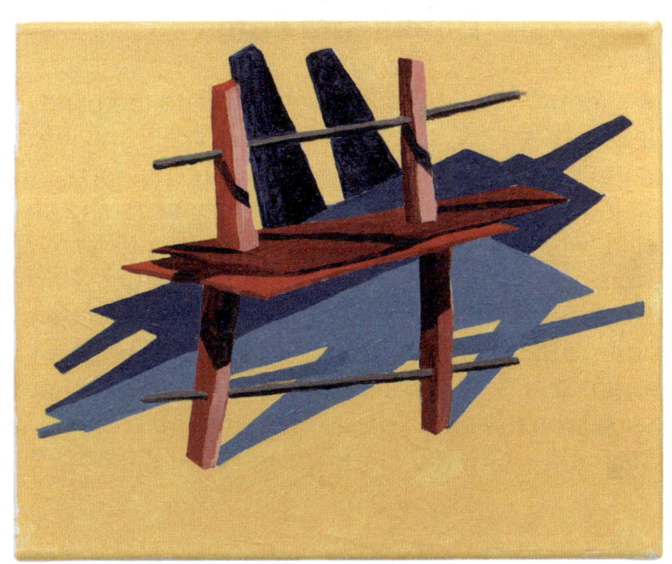

untitled: smallpainting; 12, 2022–23

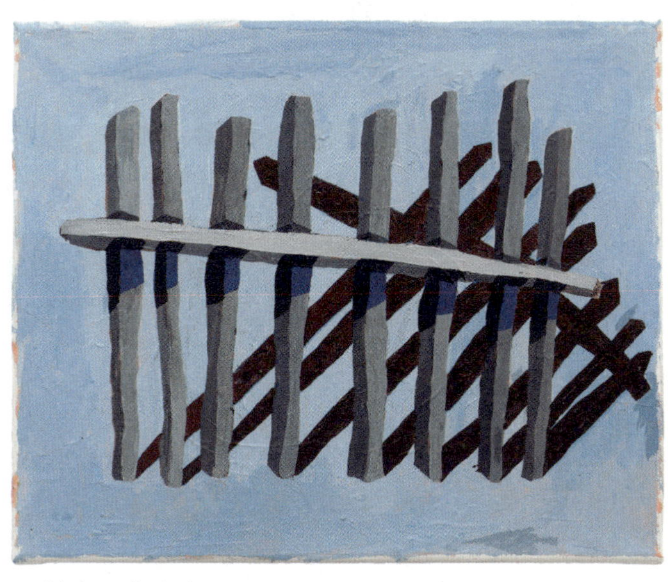

untitled: smallpainting; 9, 2022–23

Books and Films

Barlow's immersion in the art world and its long and complex history was accompanied by a lively and informed interest in literature, music, film, and the performing arts. Aside from the rich cultural experiences she enjoyed as a child, which engendered a lifelong interest in avant-garde film, classical music, and world literature, Barlow was also fascinated by popular culture and entertainment. It was her tutor George Fullard who encouraged her to find "sculptural" experiences and techniques in other art forms and who nurtured her love of animated cartoons and black-and-white slapstick movies of the 1920s.

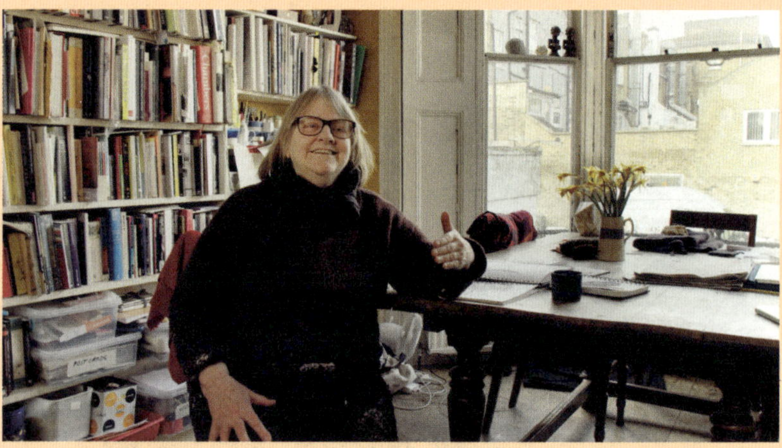

Barlow at home, ca. 2017

 Influences

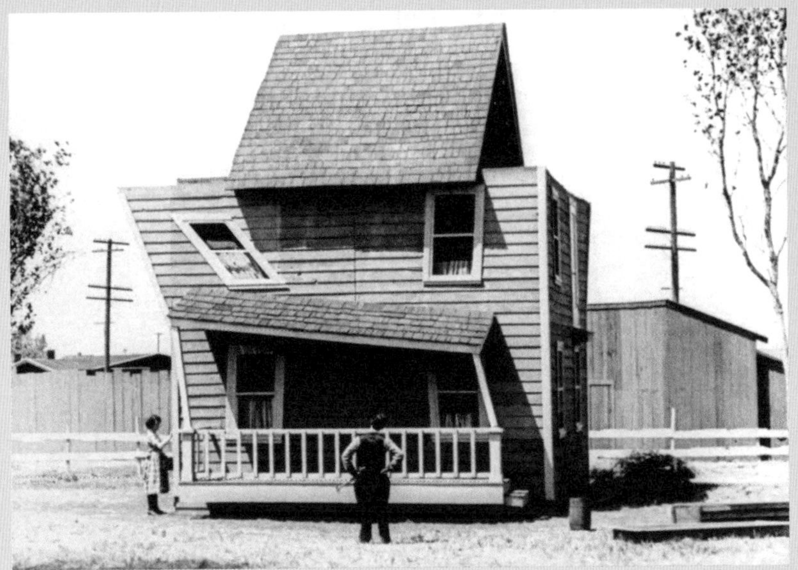

Sybil Seely and Buster Keaton in *One Week*, 1920

Buster Keaton, *One Week*

In Keaton's silent slapstick comedy, released in 1920 as his first independent production, he and Sybil Seely costar as newlyweds in small-town America attempting to construct a house from a prefabricated kit gifted to them as a wedding present but tampered with by a jilted lover. Barlow put making mistakes at the center of her own approach to making objects and saw in Keaton's extraordinary antics a demonstration of the farcical relationship we can all have with them. She often presented objects in precarious situations, poised or hanging on, tempting disaster, while piles of debris— the aftermath of disintegration—regularly feature in her installations. Barlow likened the process of making sculpture to life cycles in nature, embodying equally powerful and interlocking forces of damage and repair.

Luis Buñuel and Salvador Dalí, *Un chien andalou*

Barlow was fascinated by how interior space in Buñuel
and Dalí's *Un chien andalou* (1929) becomes a landscape
animated by strange dreamlike occurrences. A number
of her works after she graduated from the Slade were
stagelike constructions of domestic settings that she
described as informed by the work of Buñuel, the Irish
novelist and playwright Flann O'Brien, and the Italian writer
Italo Svevo. *Un chien andalou* also includes two shocking,
unforgettable short sequences, one of a hand covered in
crawling ants, the other a close-up of a woman's face as
a young man slowly and impassively slices open one of her
eyeballs with a razor blade. In Barlow's sculpture, including
untitled: double act (2010; p. 62) and several smaller
pieces, she used hard, flat forms to brutally penetrate soft,
spherical masses in ways that suggest the imagery from
this film may well have acted as an important reference.

Fernando Pessoa, *The Book of Disquiet*

This compilation of fragments of prose and poetry,
posthumously published in 1982, established the
international reputation of a hard-to-classify author
hailed as "Portugal's James Joyce." A staple of Barlow's
bedside table, typically for dipping into when she couldn't
sleep, the novel appealed to the artist for the way in
which Pessoa was "looking at the moment when a certain
combination of events comes together—the observation,
the emotional background noise that may trigger the
observation, and the aftermath of the clash between
the two, which acts as a fuse, bringing these two states
of awareness together." Barlow was also particularly
enthralled by Pessoa's idea that "every gesture is
a revolutionary act [and] every action is incomplete
and imperfect."

Poster for Luis Buñuel
and Salvador Dalí's
Un chien andalou, 1929

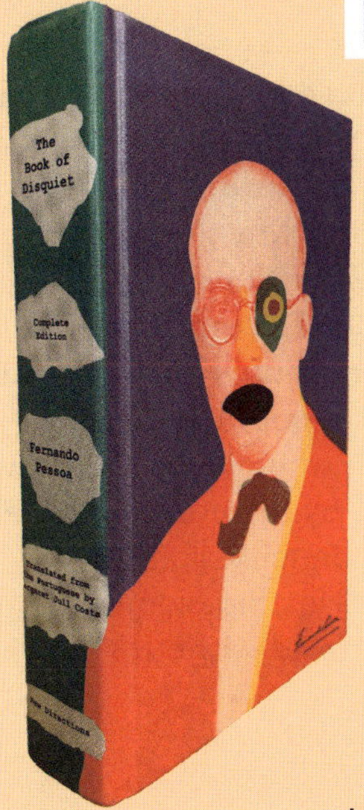

Fernando Pessoa,
The Book of Disquiet.
New Directions, 2017

Carola Giedion-Welcker, *Contemporary Sculpture: An Evolution in Volume and Space*

First published in Switzerland in 1937 and repeatedly enlarged and revised, this was Barlow's go-to book on the history of sculpture and she kept a copy within arm's reach of the kitchen table. In a 2006 lecture she described Giedion-Welcker's kind of analysis as "an almost forgotten form of critical appraisal." She frequently referred to the publication as "the big, bad, ugly book of sculpture" and spoke fondly of the European sculptors—whose work she also admiringly called "ugly"—who were represented between its covers. While Barlow disagreed with Giedion-Welcker's moralizing attitude and her emphasis on formalism, she acknowledged that the author's interests led her far beyond the conventional view of modern art.

Alain Robbe-Grillet, *Jealousy*

Robbe-Grillet is associated with the French Nouveau Roman movement, which rejected conventional literary traditions of chronology and plot. Barlow especially admired the French writer and film-maker's 1957 novel *Jealousy*. She was interested in the way the author explored his subject through descriptions of objects, surfaces, and spaces, all of which are regulated by geometry and described with precision. Robbe-Grillet was attentive to the way inside connects to outside, the way spaces are seen through windows and doorways, reflected in mirrors, and defined by furniture. He used surface and texture, weight and density, light and temperature as important scene-setting elements in present-tense narratives that exist without reference to past or present.

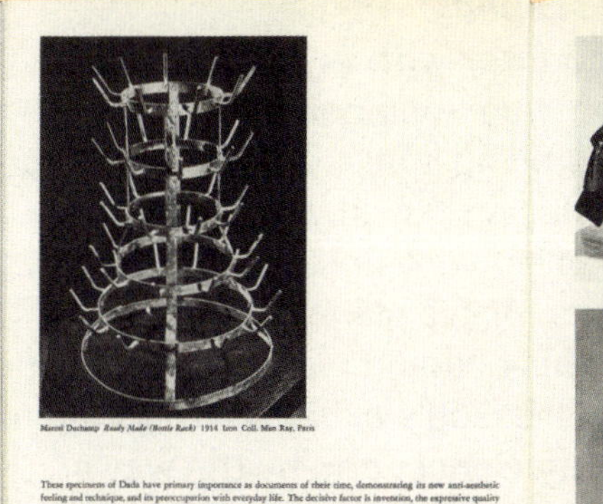
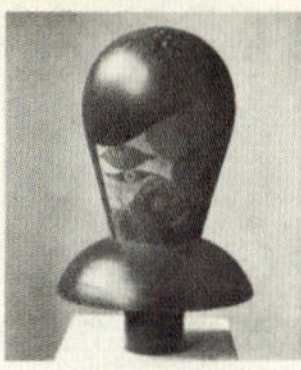
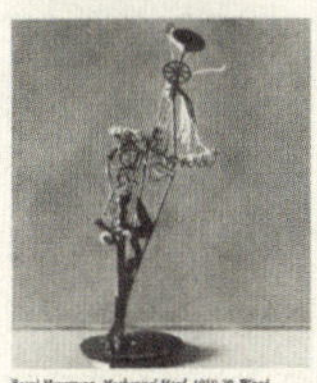
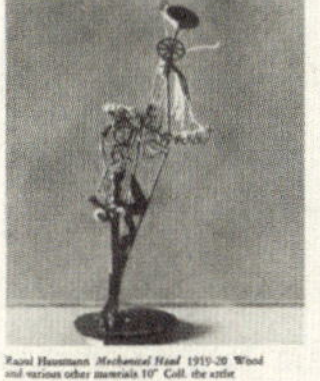
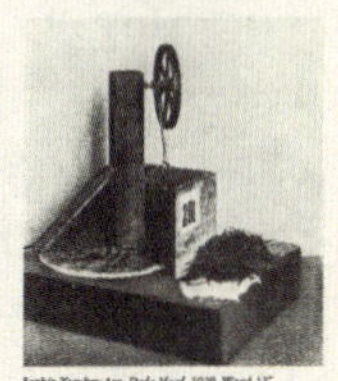

Spread from Carola Giedion-Welcker, *Contemporary Sculpture: An Evolution in Volume and Space*. Wittenborn, 1961

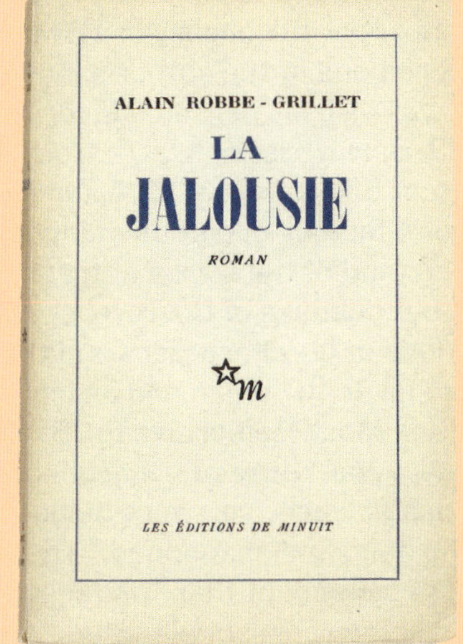

Alain Robbe-Grillet, *La Jalousie*. Éditions de Minuit, 1957

Robert Bresson, *A Man Escaped*
Barlow described her encounter with Bresson's film
A Man Escaped (1956) as a "huge epiphany." Based on
André Devigny's memoir of being imprisoned as a member
of the French Resistance during World War II, the film
is set in a claustrophobic prison cell and details Devigny's
extraordinary preparations for his planned escape
including his fashioning of his bedding materials into rope.
Barlow was fascinated by Bresson's expansive treatment
of the prisoner's limited experience, and by the way in
which every detail is imbued with profound significance.
She found in the film a grand metaphor for the artist
both trapped by their own desire to be creative and
also somehow frustratingly limited by it.

Fyodor Dostoyevsky, *The Idiot*
Dostoyevsky's portrait of Prince Myshkin—the "idiot"
of the novel's title, who returns to Russia after four years'
exile, grappling with epilepsy in a Swiss sanatorium—
is considered one of the author's more experimental
books; it was also his personal favorite.

In 2023, Barlow described *The Idiot* (1869) as "one of
the greatest books I know." She admired the work not for
the author's famous depiction of innocence confronting
corruption (and of the series of tragic events that
ensued), but because of Dostoyevsky's "almost surgical"
observations of his characters and the evenhanded
treatment given to human and animal, regardless of
their status. Most memorable for Barlow as a reader
was the very real sense of being absorbed into a narrative
with no idea of where you were being taken, of being
"led by the hand and abandoned." The actual story was for
Barlow less significant than the feeling she experienced
that the work was essentially about who *we* are now.

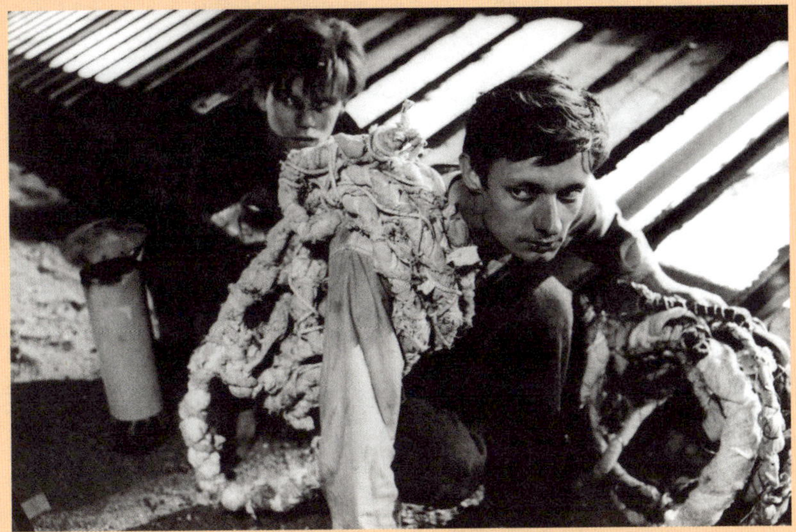

Charles Le Clainche and François Leterrier in Robert Bresson's *A Man Escaped*, 1956

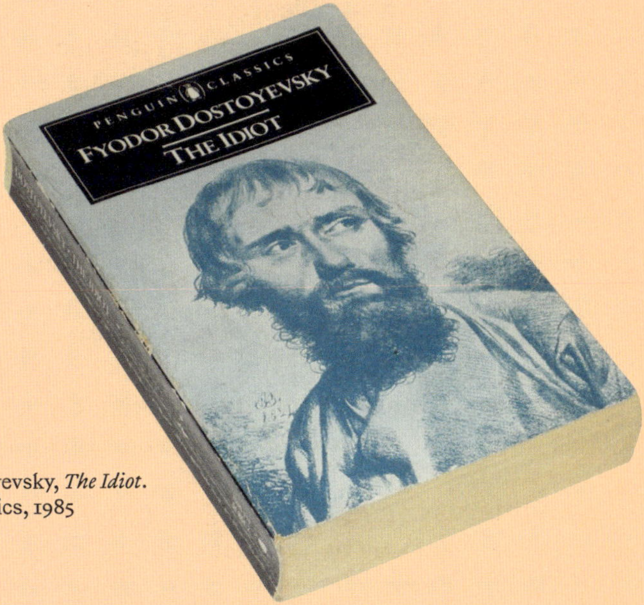

Fyodor Dostoyevsky, *The Idiot*.
Penguin Classics, 1985

Provocations

The following text, published as "Provocations for the Yorkshire Sculpture Triennial" in 2018, comprises statements that, in Barlow's words, "emerged from the two meetings … with all those involved in the Triennial," and "reflect [her] own concerns as well as addressing issues which arose from the meetings." She went on to explain: "There are two sets of statements; I have not indicated whether I agree with the statements or not."

1

- It is pointless to define what sculpture is.
- Anything can be sculptural—weather, speech, smell, temperature, darkness, light, invisibility, reflections, movement, stillness, silence, noise, chaos, order …
- All these qualities have become art and have been used as art.
- There are no surprises.
- Rothko paintings are sculptural.
- Nauman walking around his studio (video) is sculptural.
- Bernini's *Ecstasy of Saint Teresa* is film and not sculpture.
- What is "work," "labour," "effort" in relationship to "making"?
- Do moral attitudes to the above, and to the handmade, impede?
- All ways of making involve the handmade.
- There is no difference between the handmade and the fabricated/manufactured.
- Everything is appropriated.
- It is not interesting to be obsessed by invented form.
- What is invented form?

　　　The Artist's Voice

- Sculpture's silent and motionless character does not
  reflect the times we live in—politically, environmentally,
  economically, socially.
- Subject, Form, and Content dominate all creative
  processes.
- "Subject" has been the dominant concern for the past
  three decades.
- "Subject" has itself become dominated by "issues"—
  gender, sexuality, abuse, ethnicity, race, class,
  economics.
- Issues of war, migration, immigration, refugees are
  too important not to be major concerns for artists today.
- It is not viable to make art where "content" and "form"
  are more important than "subject."
- The beauty of sculpture is its relationship to failure.
- The failure of sculpture is rooted in its obduracy.
- Sculpture changes the spaces it inhabits.
- Everything changes the space it inhabits.
- Sculpture must be more concerned with time than image.
- Image destroys sculpture.
- Sculpture fails because it will always be an image.
- Truth is a fallacy in art.
- In particular, truth is a fallacy in sculpture.
- Lies, and how to lie, are a powerful imaginative force
  for both artist and viewer.

2

- "Documentary" is an art genre that goes back to
  prehistory.
- "Documentary" as an art genre includes history painting,
  portraits, memorials, commemorations, performance,
  film/video, cave drawings.
- "Modernism" is dominated by moral attitudes of good/
  bad, right/wrong.

- "Authenticity" is the new morality.
- Sculpture is inherently inauthentic.
- Making is making a comeback!
- Making is not sculpture.
- Who cares if "making" is sculpture or not?
- Art is evidence.
- Art is anthropological.
- Sculpture is the most anthropological of all the arts.
- Sculpture is as simple as digging a hole or cutting a slice of bread.
- Sculpture must not show, or tell, its labour.
- Sculpture must be effortless.
- Arte Povera changed attitudes to making more than Minimalism did.
- Arte Povera was European; Minimalism was American.
- Minimalism has edges; Arte Povera has no edges.
- Adorno refers to the shifting borders of Europe and how this influenced European culture.
- What is Yorkshire art?
- Themed exhibitions are a curse.
- Themed exhibitions are PhD-heavy.
- Themed exhibitions are more about the curators than the artists.
- Artists crave freedom.
- No, they don't.
- The word "sculptor" no longer applies.
- Sculpture will not survive as a studio activity.
- Sculpture is too expensive and requires too much space for experimentation.
- Sculpture has become design.
- Sculpture will eventually always be made by fabricators.
- Sculpture is an old-fashioned medium entrenched in convention and orthodoxy.
- Challenge is always good.

- Belief is always dangerous.
- Is everyone an artist?
- Therefore, is everyone a sculptor?
- Many people have access to a pencil and a piece of paper.
- Many people have access to phones with photography and video applications.
- Not many people have access to a lump of clay.
- Everyone has imagination.

Chronology

1944 Phyllida Barlow is born on April 4 in Newcastle upon Tyne, UK, the youngest of three siblings. Her mother is a writer and her father a doctor.

1946 The family moves to Richmond in southwest London. Barlow later recalls constructing small houses for fantasy creatures out of cardboard and matchboxes.

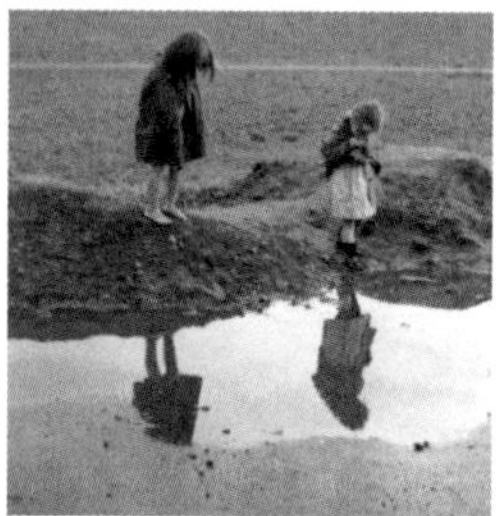

Phyllida Barlow (right) and her sister Camilla on Richmond Green, London, 1948

1951 Barlow's father begins working as a psychiatrist at St Thomas's Hospital Medical School in London.

1960–63

Barlow initially studies among traditionalists. Enter an inspiring teacher, sculptor George Fullard.

1960 Begins studying art at Chelsea School of Art, London, initially in the painting department before switching to sculpture. The teaching in both is, at first, traditional and Barlow finds it restrictive and not experimental enough.

1962 Meets her future husband Fabian Peake, a fellow student at Chelsea and son of the novelist Mervyn Peake.

1963 George Fullard becomes head of Chelsea's sculpture department and breaks with convention, urging students to take inspiration from the everyday world. With Fullard's encouragement, Barlow soon begins experimenting with clay and other soft modeling materials.

After the summer, Barlow continues her studies at the Slade School of Fine Art, London, where she makes sculptures combining geometric and biomorphic forms, using materials including resin, fiberglass, wood, paper, fabric, and paint.

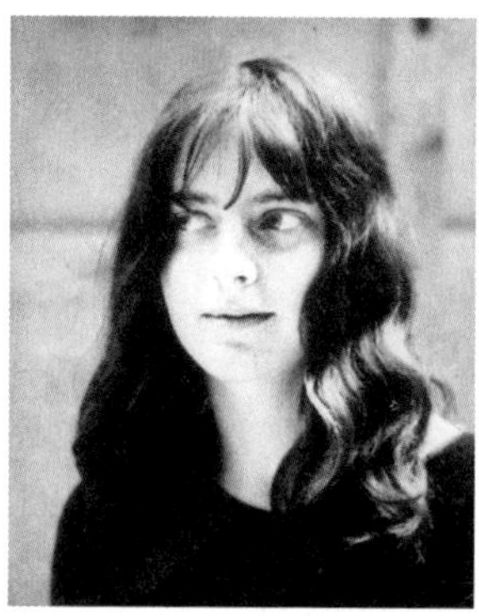

Barlow in 1964

1965 Participates in the group exhibition *Young Contemporaries* at the Institute of Contemporary Arts, London.

1966 Barlow and Peake get married.

Barlow finishes her studies at the Slade; her diploma exhibition is documented in numerous color photographs.

1966 Barlow and Peake move briefly to Norfolk, where her work is inspired by the seaside, beach huts, and boathouses.

1967 Sets up her first studio in London and secures a part-time teaching position in sculpture at the West of England College of Art, Bristol. Starts teaching sculpture part-time at Chelsea School of Art, where she will work until 1978.

1971 Takes part in two important group exhibitions: *Sculpture and Drawings* at Camden Arts Centre, London, and *Art Spectrum London* at Alexandra Palace, London.

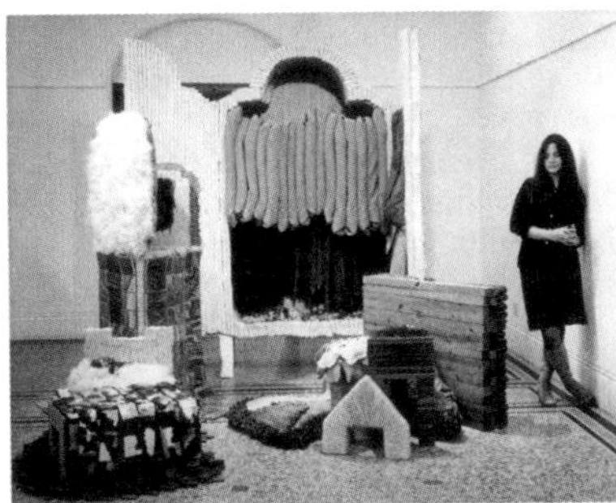

Barlow with *Wardrobe* at Camden Arts Centre, London, 1971

1972–89

Barlow begins testing methods of low-tech construction, using discarded materials in bulk to build large-scale works to be exhibited outside of traditional gallery spaces.

1972 *All and Everything* is shown in a group exhibition of sculpture at the University of Surrey.

1973 Birth of first daughter, Florence Peake.
  Stuff is included in an exhibition at the Gulbenkian Gallery, Newcastle upon Tyne.

1974 Barlow's work appears in the group exhibition *British Sculptors, Attitudes to Drawing* at the Sunderland Arts Centre.

1975 Birth of daughter Clover Peake.

1975 Exhibits the landmark work *Shedmesh* in the group exhibition *Contemporary Painting and Sculpture* at Camden Arts Centre, London.
  Gallery 21, London, presents its inaugural show, a two-person exhibition featuring drawings by Barlow and Peake.

1977 The work *Four* is part of the group exhibition *Three Sculptors in the Close* in Gloucester Cathedral.

1978 Birth of daughter Tabitha Peake.
  Leaves her teaching position at Chelsea School of Art.

1981 Birth of twin sons Edward and Lewis Peake.

1982 Begins the *Touchpieces* series, working at night in her small studio adjacent to her house. She makes these works in darkness because she wants them to be "absolutely about touch and not about image."

1983 Barlow creates *Fill* in response to an invitation by Phillip King to participate in a group exhibition of outdoor sculpture at the disused Tout Quarry in Dorset, but is asked to remove it shortly after the show's opening.

1984 Teaches sculpture at Brighton Polytechnic, where fellow teachers include Edward Allington, Eric Bainbridge, Peter Randall-Page, and Alison Wilding. She later describes her experience, largely on account of these colleagues, many of whom became close friends, as "the most brilliant year I've ever had teaching."

Installs the outdoor ensemble
Wrecks in Bayfield, Norfolk.

Abandons *Scar* in a deserted house
on Archway Road, London.

Barlow starts making large,
site-specific installations that are
dismantled after being shown.

1985 *Strangers* is exhibited in a school
playground in Finsbury Park, London,
and *Ghosts* is installed in a former
stocking factory in Hackney.

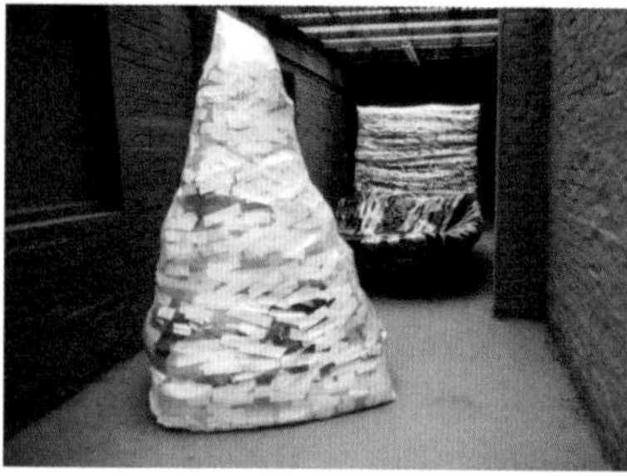

Ghosts, 1985

1986 Leaves her teaching position at
Brighton Polytechnic and secures a part-
time teaching position at Camberwell
School of Art, London, shared with the
artist Brian Catling.

Threat is part of the exhibition *Third
Generation* at the Canterbury Festival.

1987 Continues working on large-
scale installations made from recycled
materials.

Expanse is installed at Unit
7, London and *Oracle* at St Peter's
Churchyard, Cambridge.

Richard Deacon and Alison Wilding
curate the group exhibition *Casting
an Eye* at Cornerhouse, Manchester,
including Barlow's work *Engulf*.

Becomes artist in residence at
Kettle's Yard, Cambridge, where a group
exhibition, *The Shelf Show*, includes her
work *Muscle and Bone*.

1988 Leaves Camberwell and
starts teaching sculpture at the Slade
School of Fine Art, where she remains
employed for the next two decades.
Her students include artists Martin
Creed, Tacita Dean, Angela de la
Cruz, and Douglas Gordon.

The site-specific installation
Slope is presented at The Gallery,
Dean Clough, Halifax.

The group exhibition *Houseworks*,
organized by artist Mark Dunhill
in Bristol, includes the work *Fold*.

1989 A series of wall sculptures
is exhibited in *Wallworks* at Smith
Jarawala Gallery, London.

Vigil 1, a work made up of three
site-specific sculptures, is installed
in a churchyard for the Windsor
Festival, Berkshire.

1990–2001

**Barlow's works for public spaces
become smaller as she transitions
to what she calls a "private
encounter with making."**

1990 Creates *Seam* for the National
Garden Festival, Gateshead.

Collaborates with dancer Louise
Tonkin for the MAAD Festival at Kettle's
Yard, Cambridge.

1991 Becomes part-time visiting
lecturer in sculpture at Chelsea College
of Art & Design.

The work *Plantation* is
commissioned by the Business
Design Centre and the Museum of
Installation, London. The sculpture
Deep is also presented at the Museum
of Installation, London, and *Closed
(Vigil II)* is installed at the RIBA
Sculpture Court, London.

1992 Becomes a part-time visiting lecturer in sculpture at the Royal College of Art.

Appointed acting head of sculpture at the Slade School of Fine Art.

The outdoor ensemble *Things* is installed at Sydenham Hill Wood, London.

Curates the group exhibition *Three Sculptors* at the Diorama in Regents Park, London, which includes her work *Across, Around, Up*.

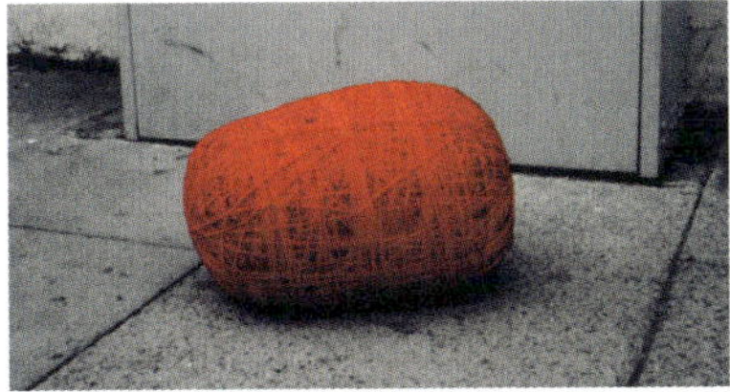

out of place: streetwork1; redwool; 1992–93

1994 Begins working on the series *Objects for . . .* , creating works that challenge preconceived notions of how artworks are expected to behave and interact with domestic spaces and the urban environment. Some of these works are commissions; some are left in the houses of friends, or abandoned in the streets of London.

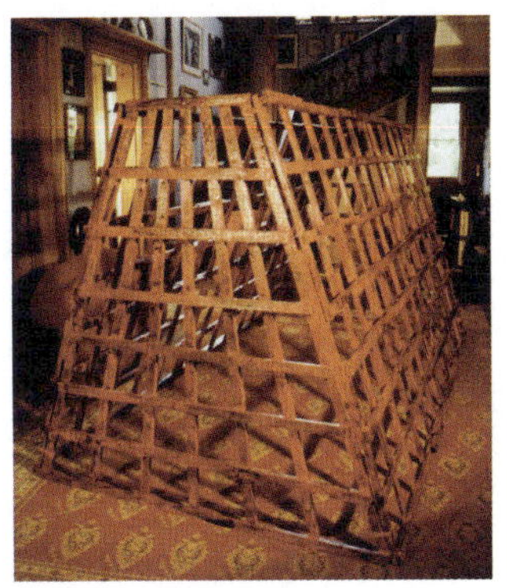

Installation for a Country House Hallway, 1994

1995 Gives the talk "The Hatred of the Object" at Central Saint Martins, London, which explores how easily the admiration demanded by highly finished objects, from sculptures to cars, can tip into loathing.

Mounts the show *Depot* at the Museum of Installation in London.

Sculptures for the Library is exhibited at the Henry Moore Institute, Leeds.

1996 *Recall* is shown at the Marshall's Mill, Dean Clough, Halifax.

Organizes two exhibitions in London: *Artist for a Day* at Flowers East and *AD HOC* at London Art Forms.

1997 Participates in *Between the Visible and the Invisible*, in Lahore, Pakistan, a workshop where, as she puts it, she is forced to confront the continuing legacies of colonialism.

Her work *Truce* is included in the group exhibition *EAST International* at the Norwich School of Art, and *Objects for a Dressing Table* features in the group exhibition *Barely Made* at Norwich Art Gallery.

Participates in the group exhibition *Musée imaginaire* at the Museum of Installation, London.

Becomes a reader in fine art and the head of undergraduate studies at the Slade School of Fine Art.

1998 The work *after dark* is exhibited at the Master Shipwright's House, London, and *time and time again* is included in the exhibition *Out of Place* at the Chapter Art Gallery, Cardiff.

1999 Is among six sculptors selected by John Maine and Alison Wilding for the Triennial Sculpture Exhibition at the Royal Western Academy, Bristol, where she presents the work *Dawn till Dusk*.

Presents *Far Away* at the group exhibition *O pas là: Surprising Spaces*

at the Lieu d'art contemporain,
Narbonne, France.

Takes part in the touring group
exhibition *Furniture*.

2000 Participates in the fifth British
Art Show with *after dark into black*.
Barlow finds this work, in retrospect,
disappointing and embarrassing,
describing it as "histrionic" and
"attention-seeking."

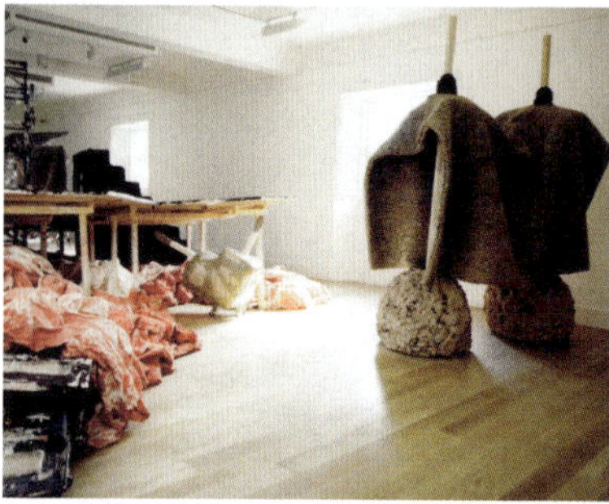

after dark into black, 2000, at the Deen Gallery,
Edinburgh

2001–9

**Following a creative crisis,
Barlow turns to large sculptural
installations that force audience
members to walk within, beneath,
and around her works.**

2001 Barlow later sees this summer
as a crisis, in which she comes to
a complete standstill in sculpture-
making. She focuses increasingly on
photography and formulaic drawing.
The resulting drawings (dubbed
"coloured drawings") would become
a basis for many sculptural works
to follow.

Creates the set design for *Knives
in Hens*, commissioned by the Attic
Theatre Company, Wimbledon
Theatre, London.

2002 Gives the lecture "Hearsay,
Rumours, Bedsit Dreamers, and Art
Begins Today" at the Whitechapel
Art Gallery, London.

Is included in the Royal Academy
of Arts Summer Exhibition in London,
curated by Alison Wilding.

2003 Is visiting artist at the University
of Texas, Dallas, and makes work for
various exhibitions in the city.

2004 Is appointed professor of fine
art and director of undergraduate
studies at the Slade School of Fine Art.

First solo exhibition in a UK public
institution, *Peninsula*, opens at the
Baltic Centre for Contemporary
Art, Gateshead.

The landmark book *Objects for . . .
and other things* is released by Black
Dog Publishing.

2005 Creates two large-scale
installations: *SCAPE* at Spacex,
Exeter, and *SKIT* at the Bloomberg
Space, London.

Participates in the group exhibition
sense of place: place of sense at the Beacon
Art Project, Sleaford.

Participates in numerous group
exhibitions in London and abroad.

2006 Participates in group shows
in Los Angeles; Guanajuato, Mexico;
and Seoul.

Commissioned to create a courtyard
sculpture for the Summer Exhibition
at the Royal Academy of Arts, London,
earning the Sunny Dupree Family Award
for a Woman Artist.

2007 *Underover*, a nine-sculpture
installation, is exhibited in Canary
Wharf, London.

Takes part in several group exhibitions
including *New Sculpture: In the Gallery
and Grounds* at the New Art Centre,

Roche Court, Salisbury, and *etc . . .* at the Amagerfaelledvej Art Project, Copenhagen. Also creates *Untitled: ramp, tower, flags* for Galería Jesús Gallarda, León, Mexico.

2008 *STINT*, an installation comprising ten sculptures, is exhibited at the Mead Gallery, Warwick Arts Centre.

STACK, FENCE opens at the Southbank Centre, London, and *Untitled*, comprising two sculptures, is exhibited at the Kilkenny Arts Festival, Ireland.

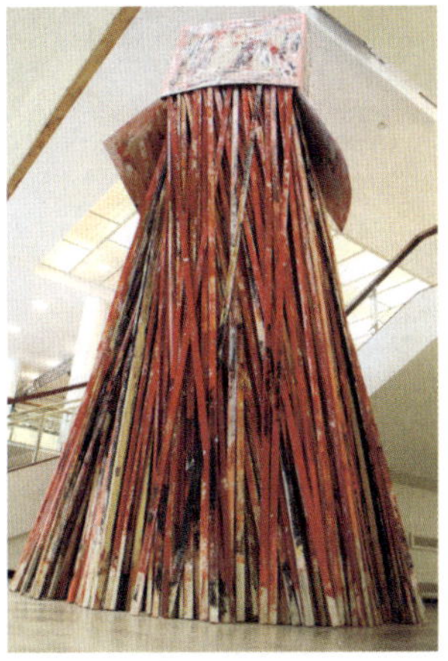

untitled: stack; 2008, at the Southbank Centre, London

2009–23

Barlow retires from her job and soon becomes an internationally celebrated artist with gallery representation. She shifts gears toward enormous installations that overwhelm the exhibition space and stretch it to its limits.

2009 Retires from her position as professor of fine art and director of undergraduate studies at the Slade School of Fine Art where she will remain as emerita professor of fine art.

Exhibits *BRAKE* at the One in the Other Gallery, London and participates in the two-person exhibition *Phyllida Barlow / Jess Flood-Paddock* at the Russian Club Gallery, London.

2010 Two solo exhibitions in London—*BLUFF* at Studio Voltaire, and *SWAMP* at V22—and one in Vienna: *STREET*, at BAWAG Contemporary.

Nairy Baghramian and Phyllida Barlow takes place at the Serpentine Gallery, London, and *Phyllida Barlow & Fiona MacDonald* at CoExist Galleries, Essex.

Barlow's work is included in the group exhibitions *Displaced Fractures* at the Migros Museum für Gegenwartskunst, Zurich, and in *Old Ideas* at the Kunstmuseum Basel.

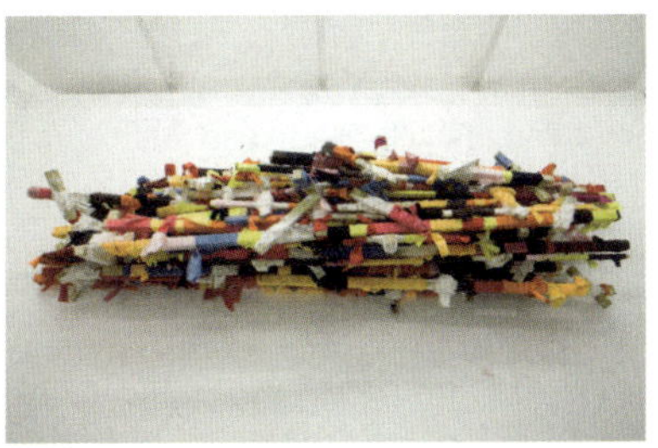

STREET untitled: broken shelf, 2010, at BAWAG Contemporary, Vienna

2011 The solo exhibition *Cast* opens at the Kunstverein Nürnberg, Nuremberg, Germany.

Participates in the group exhibition *Sculptural Acts* at Haus der Kunst, Munich, and *Before the Law* at the Museum Ludwig, Cologne.

Is appointed a Royal Academician, Royal Academy of Arts, London.

Exhibits *RIG* at Hauser & Wirth London.

2012 Three solo exhibitions: *siege*
at New Museum, New York; *brink* at
the Ludwig Forum für Internationale
Kunst, Aachen, Germany; *Phyllida
Barlow: Bad Copies* at the Henry Moore
Institute, Leeds.

Takes part in the first Kyiv International Biennale of Contemporary Art.

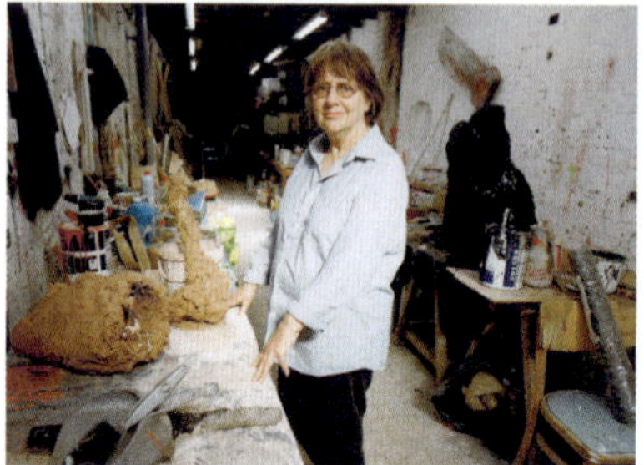

Barlow in her studio, London, 2012

2013 Several exhibitions in the
United States, with solo shows at
the Des Moines Art Center, Iowa,
and at the Norton Museum of Art,
West Palm Beach, Florida. In addition,
TIP features as a monumental
intervention in dialogue with a Richard
Serra work at the entrance to the
Carnegie International, Pittsburgh.

Barlow is a participating artist in the
main exhibition of the Venice Biennale.

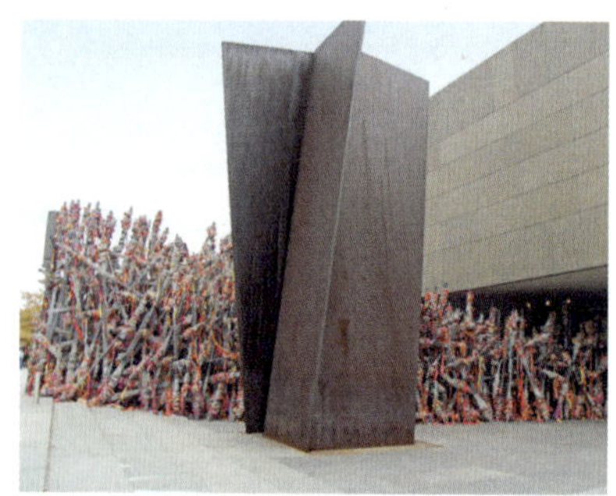

TIP, 2013, next to Richard Serra's *Carnegie*, 1985,
at the Carnegie Museum of Art, Pittsburgh

2014 In response to the Tate
Britain Commission, fills the Duveen
Galleries with her work *dock*, which
she describes as an "argument with
the space."

Fifty Years of Drawings brings together
more than two hundred of Barlow's
drawings at Hauser & Wirth London,
and *GIG* opens at Hauser & Wirth
Somerset.

Gives the William Townsend Lecture
at the Slade School of Fine Art, London,
with a talk titled "For No Reason."

2015 Two important solo exhibitions:
tryst at the Nasher Sculpture Center,
Dallas, and *set* at the Fruitmarket
Gallery, Edinburgh.

Receives a CBE for her services to the
arts in the Queen's New Year's Honours.

2016 Creates *demo* for the Kunsthalle
Zürich, which incorporates materials
discarded during the museum's
renovation. Parts of the installation
are only visible through peepholes.

2017 Represents Britain at the 57th
Venice Biennale with the exhibition
folly in the British Pavilion.

Charlotte Higgins writes a long-read
profile in the *Guardian* titled "Bish-
Bash-Bosh: How Phyllida Barlow
Conquered the Art World at 73."

2018 Installs a permanent woodland
sculpture, *quarry,* in the grounds of
Jupiter Artland, Edinburgh.

Creates the outdoor work *prop* for
New York's High Line; and presents
the exhibition *tilt* at Hauser & Wirth
New York.

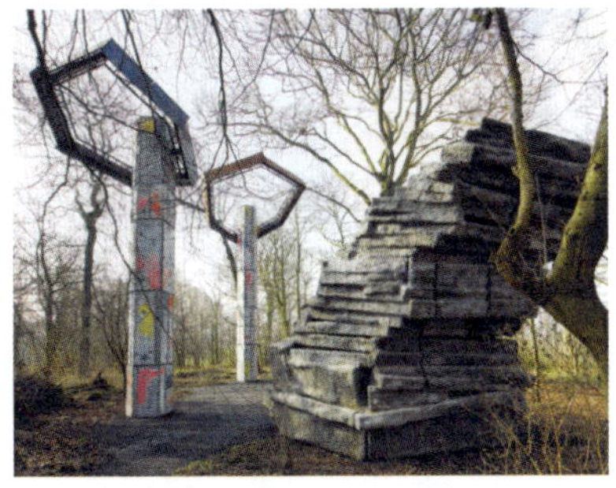

quarry, 2018, at Jupiter Artland, Edinburgh

2019 *cul-de-sac* opens at the Royal Academy of Arts, London.

2020 Barlow's work is showcased in the Artist Rooms series at Tate Modern, London.

Commissioned to design the set for the Bayerische Staatsoper's staging of *Idomeneo*.

Phyllida Barlow: Collected Lectures, Writings, and Interviews is released.

During the Covid lockdowns, Barlow works on *smallmodernart*, a series of tiny works exploring her roots in postwar European art.

Decides to remake the landmark work *Shedmesh* (1975), one of a number of "enduring" works that emerge as a separate stream of her practice.

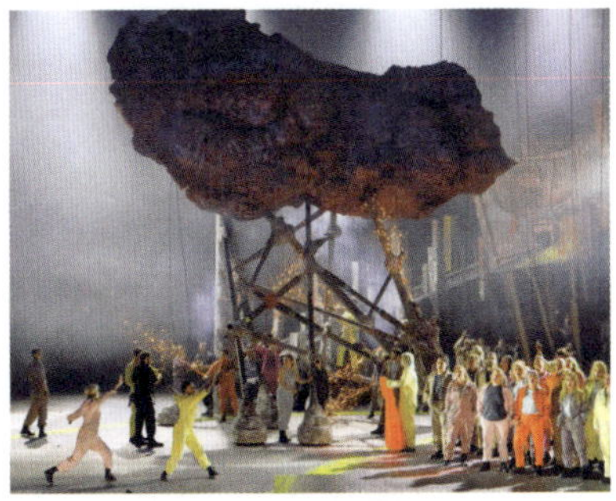

Idomeneo at the Bayerische Staatsoper, Munich, 2021, with set design by Barlow

2021 The retrospective *frontier* opens at the Haus der Kunst, Munich.

Barlow is included in *Another Energy: Power to Continue Challenging* at the Mori Art Museum, Tokyo, a group show of new work by women over seventy.

Creates *act*, a site-specific sculpture for Highgate Cemetery, London.

Is awarded a DBE for her services to the arts in the Queen's New Year's Honours.

2022 Awarded the Niedersächsische Sparkassenstiftung's 2022 Kurt Schwitters Prize.

The solo show *BREACH* opens at the Sprengel Museum Hannover, Germany.

2023 Prepares three important projects: the survey show *Eleven Columns* at the Museum of Contemporary Art, Toronto; an exhibition at the Chillida Leku museum, Hernani, Spain; and a new suite of outdoor works titled *PRANK* at City Hall Park, New York. All of them open posthumously.

Barlow dies unexpectedly on March 12 in London.

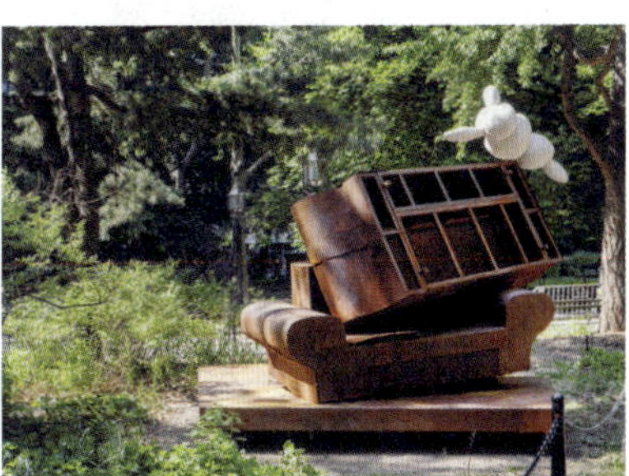

PRANK: truant; 2022/23, at City Hall Park, New York, 2023

Additional Resources

Given that so many of Barlow's works were transient by nature and that the large sculptural installations she made in the last decades of her life were, almost without exception, dismantled after being shown, documentation has a special significance in relation to her oeuvre. Her forceful insistence on physical encounters with the work in time and space makes this somewhat ironic. Nevertheless, the intellectual and emotional charge of her work comes across powerfully in photographs, books, films, and, not least, the artist's own writings and video, audio, and printed interviews.

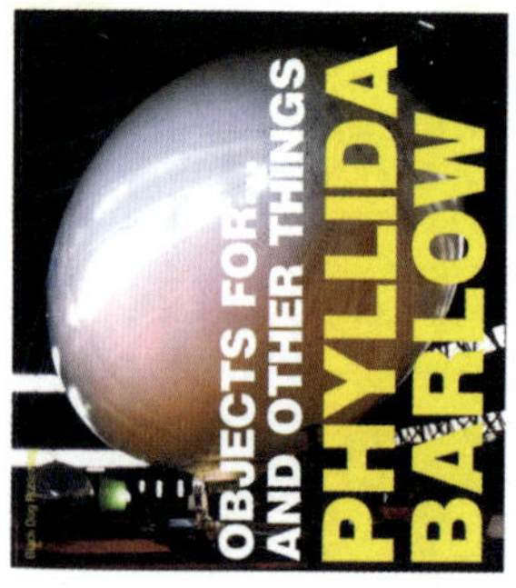

Phyllida Barlow: Objects for . . . and Other Things (2004). This ambitious and beautifully illustrated publication comprehensively documents the series *Objects for . . .* and includes key writings by Barlow as well as insightful essays on her work by Mark Godfrey and Jon Wood.

Phyllida Barlow: frontier (2021) went far beyond the exhibition at the Haus der Kunst in Munich that was the occasion of its publication. With writing by Barlow, essays by art historians, and a biography of the artist.

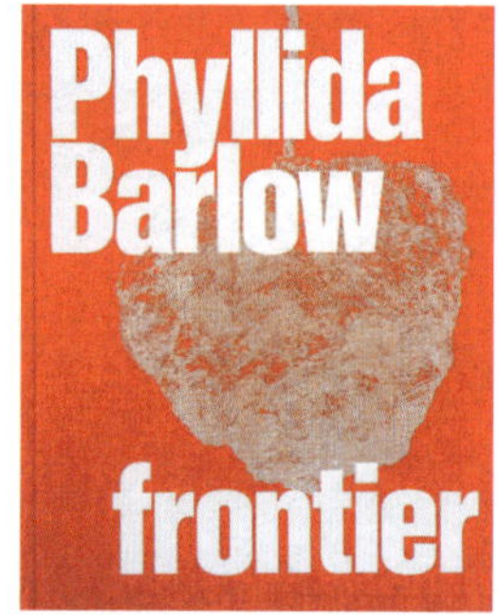

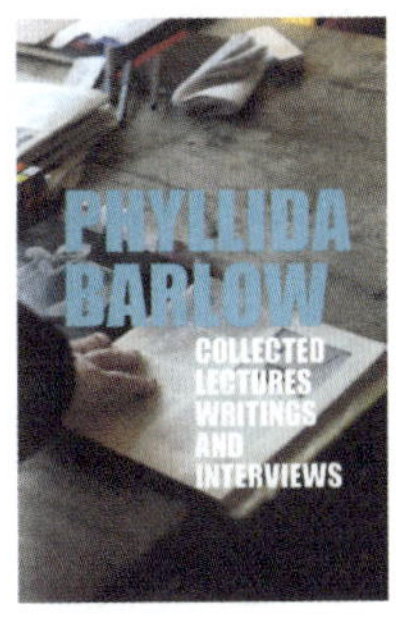

Phyllida Barlow: Collected Lectures, Writings, and Interviews (2021) is the go-to volume for anyone wishing to get a sense of Barlow's gift for talking and writing about art in general, sculpture more specifically, teaching, drawing, and more.

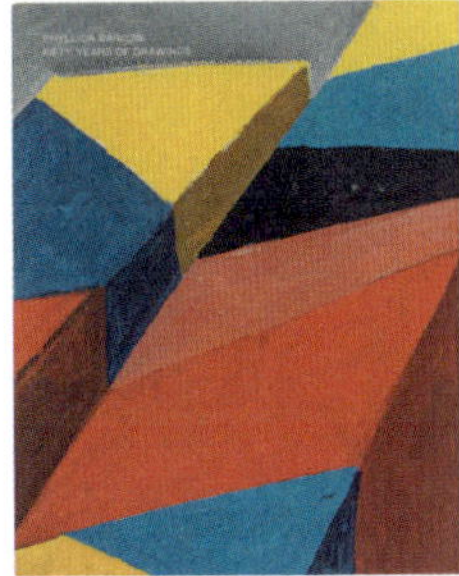

Phyllida Barlow: Fifty Years of Drawings (2014; repr. 2024) was made with the artist's involvement and takes us inside her extensive archive of drawings, dating from her days as an art student through to her late works.

Phyllida Barlow: Sculpture, 1963–2023 (2024) is an updated and expanded edition of Frances Morris's indispensable guide to the Barlow's sculptural language over six decades.

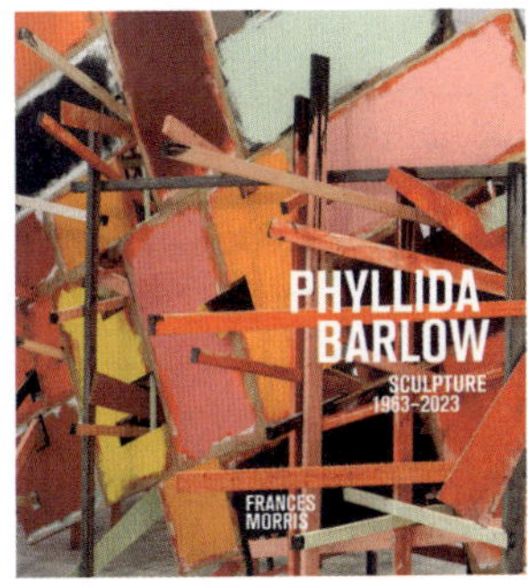

Videos of Barlow in conversation, linked above, include the Royal Academy of Art's *PHYLLIDA* (2019; p. 74) and the Barlow segment of the "London" chapter (2020) of Art21's *Art in the Twenty-First Century*. A sensitive and personal interview is documented in the Louisiana Channel's *Phyllida Barlow: Damage and Repair* (2022).

Also of note is Ben Luke's intelligent and wide-ranging conversation with Barlow on the *Art Newspaper*'s podcast *A Brush With . . .*, recorded in March 2023, just a few days before the artist's untimely death.

Additional Captions

Cover: Barlow in her studio, Bermondsey, London, 2013

pp. 4–5: Outside Barlow's studio, Bermondsey, London, 2013

pp. 6–7, 8–9: Views of Barlow's studio in Camberwell, London, 2023

pp. 10–11; 14: Artwork in Barlow's studio, Camberwell, London 2023

pp. 12–13: Barlow in her studio with maquettes for the outdoor sculptures installed at Jupiter Artland outside Edinburgh in 2018

p. 15: Barlow in her studio, Hornsey, London, September 2018

p. 16: *pompom 2014-3*, 2014

p. 17: *pompom 2014-4*, 2014

p. 73: Still from *PHYLLIDA*, 2019

p. 148: Children visiting *Phyllida Barlow: unscripted* at Hauser & Wirth Somerset as part of the Education Lab project "School Without Walls," 2024

Back cover: *untitled: sodiumlit street object; 2020, 5*, 2020

Image Credits

Sources

Most quotations from the artist are from *Phyllida Barlow: Collected Lectures, Writings, and Interviews* (Zurich: Hauser & Wirth Publishers, 2021), which includes additional source information and is henceforth cited as *Writings*.

p. 6: Pull quote from Barlow, "Because It's Not There" (2018), *Writings*, p. 110.

p. 15: Pull quote from Barlow, "Interview with John Yau" (2011), *Writings*, p. 151.

p. 25: "lies, borrowing …" is from Barlow's January 15, 2017, diary entry in the catalogue *Phyllida Barlow: folly* (London: Black Dog, 2017), p. 42.

p. 32: Pull quote from Barlow, "Louise Bourgeois: Conversation with Frances Morris" (2012), *Writings*, p. 410.

p. 46: Abridged from "Hearsay, Rumours, Bedsit Dreamers, and Art Begins Today" (2002), *Writings*, pp. 71–76.

p. 52: Hesse: Quotation from Barlow, "For No Reason" (2019), *Writings*, p. 35.
　Chillida: Quotation from Barlow, "In the Heat of the Moment" (2011), *Writings*, p. 389.

p. 56: Bourgeois: Quotation from Barlow, "Louise Bourgeois: The Sneeze of Louise" (1995), *Writings*, p. 331.
　Fullard: Quotation from Barlow, "George Fullard: Touching the Past" (1998), *Writings*, p. 337.

p. 58: Duchamp: Quotation from Barlow, "For No Reason," pp. 32, 35.
　Fautrier and Richier: Quotation from Barlow, "For No Reason," p. 32.

p. 61: "anarchic pleasure" is from "For No Reason," p. 24.

p. 70: Abridged from "The Hatred of the Object" (1995), *Writings*, pp. 51–59.

p. 84: Pull quote from Barlow, "For No Reason," p. 27.

p. 91: "faded and dejected glory …" is from Barlow's November 6, 2016, diary entry, in *folly*, p. 35.

p. 103: Pull quote from Barlow, "Conversation with Daniel Baumann" (2017), *Writings*, p. 221.

p. 106: Abridged from Barlow's February 7, 2017, diary entry, in *folly*, p. 43.

p. 115: "a network of shadows …" is from Barlow's November 26, 2016, diary entry, in *folly*, p. 36.

p. 117: "colours from the 1950s …" is from Barlow, "Interview with Hans Ulrich Obrist" (2014), *Writings*, p. 279.

p. 118: Excerpted from Barlow, "Then and Now," in *Cezanne*, edited by Achim Borchardt-Hume, Gloria Groom, Caitlin Haskell, and Natalia Sidlina (Chicago: Art Institute of Chicago, 2022), 195–96. © The Art Institute of Chicago, 2022.

pp. 124–31: "Influences: Books and Films" is indebted to Barlow's unpublished conversations with Frances Morris in 2015, Barlow's March 2023 interview with Ben Luke for the *Art Newspaper*'s podcast *A Brush with …*, and (for the Pessoa entry) the interview "The Artist's Library: Phyllida Barlow on Fernando Pessoa and *The Book of Disquiet*," *Ursula*, November 28, 2021, https://www.hauserwirth.com/ursula/35313-artists-library-phyllida-barlow-fernando-pessoa/.

p. 132: Unabridged from "Provocations for the Yorkshire Sculpture Triennial" (2018), *Writings*, pp. 17–19.

In the Studio: Phyllida Barlow
© 2025 Hauser & Wirth Publishers

All texts © 2025 the authors
Additional copyright credits on pp. 146–47

Special thanks to Phyllida Barlow's family,
in particular to Fabian Peake

ISBN: 978-3-907493-03-8
ISSN: 3042-5751
Library of Congress Control Number: 202494777

Available through ARTBOOK | D.A.P.
(North and South America) and Thames
& Hudson (all other territories)

Series design: Fraser Muggeridge studio
Printed in Italy

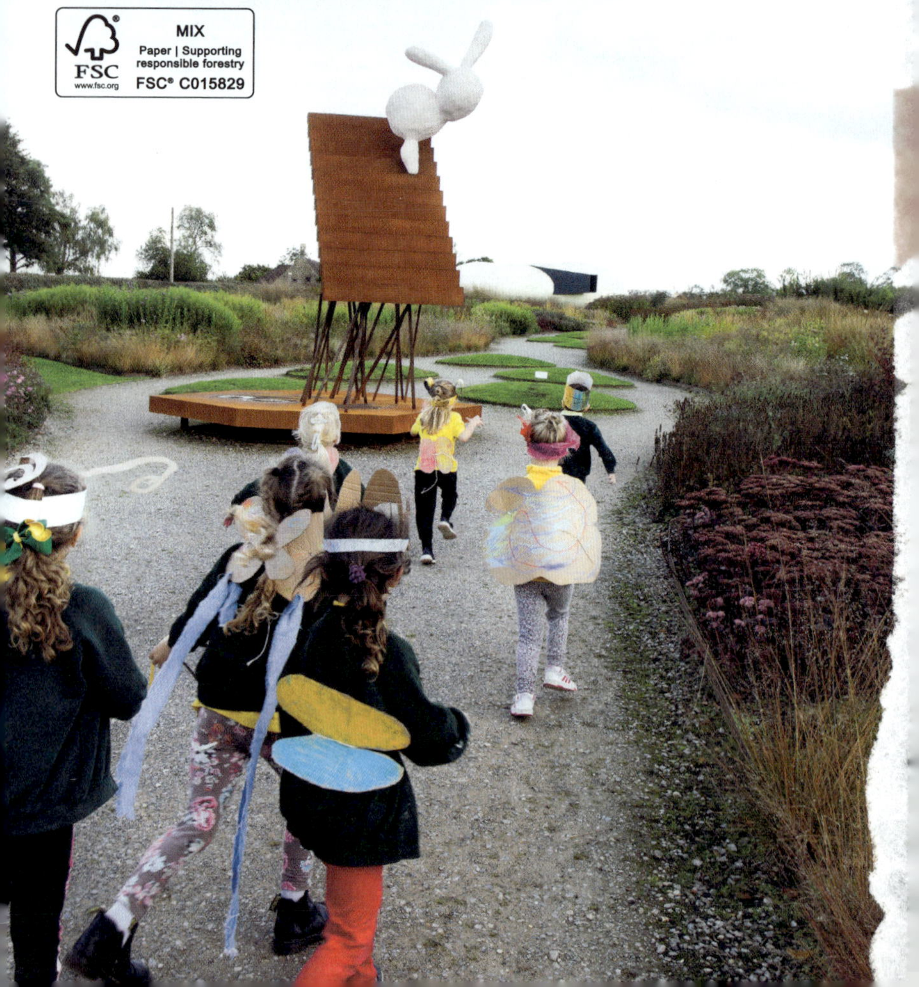